Embodying Xuanzang

Embodying Xuanzang

The Postmortem Travels of a Buddhist Pilgrim

Benjamin Brose

University of Hawai'i Press

Honolulu

Library of Congress Cataloging-in-Publication Data

Names: Brose, Benjamin, author.
Title: Embodying Xuanzang : the postmortem travels of a Buddhist pilgrim /
  Benjamin Brose.
Description: Honolulu : University of Hawai'i Press, [2023] | Includes
  bibliographical references and index.
Identifiers: LCCN 2023013328 (print) | LCCN 2023013329 (ebook) |
  ISBN 9780824895655 (trade paperback) | ISBN 9780824894900 (hardback) |
  ISBN 9780824896379 (pdf) | ISBN 9780824896386 (epub) |
  ISBN 9780824896393 (kindle edition)
Subjects: LCSH: Xuanzang, approximately 596–664—Legends. | Wu, Cheng'en,
  approximately 1500–approximately 1582. Xi you ji—Criticism and
  interpretation. | Buddhist legends—China. | Buddhism—China—Rituals.
Classification: LCC BQ8149.H787 B759 2023 (print) | LCC BQ8149.H787
  (ebook) | DDC 294.3/92092—dc23/eng/20230503
LC record available at https://lccn.loc.gov/2023013328
LC ebook record available at https://lccn.loc.gov/2023013329

Cover art: Cibei 慈悲 (Compassion). Zhang Moyi 張墨一. Digital media. 2016.

Contents

Acknowledgments

Stories about Xuanzang, that most famous of pilgrims, have traveled far and wide. It seems appropriate, then, that this book, a story about stories, has taken shape on the road. It began in Taiwan, where I spent a happy year at Academia Sinica's Institute of Modern History. Paul Katz and Liu Shufen were gracious hosts, and their deep knowledge of Chinese popular religion and the life and legacies of Xuanzang both inspired and informed this book. In Taiwan, I also benefited from the friendship and insights of Will and Kristine Zhang, Ching-chih Lin, Cheng Weiyi, and Dafu.

A research fellowship from the Alexander von Humboldt Foundation made it possible for me to continue this work over the course of two summers at the Universität Hamburg. I am indebted to Michael Zimmerman and the Numata Center for Buddhist Studies for hosting my visit. My time in Germany was further enriched by engaging conversations with Steffen Döll, Barend ter Haar, Michael Radich, and Daniel Boyarin.

Back in Ann Arbor, I am fortunate to work in a department filled with specialists in both Buddhist and Chinese Studies. Donald Lopez, Juhn Ahn, Micah Auerback, Sangseraima Ujeed, David Rolston, and S. E. Kile read through a draft of the manuscript and offered their expert advice. Susan Juster and Markus Nornes provided moral and logistical support. Our fabulous librarian Liangyu Fu never failed to locate obscure books for me, and Raymond Hsu was instrumental in securing permissions for several of the images reproduced here.

Several other friends and colleagues have assisted in ways large and small. An incomplete list includes Se-Woong Koo, Zhaohua Yang, Fabrizio Pregadio, Max Deeg, Jason Protass, James Benn, Chen Jinhua, Kurtis Schaeffer, Paul Copp, Ji Zhe, Jimmy Yu, Miranda Brown, Raoul Birnbaum, Megan Bryson, Nelson Foster, Gary Snyder, Hou Chong, and Ye Mingsheng.

Many of the ideas presented here began as talks delivered at the University of Chicago, the University of British Columbia, Universität Hamburg, Heidelberg University, Dharma Drum University, and the Institut national des langues et civilisations orientales. I am grateful to the organizers of these events and to all who attended. Additional funding for research, writing, and publication was generously provided by the Fulbright Program, the Robert H. N. Ho Family Foundation, the Chiang Ching-kuo Foundation, and the Lieberthal-Rogel Center for Chinese Studies.

At the University of Hawai'i Press, Stephanie Chun supported this project early on and saw it through to completion. Editorial assistance was provided by Kristen Bettcher and Kathi Anderson. Thanks also are due to my not-so-anonymous readers, Meir Shahar and Jeffrey Kotyk. Their learned comments and critiques made this a better book.

Finally, this book is dedicated to Wendy and Barry Brose, Cora and Jerry Iby, and my own band of fellow travelers: Jennifer, Walker, and Kalina.

Abbreviations

Biography	Huili et al., *A Biography of the Tripiṭaka Master of the Great Ci'en Monastery of the Great Tang Dynasty.*
Journey	Wu Cheng'en, *Journey to the West.* Translated by Anthony C. Yu.
MQMZ	*Ming-Qing minjian zongjiao jingjuan wenxian*
SKQS	*Wenyuange siku quanshu.*
T	*Taishō shinshū daizōkyō.*
Zhuan	Huili et al., *Da Tang da Ci'en si Sanzang fashi zhuan.*

Prologue

Xuanzang's Reincarnations

> Stories don't end, they go to sleep, and what sleeps may wake at
> any moment, or never wake at all.
>
> —Elias Khoury, *Broken Mirrors: Sinalcol*

On a cold night in the winter of 664, the revered monk Xüanzang 玄奘 (600/602–664) fell and injured his leg. Confined to bed, his body began to fail and his breathing grew labored. Knowing death was near, Xuanzang had one of his disciples compile a list of all the texts he had translated since returning from India nearly twenty years earlier. When the list was complete, he asked that it be read aloud.

> There were seventy-four volumes in 1338 scrolls. The many images [the master] had made were also recorded. [These included] one thousand images of Maitreya and ten *koṭīs* of clay images. He had copied the *Diamond Sūtra, Original Vows of the Medicine-Master Tathāgata of Lapis Light, Dhāraṇī of the Six Gates,* and other sutras ten times each. He had made offerings to over ten thousand members of the two merit fields—those pitiable and poor and those worthy of respect. He lit hundreds of thousands of lamps and redeemed countless beings.[1]

Hearing all he had accomplished, Xuanzang placed his palms together in a gesture of gratitude. Shortly thereafter, he made a vow to be reborn in Tuṣita Heaven, turned onto his right side, assumed the posture of the dying Buddha, and passed away.

The history of Buddhism in China brims with remarkable monks, but most of those who achieve some renown during their lives fade into obscurity after their deaths. Their memories are kept alive, if at all, only by a small number of monastics and scholars. Just a handful of Buddhist clerics—legendary figures like Bodhidharma, Huineng, and Jigong—have lingered in the popular imagination, their lively, colorful hagiographies often built and rebuilt on rickety scaffolds of historical facts. Xuanzang has the dual distinction of being China's best documented *and* most celebrated monk. Even now, nearly fourteen hundred years after he lived, he is studied and venerated not only in China but also in Taiwan, Japan, Korea, India, Europe, and the United States. The details of his life circulate in popular books and films; his image adorns monuments and is enshrined on altars. Works by and about him are assigned in college classrooms, and an entire university in Taiwan was recently founded in his name. Like Saint Francis of Assisi, Xuanzang has proven a remarkably pliable cleric whose life is regularly mined as an inexhaustible source of "old truths and new ideas."[2]

This book is a journey into the vast shafts of that mine in search of the stories that animate Xuanzang's many afterlives. As such, it is not so much an account of who Xuanzang was but, rather, a record of what he became for later generations of devotees. Before delving into those narratives, I begin with a few brief words about the man behind the myths.

Xuanzang's Life

Xuanzang already had attained legendary status in the decades before his death. Since his return to China in 645, he had been the preeminent Buddhist cleric in the Chinese capital cities of Chang'an and Luoyang. Famed for his nearly seventeen-year pilgrimage through Central Asia and India and lauded for his broad erudition and linguistic rigor, Xuanzang produced an astonishing number of translations, trained a generation of monks, and was a close ally of the imperial family and other high-ranking members of the aristocracy.[3] During his life, Xuanzang's stature in China was unparalleled. After his death, that influence only continued to grow.

The most detailed descriptions of Xuanzang's life come from two sources. The first is the extensive record Xuanzang made of his travels, the *Great Tang Dynasty Record of the Western Regions* (*Datang xiyu ji* 大唐西域記), published in 646. The second is the lengthy biography his disciples composed after his death, the *Biography of the Trepiṭaka Master of the Great Ci'en Monastery of the Great Tang Dynasty* (*Da Tang da Ci'en si Sanzang fashi zhuan* 大唐大慈恩寺三藏法師傳), completed in 688.[4] Together, these two works recount a truly remarkable life.

Born into an aristocratic family, Xuanzang became a monk at the young age of eleven. He spent his teenage years studying Buddhist doctrine under various teachers in the cities of Chengdu and Chang'an, major centers of monastic learning at that time. Monks of Xuanzang's generation lamented China's position on the periphery of the Buddhist world, and they strove to remain as faithful as possible to the traditions they had inherited from their Indian forebears. Access to authentic and accurate Indian Buddhist sutras and commentaries was thus essential. The first major effort to translate Buddhist texts from Sanskrit into Chinese was undertaken by An Shigao 安世高 (fl. ca. 148–180), a Parthian monk who traveled to China to spread the Dharma in the latter half of the second century. A succession of monks from South and Central Asia followed in his footsteps, laboring to make key Buddhist texts available to China's growing population of monastics and lay-people. Teams of Chinese monks, almost none of whom could read Sanskrit, assisted foreign-born clerics. By the early seventh century, these collaborations had produced an impressive corpus of Buddhist texts in classical Chinese, but divergent linguistic skills and translation styles resulted in inconsistent terminology and contradictory teachings. As a result, clerics in China, relying on divergent translations of texts written in different historical eras in support of sometimes opposing sectarian positions, disagreed on basic aspects of the teachings. They held competing views on issues as fundamental as the nature of consciousness, the status of awakening, and the process of purification. Xuanzang, like virtually every other Chinese monastic, assumed that all sutras faithfully record the actual words of the Buddha. Discrepancies among scriptures or commentaries, therefore, must be the result of an incomplete transmission—essential texts and teachings had simply not yet arrived in China—coupled with the mistakes and misunderstandings that marred existing translations. According to his disciple Huili 慧立 (b. 615), Xuanzang "often regretted that the books obtained and used by ancient sages contained miswritten words that perpetuated misunderstandings. It pained him that previous scholars heard and then passed on dubious points that compounded people's confusion."[5] Xuanzang thus resolved to travel to India, learn Sanskrit, and study the most current teachings under the most erudite monks and laymen of the subcontinent. Once he had mastered the languages and doctrines of both mainstream and Mahāyāna teachings, he would collect key Sanskrit texts, bring them back to China, and translate them into clear and accurate Chinese.

Remarkably, Xuanzang succeeded in these extraordinarily difficult tasks. Sometime between 627 and 629 (the precise date is unknown), he set off for India.[6] He navigated the barren Gobi Desert and the treacherous passes of the Tianshan and Hindu Kush mountains. Over the course of more than sixteen years, Xuanzang traveled thousands of miles, through Central Asia, across northern India, as far south as the Indian city of Chennai, and back again. Along the way, he earned the respect and support of multiple kings, visited hundreds of Buddhist sacred sites, studied Sanskrit, and learned to speak, presumably, one or more north Indian dialects. He apprenticed under the preeminent monks and lay scholars of the era and lived for nearly five years at Nālandā, the most prestigious center of Buddhist learning in India. Xuanzang eventually copied hundreds of texts and collected dozens of precious relics, statues, and images, all of which he transported to China on the backs of twenty horses. Arriving home in 645, he received a hero's welcome. For a monastic community that looked longingly to India as the original and authentic source of the Buddha's teachings, Xuanzang—who read, wrote, and spoke Indian languages and even dressed in the fashion of Gandhāran monks—was revered as *the* preeminent authority on Indian Buddhism.

After returning to the capital of Chang'an, Xuanzang composed the *Record of the Western Regions,* a work that remains the richest source for the geographies, demographics, religious traditions, histories, and cultures of seventh-century Central Asia and India.[7] Xuanzang composed the *Record* at the behest of the emperor, who was eager to acquire the most current intelligence about potential rivals and allies along Tang China's western borders.[8] Once that official obligation was fulfilled, Xuanzang dedicated the remainder of his life to teaching and translating Buddhist texts.

In Chang'an, Xuanzang headed an imperially sponsored translation team based out of the newly built, richly appointed Ci'en 慈恩 (Compassionate Kindness) Monastery. That team eventually produced seventy-five texts in a staggering 1,335 scrolls, more than one quarter of the entire Buddhist canon at the time. No translator of Buddhist texts into Chinese was more prolific than Xuanzang. Kumārajīva (344–409/413), the translator to whom Xuanzang is most often compared, translated only 294 scrolls. (Xuanzang's disciples thus compared their master to a great lake or river; previous translators like Kumārajīva were, by contrast, mere "ditches by the side of the road."[9]) Given this voluminous output, anyone who reads Mahāyāna Buddhist texts will eventually encounter Xuanzang's work. His version of the *Heart Sūtra,* to note only the most famous example, is recited daily in nearly every Buddhist monastery in East Asia.[10] Xuanzang's translations of the massive six hundred-scroll *Great Perfection of Wisdom Sūtra* (*Mahāprajñāpāramitā sūtra*), along with several important Yogācāra treatises and commentaries, also have remained central to Buddhist thought and practice to this day.

It was not only his astounding productivity that set Xuanzang apart; his translations were also famously faithful to the original Sanskrit. To give just one striking illustration, when the modern Belgian Indologist Louis de la Vallée Poussin (1869–1938) set out to translate Vasubandhu's (fl. ca. fourth or fifth century) monumental commentary on the Abhidharma (*Abhidharmakośa-bhāṣya*) into French, he relied heavily on Xuanzang's Chinese translation of the work. At that time, the Sanskrit edition was presumed lost, but a copy was later discovered in a Tibetan monastery. When the Sanskrit text was compared to Xuanzang's translation, the versions were found to be so similar that la Vallée Poussin's work required no substantial revision. The reliability, volume, and selectivity of Xuanzang's translations earned him a reputation—still undiminished after nearly fourteen hundred years—as one of the most consequential Buddhist translators ever to have lived.

That is a remarkable achievement, but readers of medieval Chinese translations of ancient Sanskrit Buddhist texts are a rather circumscribed group. Xuanzang's scholarly output and doctrinal mastery are hardly the driving force behind his global renown. His fame has always been more closely tied to his travels than to his translations or his teachings.

Xuanzang's Legend

When most people think about the historical Xuanzang, they think not of his explications of Yogācāra doctrines but of his extraordinary pilgrimage across the deserts, mountains, and rivers of what is now northwestern China, Kyrgyzstan, Uzbekistan, Kazakhstan, Tajikistan, Afghanistan, Pakistan, Nepal, Bangladesh, and India. These travels have fired the imaginations of Buddhists and non-Buddhists from the seventh century to the present day. Stories of Xuanzang's pilgrimage through the exotic and forbidding "western regions" circulated broadly soon after he returned to China, and they were embellished and enlivened in the retellings.

In later versions, the ghosts and demons mentioned briefly in earlier accounts multiplied. Monsters soon lurked in every desert, forest, and town, hell-bent on consuming Xuanzang's life-giving virgin flesh. His travel to Nālandā Monastery to study under learned Indian monks and laymen was reconceived as an otherworldly pilgrimage to the realm of buddhas and bodhisattvas. Xuanzang not only sought a clearer and more comprehensive understanding of Buddhist doctrine but, according to later legends, he also was determined to acquire and transmit the *entire* Buddhist canon and all its attendant powers from "Western Heaven" (*Xitian* 西天—one of the Chinese names for India) to the people of China. Even more dramatic and colorful than his actual travels, mythologized accounts of Xuanzang's journey gradually eclipsed more historically grounded accounts of his life.

Mythic versions of Xuanzang's pilgrimage received their most elaborate and influential expression in *Journey to the West* (*Xiyou ji* 西遊記), a long novel that has remained wildly popular since its publication in the late sixteenth century. Over the course of one hundred chapters (more than fifteen hundred pages in Anthony Yu's authoritative English translation), *Journey to the West* follows a caricature of Xuanzang who, along with four quasi-divine companions, embarks on a perilous journey from the capital of China to the land of the Buddha.[11]

In this telling, the pilgrimage is set in motion by Taizong (r. 626–649), the second emperor of the Tang dynasty (618–907). After a frightful journey through hell for his complicity in the death of a dragon, Taizong orders Xuanzang to travel to India to acquire a cache of Buddhist texts with the power to "save the dead and liberate wandering souls."[12] Xuanzang is the ostensible leader of this imperial mission, but the real protagonist of the novel is the irascible monkey Sun Wukong 孫悟空. With his shape shifting skills, his astounding martial prowess, and his unvarnished disdain for authority, Sun Wukong serves as the indispensable, if unruly, guide for Xuanzang as he traverses dangerous, demon-infested terrain. The slothful but formidable pig Zhu Bajie 豬八戒, the demon-monk Sha (Sha Wujing 沙悟净), and a dragon in the form of a horse round out the escort.

The bulk of the novel recounts the group's harrowing battles with a menagerie of ghouls and ghosts, their narrow escapes, and their plodding progress toward their goal. In the end, Xuanzang and his companions finally do encounter the Buddha and receive the sacred scriptures, which they duly deliver to the Chinese emperor. Their task complete, at the conclusion of the novel, all five pilgrims ascend to heaven, apotheosized as buddhas or bodhisattvas.

Virtually everyone familiar with the cultural traditions of East Asia knows the broad outlines of this story. They have read it in books—whether the hundred-chapter novel or its many abridgements, sequels, and spinoffs—seen it in theatrical performances, puppet shows, paintings, and sculptures, and heard it in stories and songs. In the past decade alone, the tale has been repeatedly adapted for films, television shows, cartoons, comics, and video games. The Xuanzang character from the novel, often known simply as the "Tang Monk," is a familiar feature in the cultural landscape of China and neighboring countries. He is now far more recognizable than the seventh-century pilgrim, scholar, and translator who served as his original inspiration.

The mythical Tang Monk appears to have only the most tenuous link to the historical Xuanzang. For good reasons, scholars and fans of the novel often treat the two figures as completely distinct. The character in the novel shares the same surname (Chen 陳), Dharma name (Xuanzang), and title (Trepiṭaka; Sanzang 三藏) as the seventh-century monk.[13] Some original documents, including the memorial that Emperor Taizong composed for Xuanzang in 648, are even woven into the novel, conveying at least a pretense of historical veracity. Nevertheless, other aspects of the two figures' biographies, such as the names of their respective parents and teachers, the texts they study, and even the dates and lengths of their journeys, differ. The monk in the novel, moreover, is essentially inept. Far from the courageous and brilliant man portrayed in historical sources, the Tang Monk is timid, indecisive, and borderline incompetent. Whereas Xuanzang was a prominent cleric who lived and died in the early Tang dynasty, the Tang Monk is a fictional character who appears to exist only in the timeless realm of fantasy.

That, at least, is how most people see it. It was certainly my assumption when I first started work on this project. In the early phases of research, I planned to focus only on issues related to the "real" Xuanzang: his relics, his translations, the traditions he established, and the reverence he inspired among later generations of monastics and laypeople. As a work of fiction, *Journey to the West* fell outside this scope. It was a topic better suited to scholars of Chinese literature. Indeed, over the last hundred years, dozens of books and thousands of articles have exhaustively analyzed the history and content of the novel. I was quite content, not to say eager, to sidestep this mountain of material.

It did not take long, however, for my presumptions and my plans to fall apart. I began noticing that some ceremonies involving Xuanzang's relics featured men and women dressed up as the characters from *Journey to the West*. I visited Buddhist monasteries with murals illustrating scenes from the novel set next to depictions of buddhas and bodhisattvas. In Taiwan, I found entire temples and shrines dedicated to Xuanzang's legendary companions, the monkey Sun Wukong and the pig Zhu Bajie.[14] Devotees were treating these figures as deities rather than fictional characters. It was the same in temple processions and other ritual performances. When Xuanzang appeared in these contexts, he was not depicted as the seventh-century scholar and translator but as the fantastical Tang Monk from *Journey to the West*. People seemed to be conflating fiction with history. Could it be that a secular work of literature had been transformed into a kind of sacred scripture? I started to look more carefully at the novel.

Over the last twenty-five years, scholars of Chinese religions have been exploring the richly symbiotic relationship between vernacular fiction and ritual.[15] Popular novels and their theatrical corollaries are accessible to a much wider audience than the canonical texts of Buddhist, Daoist, and Confucian traditions, all of which are typically written in abstruse classical Chinese. (Xuanzang's own translations, which are essentially impenetrable to nonspecialists, are a prime example.) Stories and dramas also are more fun to read and watch. The narratives in novels and plays are lively, full of bizarre characters, high drama, and crass humor. Their spectacular natures make them ideal conduits for the transmission of deity cults and ritual practices. As Meir Shahar has pointed out, "The body of religious beliefs and practices we now call Chinese religion (or Chinese popular religion) is inseparable from the works of fiction and drama that have served as vehicles for its transmission."[16] Novels dealing with deities were not necessarily reconceived as divine narratives, in other words, but ritual traditions did sometimes serve as source materials for aspiring authors.

Some of the vernacular novels that incorporate material from religious traditions have subsequently played an important part in preserving and broadcasting ritual practices and hagiographies. Mark Meulenbeld, for example, has shown that the Ming-dynasty novel *Canonization of the Gods* (*Fengshen yanyi* 封神演義) was constructed out of oral traditions, ritual practices, and local deity cults. *Canonization* served to synthesize and codify a diverse body of myth and legend into a single, comprehensive metanarrative that drew together disparate stories and traditions associated with the demons and deities of regional Chinese pantheons. This and other vernacular novels, Meulenbeld concludes, were "written as narrative accompaniments to ritual. By means of their full-fledged narrative cycles, novels *explain* the sacred histories (and dynamics) behind rituals and provide a comprehensive framework within which individual episodes of theatre are understood. It cannot be stated strongly enough that the novel appears on the scene long after ritual and theatre have dealt with the same subjects."[17] Certain works of vernacular "fiction," in short, are rooted in and serve as repositories for local ritual traditions.

Does the same hold true for *Journey to the West*? Although references to temples and ritual practices associated with the Tang Monk's mythic pilgrimage began to proliferate after the publication of the novel, images of Xuanzang together with a monkey attendant and a horse bearing luminous scriptures started appearing in Buddhist caves and on Buddhist stūpas several centuries earlier. By the fifteenth century, multiple "precious scrolls" (*baojuan* 寶卷)—scriptures used by largely lay religious groups—incorporated elements of the *Journey to the West* narrative into their teachings and liturgies. Exorcistic ritual dramas involving Xuanzang and his fellow pilgrims also were performed in northern China prior to the emergence of the novel.

These traditions, all of which are discussed in detail in the following chapters, demonstrate that the novel did not give rise to ritual traditions, as many observers in both China and abroad have long presumed. Instead, the circulation of the novel only enhanced the narrative's appeal and accelerated the spread of its stories and ritual forms. *Journey to the West* is just one telling of an old and amorphous tale. Other expressions of Xuanzang's pilgrimage—as liturgy, as hagiography, as scripture—preceded the novel and continue to exist and evolve alongside it. By privileging the hundred-chapter version as the sole progenitor of *Journey to the West*–inspired cults, officials and scholars overlooked the novel's indebtedness to local traditions and concluded that related rituals were parasitic on rather than symbiotic with the novel.

There are at least two reasons why these dimensions of Xuanzang's pilgrimage have passed unnoticed for so long. One is surely the overwhelming influence of the novel. Since its publication in the late sixteenth century, *Journey to the West* has been the subject of a steady stream of commentary and critique. Although initially derided as a lowbrow, vulgar, vernacular work, and, therefore, unworthy of the attention of classically trained Confucian scholars, the novel appears to have been something of a guilty pleasure among literati. Its anonymous author was clearly steeped in the poetic, literary, and philosophical traditions of the day, and people of similar training and class wrote subsequent reactions to his or her work. The novel, together with its many commentaries, critiques, sequels, abridgements, and adaptations, was published, printed, and diligently preserved for posterity. Later generations of scholars, both in China and elsewhere, have dutifully followed the paper trail. Books written by and for elites stand a fighting chance of surviving the ravages of time and thus selectively frame our understanding of the past. Popular oral traditions, handwritten liturgies, ritual manuals, performances, songs, and other ephemera, by contrast, have a way of vanishing without a trace.

As in early modern Europe, most people in late imperial China could not read. Evelyn Rawski estimates the average literacy rate in the Qing dynasty (1636–1912) at 30 to 45 percent for males and 2 to 10 percent for females.[18] These numbers, which are high compared to previous dynasties, include those with merely rudimentary or utilitarian reading levels. Benjamin Elman calculates that only 10 percent of the Chinese population had the linguistic training necessary to sit for the demanding civil service exams.[19] The vast majority of people, it is safe to say, were not reading long novels, let alone arcane scriptures or ritual manuals. Instead, most people learned about Xuanzang's adventures through stories and performances, the details of which were very rarely recorded, let alone preserved.

Even when vernacular written sources do survive, usually only by some fortuitous accident, their value is not always immediately apparent. Until relatively recently, Western sinologists shared Chinese scholars' passion for the belles lettres and showed scant interest in what they judged the cruder, more prosaic forms of cultural expression. The work of non-elites, particularly in the realm of religion, was dismissed or ignored as base superstition or ignorant attempts of uneducated peasants to emulate the higher arts. A focus on great books and great men naturally channeled scholarship on the Tang Monk's fantastical pilgrimage into the novel—its influences, its history, its author, its hidden philosophical meanings (or lack thereof)—and, to a lesser extent, the sophisticated literary and theatrical traditions the novel inspired.

Some of the most accomplished modern scholars of Chinese literature have applied their talents to these topics, producing a series of masterful studies on *Journey to the West*. The novel is now one of the most extensively studied works in the Chinese literary canon.[20] This ever-growing body of critical scholarship is invaluable, but it has had the unintended effect of overshadowing other forms of the narrative. The monumental status of the hundred-chapter novel marks it as *the* primary point of reference, but stories of Xuanzang's otherworldly pilgrimage have always circulated independent of the novel.

These little-known narratives and traditions are at the center of this book. There will be much to say about the novel, but my primary focus will be the broader complex of stories that relate Xuanzang's mythic travels to Western Heaven. To clearly differentiate these accounts from those found in the novel, I refer to the former by the title most often used in ritualized accounts: "Obtaining the Scriptures." Among this larger web of tangled and often overlapping narratives, the *Journey to the West* novel represents just one among many strands.

A second reason the ritual elements of Xuanzang's pilgrimage are not better known today has to do with the relatively marginal position these traditions occupy in the larger landscape of Chinese religious cultures. Unlike the major traditions of Buddhism and Daoism, with their voluminous canons, their elaborate doctrines and practices, their monastic and lay institutions, and their integration into the upper echelons of Chinese society, rituals involving Xuanzang and his pilgrimage were largely performed in rural villages by lay ritual specialists with no strong ties to monastic institutions or elite lay networks. Although accounts of Xuanzang's mythic pilgrimage first emerged in what we might call mainstream Buddhist contexts—monastic libraries, cave temples, and stupas—they took root and flourished primarily in the realm of "popular" religions.

Known in modern Mandarin by the neologism *minjian xinyang* 民間信仰 (the people's faith), and in English as "popular," "communal," "diffused," or "local" religion(s), these traditions are defined in opposition to their more centrally organized, institutionalized counterparts. They represent, in the words of David Palmer, "the more obscure, chaotic, ecstatic, localized, dispersed, marginal, feminine, and embodied religion, in contrast to the more public, ordered, central, masculine, civil, and government-oriented religion."[21]

Despite such distinctions, institutional and popular forms of religious expression—designated in the premodern period by binaries like "orthodox" (*zheng* 正) and "heterodox" (*xie* 邪)—never were neatly divided spheres but, rather, mutually dependent, complementary aspects of integrated, overarching cultural systems. Members of the aristocracy participated in the festivals, funerals, and other communal rituals that punctuated the rhythms of local life, just as the cosmologies, rituals, and mythic narratives created and maintained by the custodians of Buddhist, Daoist, and Confucian traditions affected and informed the lives of illiterate farmers. As part of a common cultural tradition, stories about Xuanzang and his otherworldly travels suffused all levels of Chinese society, but as far as we know, lay ritualists rather than ordained clerics or literati were the ones who performed ritual reenactments of his pilgrimage.

The label "popular religion," which I use for want of a better term, is an awkward and imprecise category. Not only does it suggest a sharp distinction between the cosmologies of elite and non-elite peoples, it also implies that communities across China adhered to a single, homogeneous system of belief and practice. Needless to say, the cultural traditions of coastal Fujian—the stories people told, the songs they sang, the rituals they performed, and the festivals they organized and attended—were distinct from those of the desert towns of Gansu or the mountain villages of Guizhou. To what extent did people in such far-flung places share a similar sense of the spirit world? Different versions of Xuanzang's mythic pilgrimage flourished throughout China as well as in the neighboring territories of Tibet, Mongolia, Korea, Japan, and Vietnam. The transmission, adoption, and adaptation of this and other mythic narratives and ritual structures across diverse geographic, linguistic, and ethnic lines suggests a degree of cultural continuity among people living in the broader Sinosphere. We might say that widely shared assumptions about ethical norms, cosmological structures, and ritual efficacy constitute, to borrow Steven Sangren's metaphor, a kind of shared language with multiple dialects. Such a language allows for infinite expressions, all of which remain distinct but still are largely intelligible within an overarching framework.[22] It is from this perspective that the many regionally distinct traditions involving Xuanzang's pilgrimage can be viewed as unique expressions constructed from a common store of symbolic forms.

As widespread as such expressions are, rituals involving Obtaining the Scriptures narratives are not well known outside of China. This may be because of their position on the periphery of more organized and integrated national cults. Transregional religious traditions often involve dedicated altars or shrines attended by committed adherents or, in some cases, ordained initiates. Their gods tend to communicate directly with devotees through possession and spirit writing, feature regularly in temple processions, and receive offerings on particular days of the year. In the imperial period, many such deities were awarded honorific titles by the court and were listed in *Canon of Sacrifices* (*Si dian* 祀典)—a register of orthodox deities endorsed by the state. The sanctified Xuanzang lacks this level of celebrity. He also is not ordinarily asked to confer wealth, to affect the weather, to heal the sick, to bestow children, or to ensure a good harvest—typical tasks for many major Chinese gods.

The Tang Monk thus does not neatly fit the mold of a conventional Chinese deity, but he is, nonetheless, tightly woven into multiple regional ritual traditions. For the faithful, he and his companions occupy pivotal positions in the heavenly pantheon and are possessed with a range of divine powers, which they can deploy on behalf of their devotees. While there is no single, static conception of the deified Xuanzang, in many traditions he mediates between the human and spirit realms, transmitting sacred texts to the human world in one direction and escorting the souls of the dead to the Pure Land in the other. Given the fraught nature of this transit, he and his fellow pilgrims typically are summoned to serve as guardians and escorts, protecting supplicants from demons and other dangers. For these reasons, devotees regularly reenact their pilgrimage during communal exorcistic festivals, collective and individual mortuary rites, and rituals involving the bestowal of divine texts. In the crowded popular pantheon, the Tang Monk might seem to cut an inconspicuous figure. But for many people in the past, as well as those in the present, the regular repetition of Xuanzang's pilgrimage—retracing the route, reenacting the travelers' trials and triumphs—is crucial for maintaining the proper relationship between humans, gods, and ghosts.

The existence and extent of these traditions will come as a surprise to most readers of *Journey to the West,* but they have not escaped the notice of scholars working in China and Taiwan. Over the past two decades, a series of path-breaking studies has introduced several new sources that situate the deified Xuanzang and his pilgrimage in an entirely new light.[23] Leading figures in this effort include Liu Shufen 劉淑芬, Hou Chong 侯沖, Cai Tieying 蔡鐵鷹, Ye Mingsheng 葉明生, Cao Lin 曹琳, and Zhu Hengfu 朱恒夫, though there are many others. Working variously with scripts, liturgies, ritual manuals, historical records, images, commentaries, oral traditions, and living communities, these scholars have shown that stories about Xuanzang occupy a prominent place in the performative and literary cultures of a range of regional communities. This book is deeply indebted to their pioneering work.

What's in a Name?

Even with the benefit of these new studies, my own efforts to track the disembodied Xuanzang across time and space ran up against two obstacles. The first is the diffuse and composite nature of the deified Xuanzang. Any attempt to document Xuanzang's afterlives risks reducing a vast, complex web of relations to a singular, self-contained figure. There is, of course, no one version of Xuanzang that endures unchanged through time, inhabiting imaginations and manifesting during rituals. There are, rather, multiple Xuanzangs, each with its own characteristics and agendas, each inextricably, often imperceptibly, entwined with an array of other deities, ritual traditions, and narrative forms. Claude Lévi-Strauss once observed that "every myth is by its very nature a translation," and myths involving Xuanzang's pilgrimage, which emerge from and merge with other hagiographies, scriptures, and legends, are a case in point.[24] Xuanzang manifests as a spirit guide in some ritual contexts, for instance, but traditions, narratives, and iconographies of psychopomps in China predate Xuanzang's assumption of this role by more than a millennium. Stories and performances of Xuanzang's efforts to liberate the dead are thus bound up with accounts of other divine intermediaries similarly committed to the salvation of spirits suffering in the netherworld. One could—and people often do—substitute one god for another without significantly altering the ritual. Explanatory accounts and appearances might differ, but the broad structure of the rite and its intended outcomes remain the same. As holds true for most Han Chinese depictions of the heavenly bureaucracy—including *Journey to the West*—a range of candidates can fill celestial offices. There are jobs that need doing; which deity performs which task is not terribly important, provided, of course, they perform it well.

The positions Xuanzang has occupied over the centuries—transmitter of divine texts, exorcist, spirit guide, prophet—are, therefore, not unique to him. Rather, he reprises established, iconic roles with their own histories, their own protocols, associations, and expectations. When Xuanzang is called to protect a community against demonic incursions, for example, he is conceived in a way that resonates with established exorcistic traditions, and his own identity is subtly remade in the process. A kind of confluence takes place, as Xuanzang and his story are incorporated into the hagiographies and story-cycles of other, functionally related deities, each expanding the capacities and narrative possibilities of the other. In thinking about Xuanzang's postmortem career, then, it is not enough to simply track the qualities of his cult and consider how representations of his pilgrimage have evolved over time. Given how little is currently known about these traditions, that kind of documentation remains valuable, and I attend to it in this book. But my broader goal is to investigate *why* Xuanzang acquired certain divine attributes—what was it about his story that compelled devotees to venerate him in these particular ways?—and *how* associations with certain ritual traditions in turn reshaped narratives about his life.

Xuanzang's postmortem identities are regularly reconceived in response to the needs and conditions of the moment, so they are not easily traced as linear or even accretive things. Such mutability is hardly unique to Xuanzang. The Finnish scholar Matti Kuusi once likened a poem to "the numerous strata of a burial mound in which many generations of men and their artefacts have been buried."[25] These burial mounds, he goes on, often have been plowed up by bulldozers. The same holds true for sacred narratives and ritual forms, but scholars have, nonetheless, attempted careful excavations of the hagiographies of Chinese deities.

Prasenjit Duara, writing about the cult of the deified Guan Yu, famously argued that versions of a god's narrative accrue over time, with earlier accounts underlying more recent adaptations. He called this process "superscription," highlighting its cumulative effect. Former versions of a deity's hagiography inform subsequent iterations, the whole contributing to a complex, richly textured narrative. "A symbol draws its power from its resonances (and sometimes its dissonances) in the culture, from the multiplicity of its often half-hidden meanings," according to Duara. "It is precisely because of the superscription over, not the erasure of, previous inscriptions that historical groups are able to expand old frontiers of meaning to accommodate their changing needs."[26] Like a palimpsest, portions of older texts, embedded with earlier ideas and interpretations, might be obscured over time, but they are never fully eradicated.

Some versions of the Obtaining the Scriptures story-cycle have, indeed, absorbed, expanded, and modified earlier accounts. The most prominent example of this process is surely the *Journey to the West* novel, and scholars have devoted a great deal of time and energy to sifting through the earlier strata of the novel's narratives. This is important work, but often it presumes the linear progression of a single master narrative that grows more complex over time. Such an approach is productive in some contexts but not in others. Cults tend not to be singular; deities and their hagiographies often exist in multiple forms, embedded in an array of narratives and contexts simultaneously. Paul Katz likens this heterogeneity and discontinuity to "punctuated evolution," whereby brief periods of diversification are followed by longer periods of stability.[27] When a cult does expand rapidly and assume new forms, the innovations do not always stem from a single cause, but can, Katz observes, be cogenerated. Various communities in different regions might nurture locally specific traditions centered on the same deity for their own particular reasons. The process is organic rather than organized, without any one authority dictating the standards of orthodoxy. Even in the case of highly standardized, state-sanctioned deities, there often is only an appearance of uniformity as different groups pursue their own idiosyncratic interests. In this varied and sometimes competitive context, the name of a deity may remain constant, but the characteristic of his or her cult will fluctuate according to the expectations, needs, and imaginations of diverse communities in particular places during specific historical moments.

This is certainly true of Xuanzang. Ritual traditions involving his mythic pilgrimage spread variously by means of texts, images, performances, and oral instructions. In the absence of a single master narrative, what these accounts share is a relatively simple and highly adaptable structure. Certain themes remain, if not constant, at least predominant, but communities were at liberty to make the story their own. Daoists might read the pilgrimage as a process for refining the elixir of immortality, for example. Buddhists could see it as an exposition on the realization of emptiness. Confucians might interpret it as a method for rectifying the mind. Writers of modern fiction could read it as a literary classic. Communists might recognize a process of revolutionary struggle, while their secular humanist comrades could envision an account of "human liberation from mystery and progress from the medieval world to the spirit of modernity."[28] New philosophical and political paradigms will surely inspire new readings. That is the beauty of a good story; it is easy to identify with. The meaning remains malleable, and audiences are always coauthors.

There is thus no single authentic message, no one authoritative interpretation of Xuanzang's pilgrimage. Constant reinvention keeps the story relevant as the very process of interpretation enlivens the story and reshapes the narrative in the image of the storyteller. As scholar of Greek mythology Sarah Johnston has noted, one of the reasons mythic heroes took on lives of their own "was precisely the fact that they could *not* be contained within any single diegetic world; they seeped beyond the boundaries of the individual myths that the poets told about them and flourished in the margins, nourished *by* particular narrators but never becoming the *property* of particular narrators."[29] Accounts of Xuanzang's journey to heaven, like all great myths and legends, are in the public domain. Anyone is free to reproduce or transform them as they see fit.

The decentralized, nonhierarchical dissemination of narratives and rituals calls to mind Gilles Deleuze and Félix Guattari's influential rhizomatic model of cultural production and transmission. Unlike the conventional image of trees that branch out from a single trunk, rhizomes have multiple points of connection, spreading underground and out of sight.[30] Traditions, according to this metaphor, similarly radiate out and, if severed or broken free from their source, can operate independently and give rise to new networks. Scholars have productively applied this model to Chinese social and religious systems, whose networks of informal relations often are composed of multiple nodes without a singular center.[31] In thinking about the evolution of Xuanzang's postmortem forms, however, the rhizome serves as a useful but imperfect analogy. Rhizomes, after all, are self-replicating and genetically homogeneous, whereas deities and their hagiographies evolve and spread not only by growth, replication, and adaptation but also through incorporation, mutation, and fusion.

We might, therefore, consider the histories of deities in the same way we think about the heritages of people. Just as we traditionally identify with a single surname, simplifying our ancestry and identity to a single strand in a nearly infinite web of interrelations, scholars have grown accustomed to tracing the history of a deity by tracking its names and titles through time. But genealogy is not the same as genetics. Individual deities are the progeny of innumerable couplings. The gods are promiscuous. Some absorb others, some combine to produce something new, and some split to form multiples. Hagiographies, likewise, are animated and informed by an array of events, tropes, characters, and plots. These move within, across, and between ostensibly distinct traditions, with each manifestation presenting a unique but always temporary arrangement. In a kind of natural selection of narrative, certain derivations will thrive while others will falter and die. As the historical Xuanzang was fond of pointing out, no condition endures indefinitely.

The notion of a singular, stable entity that persists through time is thus an illusion—albeit an often irresistible one. In this book, I often refer to the deified Xuanzang in the singular, but the reality is that multiple deities bearing the same or similar features always are adapting and evolving within the contexts of their particular environments. To link a deity's history to a name (or set of names) is to highlight coherence and stability at the expense of multiplicity and flux—a very un-Buddhist kind of approach.

Is it possible to acknowledge and appreciate this complexity without abandoning all attempts to study the historical evolution of a deity? The name "Xuanzang," after all, is not merely a floating signifier without *any* coherence preserved over time. Some qualities do endure; certain traits turn out to be dominant. Like the fabled ship of Theseus, the components of Xuanzang's iconography and hagiography inevitably change over time as each community and each generation cobbles together their own narratives from the materials at hand, but the broad outlines of his story retain a degree of continuity—a kind of family resemblance that remains recognizable even over centuries.

In this book, I focus on those traits that, although rarely perfectly reproduced, appear to define the deified Xuanzang, distinguishing him from other figures in the pantheon. These include the conviction that Xuanzang serves as an intermediary between the imperfect and dangerous human world and the perfect heavenly realm of buddhas and bodhisattvas. He has a reputation, maintained and strengthened through time, of guiding those who seek passage to the pure land and protecting his devotees from the ghosts and demons who would obstruct their progress. As an envoy of the Buddha, Xuanzang also is frequently summoned to convey divine texts and technologies to the people of China. These tasks, accomplished in the past, must be regularly repeated in the present. Xuanzang is thus on a perpetual pilgrimage, constantly cycling between heaven and earth for the benefit of all beings. While these overlapping roles do not encompass the entirety of Xuanzang's postmortem identities, they all were once broadly known in China. Some of these rituals still survive, though they are fading fast. The rarity of these traditions can make them seem like anomalies or strange mutations, but they are, in fact, core components of the deified Xuanzang's DNA.

The Myth of *Journey to the West*

The second challenge of this study is closely related to the first. It has to do with the fluidity of form and function in narratives like Obtaining the Scriptures. How should we read these stories? Ever since the Qing dynasty, literary versions of Xuanzang's otherworldly journey have been categorized as *xiaoshuo* 小說, a word that translates literally to "minor speech." Translators conventionally render *xiaoshuo* into English as "fiction," but it originally referred not to content that was less real or true than other historical accounts but merely to works that were not considered official or orthodox. According to David Rolston, "Fiction was . . . seen as a supplement to history, carrying historiographical techniques into new or unorthodox realms. The fiction writer was the 'historian of the unhistoried.'"[32] In the modern era, Obtaining the Scriptures narratives, especially *Journey to the West*, have been described either as fiction—in the seventeenth-century European sense of literature composed of events and characters that are entirely and obviously imaginary—or as folklore or fairy tale in the vein of Aesop or the Brothers Grimm.

In this book, however, I treat these narratives as myth, defined not in the popular pejorative sense of a false or intentionally deceptive story but, following Wendy Doniger, as "a story that is sacred to and shared by a group of people who find their most important meanings in it; it is a story believed to have been composed in the past about an event in the past, or, more rarely, in the future, an event that continues to have meaning in the present because it is remembered; it is a story that is part of a larger group of stories."[33]

Unlike folklore and fairy tales, whose anonymous characters tend to have generic qualities, myths typically relate the dramas of named figures with distinct histories and personalities. The protagonists in myths often have elaborate hagiographies. They also may have, as in the case of Xuanzang, a verifiable historical basis. While works of fiction depict events that both the author and the audience know never occurred, myths relate a sacred *history*. The figures they feature usually are understood to have existed in the distant past and, in many cases, to still exist in the present. Myths are, moreover, collective works, not the property of any single author. If the so-called orthodox histories (*zheng shi* 正史) of China were "written by officials for officials," mythic narratives were composed by ordinary people for ordinary people.[34] They drew on themes, character types, and imagery already in broad circulation. As accessible and affective accounts of the world, they were no less real and no more imaginary than officially sanctioned forms of history.

To be sure, the historical Xuanzang's translations, his *Record,* and his *Biography* kept his memory alive for later generations, but it was the mythologized accounts of his epic pilgrimage that transcended the mundane, specific details of his life to evolve into archetypes. Such stories fit a recognizable, if not predictable, pattern. Nearly all the recurring character types famously identified by the Russian folklorist Vladimir Propp, for instance, have their corollaries in Obtaining the Scriptures narratives.[35] There is the *dispatcher* (Emperor Taizong) who sends the *hero* (Xuanzang) on a mission to obtain some *prize* (scriptures). The hero is aided by a team of *helpers* (Sun Wukong, Zhu Bajie, Sha Monk, and the Dragon Horse) and a *donor* (the bodhisattva Avalokiteśvara), who conveys magical implements and subjects the hero to a series of tests. There are also the requisite *villains* (ghosts and demons), who try to block the hero's progress. The characters and their respective roles are recognizable across time and place even if their specific identities are unfamiliar to outsiders. Indeed, Henk Versnel, describing the recurring theme of "primordial crisis" in ancient Greek and Roman myths, could just as easily have been summarizing the basic plot structure of Obtaining the Scriptures narratives: "leaving the relative safety of the familiar environment—setting out for sheer superhuman enterprises and unspeakable dangers in a marginal landscape marked by monsters and every sort of nameless terror, often to the very limits of death—returning in triumph."[36]

Xuanzang was not Odysseus, but stories of heroic men embarking on dangerous journeys encapsulate fundamental human experiences, anxieties, and desires. The transformation of historically specific individuals and events into idealized character types and narrative arcs opens up accounts like Obtaining the Scriptures to diverse communities and cultures. One need not be Buddhist or Han Chinese to identify with Xuanzang and his story. We are all moving through space and time, navigating difficult passages, lured forward by the prospect of some reward. This basic human experience is surely one of the reasons why accounts of epic pilgrimages resonated with people in the premodern, rural villages of Shanxi province as well as those in the theaters of midtown Manhattan. People everywhere, it seems, are able to see themselves reflected in these kinds of stories.

Accessibility and mutability, however, do not homogenize meaning; they multiply it, and it is in this regard that context becomes critical. *Journey to the West* is not just a Chinese variation on the *Rāmāyaṇa* (despite some arguments to the contrary). Related in different settings, even the same myth will function in very different ways. A scene from Xuanzang's otherworldly pilgrimage enacted at a funeral, for example, carries a completely different valence from the same scene performed by students in a high school drama club. Who Xuanzang is at any given moment— what he symbolizes, what he is capable of—depends on who it is that invokes or embodies him. To the extent that the audience animates the story, devotees determine the qualities of Xuanzang and infuse his westward journey with meaning.

The message may be inherent in the medium, but the contexts in which Obtaining the Scriptures narratives were depicted, recited, and performed prior to the twentieth century are often obscure. The historical record is simply too sparse when it comes to non-elite, vernacular traditions. In those cases where intentions are explicitly known or can be circumstantially inferred, however, Xuanzang's pilgrimage frequently manifests as mythic history and/or ritual process. The French philosopher and sinologist François Jullien once remarked that "the novel *The Journey to the West* is superior, from the standpoint of the revelation of religious intuition, to all the canons of Buddhism and Daoism."[37] The compelling characters, the dramatic plot, the humor, and the philosophical depth of the novel, in other words, constitute a complete and coherent cosmological and soteriological system. For many readers, *Journey to the West* was not merely engrossing and accessible, it was revelatory. It had, accordingly, a range and a reach that exceeded that of most canonical Buddhist or Daoist texts, which tended to require rather than inspire faith. Narratives of Xuanzang's pilgrimage were appealingly ambiguous, offering up a range of moral and ideological possibilities. As we will see, they could be marshaled in support of everything from self-restraint to armed insurrection.

Audiences naturally refracted these narratives through the lens of their experiences, just as regular encounters with these and other stories molded their experiences. Versions of Xuanzang's mythic pilgrimage circulated in print, oral accounts, songs, images, and rituals in registers ranging from solemn to raucous, simple to spectacular, recreational to ceremonial. People experienced these stories in different forms, in different places, and in different contexts over the course of their lives. Repeated exposure to popular narratives like Obtaining the Scriptures reinforced a commitment to their content.

Engrossing narratives are easily internalized and infuse a person's sense of the world and its possibilities.[38] Repetitive reading, hearing, discussing, seeing, and imagining scenes and characters from stories trains us to experience and interpret the world in particular ways. Joshua Landy, a scholar of comparative literature, refers to the effect of narrative on perception as a "formative circle," noting how carefully constructed, engaging works of literature shape readers' sensibilities. Such works "fine-tune our mental capacities . . . They present themselves as spiritual exercises (whether sacred or profane), spaces for prolonged and active encounters that serve, over time, to hone our abilities and thus, in the end, to help us become who we are."[39] Conceptions of history, cosmology, agency, morality, and divinity are forged and nurtured through narrative, and few narratives in China have been as influential and as formative as Obtaining the Scriptures.

During the late Qing and early Republican periods, officials often lamented the fact that those who venerated the Tang Monk lacked the sense to distinguish between fantasy and reality, but the insistence on such subjectively delineated and value-laden categories may be the real fiction. The mythic qualities endemic to Xuanzang and his story are both as real and as fantastic as other stories we tell ourselves about who we are, where we come from, and what it is we are supposed to be doing. Like all good stories, accounts of Xuanzang obtaining the scriptures offer a means for making sense of what might otherwise seem a senseless existence. They conjure a world in manageable miniature, a self-contained, ordered place where the forces of good may be threatened but always prevail. It is a comforting prospect, an appealing microcosm to project onto the larger, messier, morally ambiguous realm of ordinary life.

Overview

Temporally, this book covers a period of roughly eight hundred years, beginning with the first appearances of Xuanzang as a deity and extending into the modern era. Although my approach is largely historical and text based, I touch on several contemporary ritual traditions involving the pilgrimage of the Tang Monk and his divine companions. These traditions are not perfect replicas of earlier rites, of course, but they do represent the tail end of a continuum that stretches back several centuries. As such, modern exorcistic and mortuary rites are heirs to traditions that once were more widespread. The ritual forms that survive give some sense of how these traditions might have operated in the past at the same time they demonstrate how Xuanzang's story continues to convey meaning in the present.

Geographically, this book spans much of mainland China, with some excursions into Central Asia, Taiwan, Korea, Japan, and Southeast Asia. Source materials are similarly wide-ranging. They include murals, sculptures, scripts, prompt books, commentaries, precious scrolls, spirit books, songs, liturgies, ethnographic reports, official and unofficial histories, and ritual manuals. Given the long historical sweep, the diversity of regional cultures, and the heterogeneous nature of the sources, there is a risk of sacrificing breadth for depth. While each of the many traditions described here is worthy of stand-alone studies, here I merely attempt to locate some of the broader patterns and continuities that tie individual instances of Xuanzang's legend to larger, collective processes.

As broad as this coverage is, it is far from comprehensive. I have limited my discussions to those instances where Xuanzang is depicted or made manifest as a deity, paying particular attention to ritual traditions that reenact his mythic pilgrimage. The specificity of that focus means that many other tangentially related issues are not addressed here. The various ways people have venerated and memorialized Xuanzang in East Asia as the translator of the *Perfection of Wisdom* literature and as a patriarch of the Yogācāra tradition, for example, fall outside the scope of this study. The same is true of his influence on the European archaeologists, explorers, Indologists, and Buddhologists and his role in the political machinations of contemporary China. Many of the most familiar aspects of the *Journey to the West* tradition—the content of the novel itself and the operas and images it has inspired—also are treated only in passing.

The history of the novel and its enduring influence, however, do have a direct bearing on the ritual forms at the core of this book. In the modern era, interpretations of *Journey to the West* that emerged during the twentieth century have shaped most peoples' understanding of Obtaining the Scriptures narratives. The first chapter of this book, then, begins with an overview of the reception and reinterpretation of the novel in the late nineteenth and the early twentieth centuries. I focus on the writings of two groups of people active in China during this period. The first are American, British, and French missionaries and scholars living primarily in southeastern China. In their publications and correspondences, these men consistently described *Journey to the West* as a kind of scripture, documenting with fascination (and sometimes disdain) the veneration of the Tang Monk and his mythical companions as deities by ordinary and, according to many missionaries, irredeemably ignorant peasants. The second group of writings come from Chinese intellectuals and officials who bemoaned the pernicious influence of the *Journey to the West* novel on the common people and who recommended the text and its performance be either banned or radically reformed.

The efforts of both Western missionaries and Chinese intellectuals encouraged and eventually entrenched a new reading of *Journey to the West* that denied or downplayed its religious significance. What emerged, instead, was a book framed as a strictly aesthetic, secular work of fiction. This is the view that informed Arthur Waley's celebrated *Monkey: Folk Novel of China,* still one of the most influential abridgements of the novel in English. The modern reception of *Journey to the West* in Europe, America, and East Asia as a literary classic rather than as hagiography or scripture is thus closely linked to the forces of globalization and the ensuing social-political reforms instituted in China during the late imperial and early Republican periods. As a small part of this much larger process, the Tang Monk was transformed from a formidable deity into a fictional character.

From these proximate contexts, subsequent chapters move back in time to consider how stories of Xuanzang's pilgrimage were initially embellished and woven into larger tapestries of mythic narratives and ritual traditions. Chapter 2 explores the early apotheosis of Xuanzang in China, tracing his evolution from court cleric to disembodied spirit. By the twelfth century, texts, paintings, and sculptures across China depicted Xuanzang as an intermediary who crossed into the realm of buddhas and bodhisattvas to acquire and deliver divine scriptures. The earliest examples of nascent Obtaining the Scriptures narratives come from a series of bas-relief sculptures and murals at Buddhist cave sites in north, northwestern, and southwestern China. These works show a beatified Xuanzang together with an attendant, in either monkey or human form, and a horse laden with luminous scriptures. In all but one case, this trio stands in the presence of the bodhisattva Avalokiteśvara (Ch. Guanyin). The meaning and function of these scenes remain matters of debate, but circumstantial evidence suggests they were commissioned as offerings to the deceased ancestors of the caves' donors.

Around this same time but seventeen hundred miles distant, in the coastal cities of southeastern China, textual accounts described Xuanzang's passage from China through a demon-infested wasteland to meet the Buddha in Western Heaven. In these vernacular stories, Xuanzang brings the scriptures he receives to China on the fifteenth day of the seventh lunar month: the date of the annual communal mortuary rite known as the Ghost Festival. The special qualities attributed to Xuanzang in these early texts and images—his direct access to buddhas and bodhisattvas, his and his companions' ability to ward off demonic attacks, and his transmission of texts with the power to protect the living and liberate the dead—would remain central to later ritual traditions centered on his pilgrimage.

The ritual applications that are obliquely implied in the earliest sources grow more explicit in later periods. The third chapter considers the exorcistic qualities of the deified Xuanzang and his fellow pilgrims. Today, Xuanzang's mythic pilgrimage is reenacted in ritual dances throughout China and is recited as liturgy in some areas of Jiangsu province. While each tradition is unique in its particulars, they all share the same goal of protecting communities from demons, diseases, and other dangers. Xuanzang and his companions famously subjugated or destroyed a host of ghosts and fiends over the course of their travels in the past, and they are consequently recalled to perform the same tasks for their devotees in the present.

Xuanzang—both the historical figure and the deified saint—is perhaps best known as a transmitter of exotic objects. The seventh-century monk is credited with introducing a stunning range of foreign products to China, from texts and images to tea leaves, bamboo seeds, chicken eggs, tree saplings, and rhinoceros horns.[40] Association with Xuanzang served to authenticate the Indian origin of a thing. In the context of ritual, the divine provenance of a text, implement, or procedure also was a testament to its efficacy, and accounts of the Tang Monk's pilgrimage to "Western Heaven" to acquire and transmit the teachings and technologies of buddhas and bodhisattvas made compelling origin stories.

This was particularly true for mortuary rites, the topic of chapter 4. Throughout contemporary China and Taiwan, alternate and abbreviated versions of Obtaining the Scriptures story-cycles are chanted or performed as part of elaborate funeral ceremonies. The explanation given both in liturgical manuscripts and by contemporary funeral troupes for the incorporation of Xuanzang's pilgrimage into these ceremonies is two-fold. First, Xuanzang successfully crossed from China to the western Pure Land. As an experienced and reliable guide, he and his retinue are summoned to protect and lead the spirits of the dead as they pass from the world of the living to a heavenly paradise. Second, Xuanzang obtained the means and methods for liberating the dead from purgatory and securing their rebirth in the Pure Land. These techniques are now deployed during mortuary rites and Xuanzang's contribution to the rituals are accordingly acknowledged. The modern funerary rituals featuring the Tang Monk and his companions that can be seen today in Taiwan and elsewhere thus belong to a long tradition of identifying the ultimate destination of Xuanzang's pilgrimage as a heavenly paradise located in the distant west.

The fifth and final chapter surveys several precious scrolls, commentaries, and court documents dating from the sixteenth through the early twentieth centuries. Many of the scriptures and liturgies of lay salvationist associations depict Xuanzang as a divine prophet sent by the Buddha for the salvation of humankind. The leaders of these movements drew heavily from orthodox Buddhist and Daoist teachings as well as from local ritual and performative traditions. The scriptures they authored were presented as celestial dispensations and likened to the cache of Buddhist texts that Xuanzang brought back from India in the seventh century. Some of the patriarchs of these new sects claimed to be Xuanzang's reincarnation, and many of their teachings prescribe practices whereby devotees can transmute their ordinary, mortal bodies into the extraordinary, immortal form of the Tang Monk. In these versions of the narrative, several of which predate the publication of the *Journey to the West* novel, Xuanzang's pilgrimage becomes an allegory for the transformation and liberation of the body and mind.

The conviction that Xuanzang and his companions were deities capable of manifesting in the bodies of human beings implicated Obtaining the Scriptures narratives in some of the sectarian uprisings that threatened the imperial court during the late Qing dynasty. Some salvationist sect leaders and members claimed to be possessed and empowered by the spirits of Xuanzang and his companions who had returned to earth to dispel the demons of the present age and usher in a new era of peace and prosperity. In these highly charged and sometimes bloody confrontations, Xuanzang's journey was understood in prophetic and apocalyptic terms as mythic battles from the narrative were reenacted in real time in an effort to overthrow Manchu rule. Such uprisings contributed to a growing unease among government officials that Obtaining the Scriptures were sources of civil unrest. This was the context in which Christian missionaries and Chinese intellectuals reacted against popular belief in the power of Xuanzang's otherworldly pilgrimage at the turn of the twentieth century, the topic of the first chapter. Like many long journeys, this book concludes where it began.

A few years after the historical Xuanzang died, his friend and a former member of his translation team, the eminent monk Daoxuan 道宣 (596–667), reportedly had a vision. A spirit who identified himself as the son of the celestial general Skanda appeared and explained that he was now the deity in charge of ghosts and spirits. After castigating Daoxuan for his poor grasp of the Buddhist teachings, the apparition pointed out that Xuanzang's understanding was, by contrast, flawless. Because of Xuanzang's good work over the course of many incarnations, he was now dwelling in Tuṣita Heaven at the inner court of the future buddha Maitreya. Xuanzang, the spirit revealed, would soon become a saint (*sheng* 聖) and would never again be reborn among humans.[41]

As far as prophecies go, this one was only partially accurate. It is true that Xuanzang was sanctified after his death, but he has not remained quietly in Tuṣita Heaven. As a deity endowed with the power to subdue demons and to pass between heaven and hell, he repeatedly returns to the human realm. Xuanzang, greatest of pilgrims, remains on the move, passing through strange territories to transmit the divine teachings of the Buddha and alleviate the suffering of all beings. What follows is a partial record of his postmortem travels.

1 Fiction

We like strange stories but believe only a few.

—Adam Gopnik, *Angels and Ages*

In Arthur Waley's introduction to his abridged English translation of *Journey to the West*, he explains that the story was inspired by the real travels of the seventh-century Buddhist monk Xuanzang.[1] It was only later that the historical events of Xuanzang's life were spun into a cycle of fantastic legends culminating, more than nine centuries later, in the *Journey to the West* novel. Waley describes the novel as a long fairy tale comprised of folklore, allegory, religion, history, anti-bureaucratic satire, and poetry. The Xuanzang character in the story has been so transformed that he is no longer recognizable as a historical figure. Instead, he has become, according to Waley, an allegory for "the ordinary man, blundering anxiously through the difficulties of life."[2] Waley's widely celebrated work, first issued in 1942 under the title *Monkey*, included an introduction by prominent Chinese scholar and statesman Hu Shih (1891–1962). Hu Shih famously characterized the book as a work of "good humor, profound nonsense, good-natured satire and delightful entertainment."[3] In the United States, the book was accordingly promoted as a lighthearted, amusing classic of Chinese literature. A review in *The Nation* described it approvingly as "a combination of picaresque novel, fairy tale, fabliau, Mickey Mouse, Davy Crockett, and *Pilgrim's Progress*."[4] Waley's translation was praised as eloquent and accessible. Foreign-sounding names were made more familiar; the Tang Monk's cannibalistic companion, the demonic pig Zhu Bajie, became "Pigsy"; Sha Monk became "Sandy"; and Sun Wukong became the eponymous "Monkey." Other partial English translations of the novel were published before and after *Monkey*, but none of these ever has rivaled the popularity of Waley's abridgement. *Monkey* has remained in print for eighty years and is still a staple of Chinese literature courses in anglophone universities. Generations of college students and casual readers have enjoyed the book as an imaginative comic fantasy, the Chinese equivalent of *Don Quixote*.

The same year Waley's *Monkey* was published in England, very different versions of the same story were read and performed throughout China. In some areas, accounts of Xuanzang's pilgrimage served as scripture, recited to protect communities or to help the dead cross from the earthly to the heavenly realm. In rural villages, masked ritual specialists dressed as the figures from *Journey to the West* performed exorcistic dances to drive away demons and ghosts from homes and fields. In small temples scattered across mainland China, Taiwan, Singapore, and Malaysia, Sun Wukong descended into the bodies of spirit mediums and spoke through their mouths.[5] Scenes from the story were painted on temple walls and carved on pillars. Entire temples and shrines were devoted Sun Wukong and Zhu Bajie, and the spirits of all five pilgrims were summoned to observe and participate in a range of public and private rites. As readers in the United States were reading the novel as exotic, entertaining fiction, many people in China understood it either as a liturgical text or as a roster of guardian spirits and dangerous demons. For these people, the Tang Monk and his companions were deities, not Disney characters.

Waley, to be fair, had not witnessed any of this. An autodidact, he taught himself to read and translate classical Chinese and Japanese poetry and literature, but he never visited East Asia and did not speak Chinese or Japanese. He did, however, have an abiding appreciation for the literary traditions of China and Japan—a rare empathy in the midst of the anti-Asian prejudice rampant in Europe and the United States during WWII. Waley had access to earlier translations and summaries of some sections of *Journey to the West*, which by 1942 had been available, first in French and later in German and English, for over eighty years. He was, therefore, aware that his translation situated the novel in a new—and in his view more accurate—context.

Prior Western translations and synopses of *Journey to the West* had categorized the text variously as folklore, fairy tale, or mythology, but most commentators were in agreement about a few crucial details. First, they accepted the conventional attribution of the novel to a Yuan dynasty (1271–1368) Daoist priest named Qiu Changchun 丘長春 (a.k.a. Qiu Chuji 丘處機, 1148–1227).[6] Second, they recognized that the narrative played an influential role in the popular religious cultures of China. And third, they lamented that many Chinese regarded the account as factual rather than fictional. Waley's *Monkey*, in contrast, framed the work as a literary masterpiece. The real author of *Journey to the West*, he revealed to his English readers, was not a Daoist priest but a scholar and poet named Wu Chengʼen 吳承恩, who lived sometime between 1500 and 1582. The allegorical elements of the book, moreover, were purely psychological. The characters were not deities but represented qualities like "the instability of genius," "physical appetites, brute strength," and "whole-heartedness." For Waley, *Journey to the West* was nothing more and nothing less than the creative expression of a gifted writer who seamlessly blended "beauty with absurdity" and "profundity with nonsense."[7]

Whether he realized it or not, Waley's folksy, funny, and earthy *Monkey* was taking sides in a centuries-old debate in China regarding the nature and value of vernacular novels like *Journey to the West*. Were these books reflections of religious belief, or were they amusing diversions intended only for entertainment? Did their fantastic stories of gods and ghosts, rebels and bandits undermine social order, or did they constitute valuable contributions to China's literary and artistic heritage? By presenting *Monkey* as fiction in the vein of early modern European novels, Waley indelibly shaped the way generations of Western readers would conceive of Xuanzang and interpret *Journey to the West*.

Not until Anthony Yu (1938–2015) published his complete, four-volume translation of the text in the late 1970s and early 1980s would the depth of the novel's religious symbolism begin to be appreciated. Yu undertook his translation in part to "rectify the distorted picture provided by Arthur Waley's justly popular abridgement" and to "redress the imbalance of emphasis championed by Dr. Hu Shi."[8] In his lengthy and erudite introduction, Yu presented a careful analysis of the allegorical elements woven throughout the book. By that time, though, the die had been cast. Although Yu's annotated translation and his subsequent studies of the religious significance of *Journey to the West* changed the way many scholars and specialists read and thought about the novel, these insights have been slow to reach the general public.[9] Readability often trumps accuracy, and Waley's *Monkey* still vastly outsells Yu's own abridgement of the novel, *Monkey and the Monk*.

Generations of Americans and Europeans have read Waley's *Monkey*. The original English version was subsequently translated into Spanish, Swedish, German, Dutch, French, and Italian. Those who have not read some version of the book probably are familiar with one or more of the many literary adaptations, television shows, cartoons, or theatrical productions inspired by Waley's translation. In the United States, Sun Wukong even appeared on *Sesame Street* in the 1980s. The great puppeteer Carol Spinney, who played Big Bird, dubbed the Monkey King "the Bugs Bunny of China." My own kids, growing up in southeastern Michigan, were taught the story in elementary school and became fans of an Australian-made adaptation on Netflix. Even people with only the vaguest impressions of *Journey to the West* and its plot know Monkey as a kind of trickster figure and the Tang Monk as a well-intentioned but ill-equipped everyman.

It is no accident that accounts of the Tang Monk's pilgrimage now are presented as works of fiction and fantasy. This packaging is part of a concerted campaign to reframe the story as an entirely secular fable. Subsequent chapters of this book address the deification of Xuanzang and the emergence of rituals centered on his pilgrimage—the very traditions modern critics either consciously effaced or reflexively ignored. In this chapter, I consider two distinct but interrelated processes that culminated in Waley's *Monkey*. The first is the early history of translations of *Journey to the West* into European languages. Waley's abridgement marked an important turning point in a long tradition of interpreting the novel for Western audiences. Prior to Waley, most translators remarked, with either curiosity or exasperation, on the novel's influence on popular religious practice and belief. Following Waley, however, the novel was consistently portrayed as a work of fiction, and its religious imagery was downplayed or dismissed as inconsequential. The second and more influential process was spearheaded by late-nineteenth- and early-twentieth-century Chinese intellectuals who sought to enlist *Journey to the West* in their vision of a new, modern, and secular China. The assessments of these scholars and officials, influenced to a degree by Western missionaries, directly informed Waley's reading of *Journey to the West* and established an interpretive framework for the Tang Monk and his otherworldly travels that remains conventional to this day.

Both Western translators and Chinese reformers were concerned about the corrosive effect stories about the Tang Monk and his companions appeared to be having on the people of China. They were disturbed by the power fictional characters held over their devotees. The work of men like Hu Shih and Arthur Waley belonged to a broader effort to rein in that power and to transform disruptive, potentially dangerous deities into harmless fictional characters. But as all readers of *Journey to the West* know, the Tang Monk and his band of pilgrims are not so easily contained.

Translating *Journey to the West*

M. Théodore Pavie (1811–1896) introduced *Journey to the West* to the Western world in 1857. Pavie, a restless and gifted polymath and professor of Sanskrit at the Collège de France, had traveled widely but, like Waley, had never been to China.[10] He was, nevertheless, intrigued by the myths and legends of China, because he felt that popular stories, rather than the official histories and classical texts produced by and for the elite, were the most authentic expressions of the common Chinese worldview.[11] In the introduction to his "Étude Sur le Sy-Yéou-Tchin-Tsuén, Roman Bouddhique Chinois" (Study on the *Xiyou zhenquan*, a Chinese Buddhist Novel), Pavie argued that works like *Journey to the West*, although dismissed by European sinologists as unrefined and inconsequential, preserved accounts that were eagerly embraced by a people long subjected to a strict, dogmatic philosophical regime. Just a few years earlier, Goethe had concluded that Chinese culture was characterized by admirable moderation, and that Chinese literature was concerned only with "what is moral and proper," but Pavie saw the stringently rational, austerely moral Confucian tradition as stifling.[12] Supernatural stories like those recorded in *Journey to the West* thus provided a necessary counterbalance. Echoing Marx, Pavie explained that Buddhist novels "intoxicate as with opium the Chinese populations gathered in the cities and huddled in the countryside." Like a drug or a dream, these enchanting fables transported the oppressed to a more colorful, more bearable world.[13]

Pavie's very loose translation focused on the opening chapters of the novel, which relate the birth and early life of Sun Wukong. He relied on an edition of the text—*The True Meaning of the Journey to the West*—that included a commentary by the late seventeenth-century Daoist master Chen Shibin 陳士斌 (fl. 1696).[14] At the end of each chapter, Chen Shibin appended an interpretation of the narrative as an esoteric guide to the practice of internal alchemy as taught by the Complete Perfection (Quanzhen) tradition of Daoism. These highly coded commentaries were not included in Pavie's translation, and he may not have realized the explicitly Daoist nature of the edition he was reading. Even so, he had every reason to conclude that *Journey to the West* was a wellspring of popular Chinese belief.

Pavie's intuitions about the religious relevance of the narrative would later be borne out by his compatriot, the French Jesuit missionary Henri Doré (1859–1931). Unlike Pavie, Doré had spent much of his adult life living and traveling in China. He set himself the task of documenting the "superstitions" of the people he encountered, and he was by turns fascinated and appalled by what he observed. In the eighth installment of his sixteen-volume opus *Recherches sur les Superstitions en Chine,* Doré included a section on "Buddhist Worthies and Saintly Monks." There, he noted that images depicting the characters from *Journey to the West,* which he described as a Daoist work that dramatized the introduction of Indian Buddhist texts to China, were "printed and distributed by the million and there is not a single pagan family that has not one or two of them pasted up in the home."[15] Doré added that some of the figures from the novel, particularly the monkey Sun Wukong, even were treated as gods and worshiped in temples.

Around the same time Doré was encountering the Tang Monk and Sun Wukong in shrines and temples in mainland China, George Taylor, a lighthouse keeper stationed on the southern coast of Taiwan, was likewise marveling that even educated men did not seem to realize that *Journey to the West* was a work of fiction. "Grave scholars," Taylor reported, "have been actually known to ask travelled acquaintances, if ever in their journeyings they had seen such scenes and peoples as are described in this work."[16] Convinced of the importance of what he described as Chinese "folk lore," Taylor published one of the earliest partial English translations of *Journey to the West* in 1887.[17]

Taylor was a customs official with a personal interest in the cultures of Taiwan and China, but many later translators of *Journey to the West* were Protestant missionaries more concerned with the imperiled state of Chinese souls. Proselytizing efforts in China accelerated after the signing of the Convention of Peking (Beijing tiaoyue 北京條約) in 1860, which gave missionaries the legal right to live and work throughout the country. Protestant missionaries, the vast majority of whom were British or American citizens, flooded into China, increasing in number from roughly fifty in 1860 to nearly two thousand five hundred just forty years later.[18] Some of these missionaries read popular Chinese works like *Journey to the West* as a means of understanding, in the words of the English Methodist George T. Candlin, how "religious beliefs have lived in the Chinese mind."[19] Candlin and his fellow evangelists knew that the doctrines of Buddhism and Daoism were recorded in canonical scriptures and commentaries, but, like Pavie, they recognized that vernacular works spoke to much larger audiences and played an outsized role in shaping popular belief. *Journey to the West* and other works of supernatural fiction, Candlin argued, offered unmediated access to the "inextricably twisted jungle-forest of superstition which chokes and shadows the Chinese mind."[20] To understand the strange faith of potential converts, missionaries would need to understand and refute the false gods and demons that populated works like *Journey to the West*.

The danger posed by this kind of literature, according to many Western observers, was that most people in China were unable to distinguish reverie from reality. This childlike ignorance was particularly worrisome to a Presbyterian missionary from Kentucky named Samuel Isett Woodbridge Sr. (1856–1926). By the time the reverend Woodbridge published his translation of the tenth and eleventh chapters of *Journey to the West* in 1895, he had been living in China for thirteen years— long enough to form some trenchant opinions about Chinese culture. In the introduction to his translation, which he titled the *Golden-Horned Dragon King* (named after the dragon in the novel whose beheading results in Emperor Taizong's brief sojourn in hell), Woodbridge complained: "While comparatively few people study Confucius, all classes, men and women, old and young, rich and poor, eagerly devour and digest stories like the 'Golden-Horned Dragon King.' For centuries this assimilation has been going on until the popular thought has crystallized in the most grotesque and inconceivable shape."[21] Through their long immersion in imaginary realms, the readers of Chinese novels had come to see the world refracted through the distorted lens of bizarre fiction and fable. Woodbridge blamed Buddhist and Daoist priests for propagating these stories and thereby corroding the foundations of Chinese society. "One can truly believe," he wrote, "that certain deficiencies of character in the men and women of China are due to the fright they receive when their parents first took them as little children to the city temples. The tenets of Buddhism and Taoism, their ethical teaching and moral sayings, may be very refined and admirable, but the practical effect is degrading to human life."[22]

Acerbic critiques of Buddhist and Daoist clerics by Protestant missionaries were nothing new, of course, but Woodbridge was pointing out that people were indoctrinated into systems of belief through immersion in popular culture—vernacular fiction, images, stories, songs, and theater. Through constant exposure, people came to believe the stories in *Journey to the West,* Woodbridge wrote, just "as thoroughly as we do the history of George Washington."[23] But whereas George Candlin maintained a degree of optimism that the people of China, if properly nurtured, would eventually embrace Christianity, Samuel Woodbridge, after reading *Journey to the West,* appears to have lost all hope. Superstition had blinded the Chinese to the truth and irreversibly impaired their character. "If their objects of worship are confessedly so dishonest," he wondered, "what can we expect from the Chinese but craftiness and deceit in every department of life?"[24]

Not every missionary who encountered *Journey to the West* saw it as a sign of intellectual torpor and moral decay. Some, like the Reverend James Ware (1859–1913), in fact, detected the divine traces of Christianity in the novel. From his home base in Shanghai, Ware, an English missionary who had lived in China since 1880, was employed by the American Bible Society to revise the Chinese translations of the Old and New Testaments that missionaries distributed.[25] In his spare time, Ware also translated Chinese literature and poetry into English. Given his immersion in biblical texts, it is no surprise that his translations of some passages from *Journey to the West* seem to be lifted straight out of the King James Bible. ("He who subdueth his body, shall be exalted; and he who mortifieth his body, shall have his body preserved.")[26] Ware's turn to biblical language and imagery, however, was not merely stylistic. He suspected that *Journey to the West* contained hidden references to biblical scripture.[27] Ware never claimed *Journey to the West* was actually authored by a Christian, but he was intrigued by what he perceived as the Christian message concealed in the work. He considered that, perhaps, the novel and the Bible derived from some common source. Ware noted that *Journey to the West* was sometimes categorized as a "leisure book," but he argued that such a characterization was misleading. The book may be full of fantastic ghosts, demons, and spirits, he explained, but "it contains no more than the average Chinaman really believes to exist, and his belief in them is so firm, that from the cradle to the grave he lives and moves and has his being in reference to them."[28] In Ware's view, *Journey to the West* was, in terms of both influence and content, strikingly similar to Christian scripture.

Just a few years after James Ware published his partial translation and interpretation of *Journey to the West,* a Welsh Baptist minister living in Shanghai made what he would later describe as a "most momentous discovery." Timothy Richard (1845–1919) had been working to spread the gospel in China through translation and relief work for over forty years. To be successful in establishing Christianity in China, he felt he needed to steep himself in Chinese culture. Richard thus wore his hair in a queue, dressed in Chinese robes, and went by the Chinese name Li Timo-tai 李提摩太.[29] He also made a point of familiarizing himself with popular Chinese books, and it was while reading *Journey to the West* that Richard finally confirmed what he had long suspected: Chinese Buddhism was, in fact, a vestige of Nestorian Christianity.

Richard decided to translate and publish an abridged version of *Journey to the West* to share this good news. In the longer-is-better style of the day, he titled his translation:

A JOURNEY TO HEAVEN

BEING

A CHINESE EPIC AND ALLEGORY

DEALING WITH

The Origin of the Universe: The Evolution of Monkey
to Man: The Evolution of Man to the Immortal:

AND

Revealing the Religion, Science, and Magic,
which moulded the Life

OF

THE MIDDLE AGES OF CENTRAL ASIA

And which underlie the civilization of the Far East
to this day.

By

CH'IU CH'ANG CH'UN. A.D. 1208–1288,

Born 67 years before Dante

Richard's unwieldy title explicitly likens *Journey to the West* to Dante's *Divine Comedy*, not just because both were epic vernacular accounts of man's journey from the depths of hell to the splendors of heaven but because he was convinced that both were written by Christian authors.[30]

In the introduction to his translation, Richard explains that he first recognized the novel's Christian roots in the book's "description of creation in seven days, by the distinct avowal that it taught personal immortality, that it did not believe in Nirvana of personal annihilation, that it did not believe in Primitive Buddhism or Buddhism proper which is atheistic, that it did believe in God and His Incarnate

One as the true Model for men to copy, that it taught that the Holy Spirit was in every instance the chief agent in producing conversion, and that prayer was the source of power."[31] Richard knew that Nestorian Christians had lived in the Chinese capital during the Tang dynasty (618–907), and he concluded that the author of *Journey to the West,* who he, following convention, identified as the thirteenth-century Daoist adept Qiu Changchun, must have been a Christian convert.[32] *Journey to the West* was, therefore, only superficially about Daoism or Buddhism. At its core it was a "Pilgrim's Progress" of Nestorian Christianity.[33] The idea was so unprecedented that Richard had to invent a new term—Mahāyāna Christianity—to describe it.[34]

His suspicions thus aroused, Richard started to note other uncanny parallels. Xuanzang, for one, was strikingly similar to Jesus Christ. Like the "Angel of the Covenant," Xuanzang had descended from heaven multiple times for the salvation of mankind.[35] Richard further observed: "The demons also very frequently desire to eat the flesh and drink the blood of the Religious Master, as a sort of mystic magic sacrament, in order that they might thereby become immortal. Jesus said, 'Whoso eateth my flesh and drinketh my blood hath eternal life.'"[36] The many scenes in the novel where monstrous demons attempt to murder and devour Xuanzang were thus read by Richard as veiled references to Christian communion. In this and numerous other ways, Richard contorted the novel's Buddhist and Daoist imagery into more recognizably Christian forms. As a result, Richard's *Journey to Heaven* does, indeed, read like a Christian parable, with Xuanzang as Christ and Sun Wukong as an apostle.[37] Refracted through the lens of Richard's idiosyncratic translation, *Journey to the West,* like Richard himself, was revealed to be a Christian body dressed in Chinese robes.

Richard's reading appears extreme in hindsight, but it was influential in its day. The former premier of Japan and founder of Waseda University, Ōkuma Shigenobu 大隈重信 (1838–1922), was apparently so taken with Richard's interpretation that he had the introduction to *Journey to Heaven* translated into Japanese.[38] Richard's reading also was promoted by later American and European writers eager to reconcile the Buddhist traditions they encountered in China, Japan, and Korea with their deeply held Christian faith.

In the fifty-six years between Pavie's first translation of chapters from *Journey to the West* and Richard's abridgement, eight other partial translations or synopses of the work were published. Some read *Journey to the West* as an authentic, if misguided, expression of Chinese belief. Others saw it as a confirmation of Christian universality. What virtually all early Western interpreters and translators of the novel shared was the conviction that, for better or worse, *Journey to the West* was inextricably woven into the fabric of China's religious culture.

Reforming the Narrative

The handwringing over novels like *Journey to the West* was not limited to foreigners or Christians in China. Chinese officials and scholars had long been distressed that uneducated peasants were worshipping disreputable characters as deities and having their social and political views shaped by the perverted values and seditious narratives found in novels like *Journey to the West*. The patronizing publications of critical foreigners only added fuel to an already smoldering fire. Western missionaries may have been anxious about the future of Christianity in China, but Chinese intellectuals were worried about the future of China itself.

Such concerns were neither unprecedented nor wholly unwarranted. The veneration of unorthodox deities had long been a cause for concern among Chinese authorities, and during the Qing dynasty, figures from *Journey to the West* narratives were often disparaged as heterodox deities. According to the scholar You Tong 尤侗 (1618–1704), for example, "The people of Fuzhou all venerate the novice Sun [Wukong] at their home altars. They also set up beautifully adorned temples to the Great Sage Equal to Heaven."[39] Despite his own penchant for communing with spirits, You Tong was dismissive of these traditions. Like many of his peers, he viewed *Journey to the West* as a work of fantasy (*zixu* 子虛) with no basis in reality. To worship the story's characters as deities was foolish at best, dangerous at worst. "If heterodox shrines are not destroyed," he warned, then "false views will continue to be passed down" to later generations.[40]

In a sweeping effort to curb the spread of these unsanctioned traditions, hundreds of "licentious shrines," including temples to the Great Sage Equal to Heaven, were razed by the prefect of Fuzhou during the late seventeenth century.[41] Sporadic campaigns to eliminate popular, unorthodox temples and shrines continued throughout the Qing and into the Republican era, and sites associated with Obtaining the Scriptures narratives frequently ranked among the targets.[42] Despite such efforts, by the turn of the twentieth century, Sun Wukong still perched atop temple altars throughout China, from Chengdu to Taiwan, and as far afield as Tibet.[43] Like the character in the novel, he emerged unscathed from every attack.

If the Tang Monk and Sun Wukong were gods, *Journey to the West* was their gospel. During the late imperial period, certain vernacular novels—with their richly described heavens and hells, gods and demons, heroes and villains, origin stories and prophecies—enjoyed the status of scripture. According to the imperial scholar Qian Daxin 錢大昕 (1728–1804), vernacular fiction (*xiaoshuo*) constituted a new kind of teaching (*jiao* 教). "Among gentry, peasants, workers and merchants," he wrote, "there is no one who does not practice it. Even children and women—illiterates—frequently see and hear (it performed). It is their teaching, and compared with Confucianism, Buddhism, and Daoism, it is more widespread."[44]

As accessible, entertaining, and cosmologically comprehensive accounts, novels like *Journey to the West* rivaled or superseded more conventional forms of canonical scripture. This was true not only for peasants but also for many officials, Buddhist monks, and Daoist priests. Even You Tong, who worked to destroy shrines to Sun Wukong, saw the novel as akin to classic Buddhist sutras. "Those who record the *Journey to the West*," he wrote, "transmit the heart of the *Avataṃsaka Sūtra*'s teachings."[45] In another commentary on the novel, the nineteenth-century Buddhist monk Huaiming 懷明 described it as a "heavenly book" (*tian shu* 天書) that encapsulates the essential teachings of both the Buddhist and Daoist traditions.[46] The Quanzhen Daoist master Liu Yiming 劉一明 (1734–1821) went even further: *Journey to the West* was not just one among many divine texts, it was *the* quintessential scripture:

> Wherever this book resides, there are heavenly deities standing guard over it. The reader should purify his hands and burn incense before reading it, and it should be read with the utmost reverence. . . . The acquisition of the true scriptures by means of the journey to the West actually means the acquisition of the true scripture of the *Journey to the West*. Apart from the *Journey to the West*, there are no other true scriptures to be acquired. The *Journey to the West* is transmitted through the story of the transmission of the scriptures by the Tathāgata Buddha, that is all. If one can truly understand the *Journey to the West*, then the three baskets of true scriptures will be found within it. Only he who knows this can read the *Journey to the West*.[47]

For those able to comprehend the real meaning of Xuanzang's pilgrimage, all other scriptures were superfluous. Like the *Lotus* or the *Avataṃsaka* sutras, *Journey to the West* is not just an account of how the Buddha's teachings were transmitted; it contained within itself the totality of the Buddha's transmitted teachings.

The exalted status of *Journey to the West* and other popular novels concerned some Chinese officials and scholars. Critiques of vernacular literature date to the late Ming and early Qing dynasties, when anxieties over "improper reading" (*bushan du* 不善讀) gripped some literati.[48] If, as Zhou Dunyi 周敦頤 (1017–1073) famously remarked, "Literature is a vehicle for the Way" (*wen yi zai dao* 文以載道), then certain novels were leading readers down some dark and debauched paths. Rather than immersing themselves in edifying Confucian classics and histories, with their refined language and clear ethical standards, people were turning, instead, to the unpolished prose and morally ambiguous messages found in popular novels. When read without the proper guidance, these works could corrupt their readers' character. "*The Water Margin* could incite violence and rebellion; *The Three Kingdoms* could incite intrigue and subterfuge; and the *Journey to the West* could incite strange fantasies."[49] The situation was dire. Improper readers, according to one scholar's estimate, outnumbered "proper" readers by one hundred to one.

The problem was particularly pernicious because most people were exposed to these stories through oral traditions and dramatic performances at a young and impressionable age. The colorful characters and the spectacular scenes in narratives subliminally shaped the way people interacted with and interpreted the world. Many of these works championed the marginalized and mocked the elite. They celebrated sexuality and valorized rebellion, creating what Meir Shahar has called an "upside-down world," where social norms were subverted and the authority of the court was flaunted.[50] The most effective way to improve the lives of peasants and reestablish allegiance to the state, according to some, was to do away with problematic novels altogether. "It is better not to read than to read improperly," wrote the Qing-dynasty official Liu Tingji 劉廷璣 (fl. 1706). "If you do not want people to read, it is better if [the books] did not exist."[51] Qian Daxin's proposal was more blunt: "Those whose responsibility it is to enlighten and guide the people would do better to annihilate this literature by burning it."[52]

Elite concerns about the baleful influence of popular novels, already pronounced in the seventeenth and eighteenth centuries, grew more heightened around the turn of the twentieth. The critiques of popular religion and vernacular novels were familiar, but the language used to define the problem and expedite its solution was new; it drew on the categories and critiques of Western missionaries and scholars. Instead of distinguishing between "orthodox" (*zheng* 正) and "heterodox" (*xie* 邪) teachings, for example, critics labeled many popular religious traditions "superstition" (*mixin* 迷信), which stood in opposition to proper "religion" (*zongjiao* 宗教)—Christian categories that only recently had been introduced to China by way of Japan. Narrative accounts of gods and demons, previously categorized simply as "*xiaoshuo*" or "*zhiguai*" (志怪, accounts of the strange), were now frequently described as "myths" (*shenhua* 神話) or "fairy tales" (*tonghua* 童話, literally "children's stories"), more neologisms imported from the West.[53]

By the early twentieth century, Chinese officials, like Western missionaries, were blaming *Journey to the West* for corrupting and confusing Chinese society.[54] In the aftermath of the rebellions and uprisings that were crippling the Qing dynasty, some officials blamed the violence not on widespread poverty or government failures but on the pernicious influence of vernacular novels. Because the majority of rebels and insurgents were young peasants, their religious fervor was deemed a product of ignorance. Without the benefit of a proper education, they knew only what they had heard from popular legends or had seen inside rural temples. They falsely assumed the stories they had been told about gods and demons were actually true. Eliminate these kinds of coarse, heterodox narratives, the reasoning went, and uprisings would be deprived of their ideological fuel.

Rehabilitating the Tang Monk

Given the ubiquity of accounts known from popular novels, which circulated in alternate literary versions, oral traditions, theater productions, and images, most officials pursued a more pragmatic approach. They reasoned that vernacular stories and their offshoots could not realistically be eradicated but they could be revised or reinterpreted in ways that would neutralize their antisocial themes and encourage more ethical, patriotic behavior. The prominent scholar and poet Xia Zengyou 夏曾佑 (1863–1924), for instance, proposed that the backwardness of the people in China's impoverished regions might be corrected if the novels that formed the basis of their religious culture were reformed.[55] If novels like *Journey to the West* already were responsible for shaping popular belief, they could be co-opted in the service of social rehabilitation.

Liang Qichao 梁啟超 (1873–1929), the influential journalist, philosopher, and advocate of political reform, produced one of the more insightful analyses of the effect of literature on thought and behavior. Liang had once served as Timothy Richard's secretary, and he shared his boss's conviction that literature was the most efficient means of initiating reform. In his essay "On the Relationship between Fiction and Government of the People," published in 1902, Liang pointed out that it is because fiction is so effective at drawing the reader into its world that it has such a powerful effect on readers' experience. "All readers of novels often feel that they have entered a state of self-transformation and that they themselves become the principal characters once they are engrossed in them."[56] Readers identify with the protagonists in novels, and they thus unconsciously begin to conflate the imaginary world conjured in fiction with the real world. This confusion, according to Liang, has a disastrous effect on society. It obstructs material progress, drains the economy, wastes time, and, in extreme cases, incites rebellion.[57] As Liang saw it, the very survival of the Chinese nation was at stake, and novels were both the problem and the solution. "The reformation of the government of the people must begin with a revolution in fiction," he concluded, "and the renovation of the people must begin with the renovation of fiction."[58]

Calls to re-envision vernacular literature were part of widespread, government-led campaigns to harness the power of traditional, popular art forms for the purpose of modernization and nation building during the Republican period. Reframing the *Journey to the West* narrative, a small part of this larger movement, was begun in earnest by Lu Xun and Hu Shih in the 1920s.[59] In a landmark study, Hu Shih argued that the Ming-dynasty scholar Wu Cheng'en was the novel's real author. Not only was the traditional attribution to the Daoist Qiu Changchun wrong, according to Hu, but the many attempts over the centuries to read *Journey to the West* as a religious text also were completely misguided. Hu presented the novel as evidence that Chinese literature had evolved in ways that closely paralleled or even surpassed the literary traditions of Europe. Like the transition from Latin to local vernaculars in Italy and Germany, the shift from literary to vernacular Chinese represented an evolution to more modern forms of literary expression.[60] *Journey to the West* and other Ming-dynasty novels may have had their roots in simple stories told by uneducated storytellers, but eventually:

> After centuries of such unconscious processes of evolution, these legends suddenly caught the imagination of some great masters of literature who took them out of the hands of the people and retouched them with the brush of intelligence and artistic genius. The legends remained, but the plots were re-cast, the dialogues greatly improved, the characters ennobled, and the conception elevated. Thus retouched and improved by the great masters of the literary art, these historical and mythological recitals emerged in the sixteenth and seventeenth centuries in their final form as the first masterpieces of Chinese fiction.[61]

Hu believed that Chinese fiction was born of myth—particularly Indian Buddhist myth—but that it came of age at the hands of "intelligent" and "artistic" literati who kept their work free from all religious sentiment. This, in part, was precisely what it meant to be modern. China was on the verge of freeing herself from the grip of feudal religions, a process that Hu, who had once called for the destruction of Buddhist icons and the execution of Buddhist monks, was eager to accelerate.[62] His drive to purge what he saw as the deleterious elements of traditional religion from modern Chinese culture is evident in his insistence that novels like *Journey to the West* have "no philosophical thesis to present" and "no social reform to advocate." Their sole objective was simply to "fascinate and to delight the hearer and the reader."[63] The very idea that the founding classics of Chinese fiction could be distorted by "the superstitions of the ignorant" was deeply unsettling. For intellectuals eager to establish a history of secular, humanist literature and aesthetics on par with post-Renaissance Europe, the teachings of Buddhists, Daoists, and Confucians were embarrassing relics of a bygone era that stood as obstacles to social and artistic progress. Religious interpretations, Hu declared, "are the great enemies of the *Journey to the West.*"[64]

In Hu Shih's preface to Arthur Waley's *Monkey*, he expressed only praise for the creativity and literary skill of the novel's purported author, Wu Cheng'en. He elected not to dwell on what he saw as the serious shortcomings of the work. Good novels, in Hu's estimation, had characters that underwent a transformation over the course of the narrative. A proper conclusion should offer a satisfying resolution to the tensions that drive the plot. *Journey to the West* seemed to have neither character development nor resolution. The Tang Monk, for example, is just as inept at the beginning of the book as he is at the end. After the pilgrims deliver their cache of Buddhist sutras to the Tang emperor, the book concludes with their ascent to heaven. This may be a fitting end for a hagiographical account, but Hu Shih's model was European literary convention, not Chinese liturgical traditions. *Journey to the West* deserved a better conclusion and so Hu decided to write one.[65]

In his rewrite of the ninety-ninth chapter of the novel, Hu Shih jettisoned the original story, which told how the pilgrims encountered a final trial in the form of a giant turtle that offers to ferry them across a river only to submerge the group and their texts in the water. Instead, the culminating scene in Hu's version brings the narrative to a dramatic climax, illustrating the conversion of the Tang Monk from a timid cleric into a heroic bodhisattva willing to sacrifice himself for the salvation of all beings. Before slicing off his own flesh to feed the ghosts and demons that have been killed by Sun Wukong and Zhu Bajie during their travels, the Tang Monk uses his own blood to write a farewell note to the Tang emperor, stating that he is offering up his life "to deliver the spirits of those who have died in vain" and "to pray for the long-lasting reign of the State."[66] For someone who foreswore any allegorical interpretation of the novel, Hu Shih's rewrite sounds suspiciously like a parable for a patriotic citizen enduring hardship and giving his life for the good of the Nation.[67]

Hu Shih's alternative ending to *Journey to the West* never supplanted the original, but his take on the entirely secular quality of the narrative did eclipse readings of the text as liturgy, as hagiography, or simply as religiously relevant. The celebrated author Lu Xun, a friend of Hu Shih's and a leading proponent of the literary reform, likewise sought to liberate China from the shackles of traditional religion. In his *Brief History of the Chinese Novel*, completed around the same time as Hu Shih's study, Lu argued that the Daoist and Buddhist imagery in *Journey to the West* was merely superficial. The novel, he explained, was meant only to entertain. It "arose from playfulness and not from discussion of *Dao*."[68]

By the 1930s, this had become the standard interpretation of the book. The same year Lu Xun published his *Brief History*, the American Helen M. Hayes completed her abridged translation of *Journey to the West*, which she titled *The Buddhist Pilgrim's Progress*.[69] This was the first English translation produced after the publication of Hu Shih's influential study, and in her introduction, Hayes signals her indebtedness to Hu Shih. She then explains that the main character, the monk Xuanzang, was "that Principle inherent in man which understands its oneness with all life and is willing in its devoted love to spend and be spent."[70] The pilgrim's journey, she reveals, was an allegory of "the Epic Pilgrimage of Man from the Actual to the Ideal."[71] While this vaguely theosophical take (described by Arthur Waley as "accessible, though very inaccurate") did not dispense with allegory, it did divorce the novel from any recognizable Chinese religious context.

Three years later, in Paris, Ou Itaï 吳益泰 (fl. 1933) published a survey of Chinese novels in which he explained that to truly appreciate the purely literary character of *Journey to the West*, it is necessary to "make a clean sweep" of all religious interpretations.[72] That same year, in China, Zheng Zhenduo 鄭振鐸 (1898–1958), one of the most prominent literary historians of the Republican period, likewise concluded that the author of *Journey to the West* had very little knowledge of either Buddhist or Daoist teachings. Those who read religious meaning into the text could, therefore, be dismissed as people who see the world through colored glasses.[73] Any concerns that *Journey to the West* might be mistaken for a religious text, it seems, had finally been put to rest.

With the publication of Arthur Waley's *Monkey* just nine years later, English readers were presented with an interpretation of the novel that had many influential proponents in China, if little historical precedent. The work Waley characterized as a mix of beauty and absurdity had more often been viewed either as ignorant superstition by detractors or as divine revelation by devotees. But Waley's *Monkey* belonged to a broader movement. It was published two decades after Hu Shih made his revelations regarding the novel's authorship and objective; ten years after Ou Itaï called for sweeping away all religious interpretations; and just one year after the Wan brothers released *Princess Iron Fan* (Tieshan gongzhu 鐵扇公主)—the first animated film produced in China—whose story was based on *Journey to the West* but whose style was modeled on Walt Disney's *Snow White and the Seven Dwarves* (see figure 1.1). The producers of *Princess Iron Fan* knew that their adaptation would take some of their viewers by surprise. In a prologue, they explained that *Journey to the West* was originally a fairy tale for children but was later mistakenly read as a novel of spirits and demons.[74] Their film was thus presented not as an innovation but a restoration of original intent.

Such pointedly secularized versions of the story never completely replaced those rooted in myth and ritual, but, during the early twentieth century, they did come to overshadow them. From 1926 to 1928, no fewer than fourteen films depicting scenes from *Journey to the West* were produced in China. Whereas premodern theatrical versions of the narrative often were performed on temple stages during festivals as offerings to gods, these silent films were screened in ornate Western-style theaters, with showings held at convenient times over an extended period, and they were marketed as new, modern forms of leisure.[75] Spectacular productions created by profit-driven studios further distanced *Journey to the West* from its ritual contexts, even if movies were in some sense just an extension of commercial theater productions that had long been popular in Chinese cities.

As we will see in the following chapters, prior to the 1920s, the vast majority of people in China were exposed to Xuanzang's otherworldly travels as an expression of living religious cultures. Chinese officials and Christian missionaries both

Figure 1.1. Advertisement for the animated film *Princess Iron Fan,* 1940. Li, *Wan Laiming yanjiu,* 73.

were dismayed that such crass and outlandish stories could influence the beliefs and practices of so many people. They both were frustrated by the reluctance of some people to trade old traditions for new realities—to replace traditional Chinese mytho-histories with Christian narratives, on the one hand, or to exchange gods, ghosts, and ancestors and for psychology, aesthetics, and patriotism, on the other. Over time, mass-market adaptations of the novel normalized secular interpretations of *Journey to the West.* Just as reformers had envisioned, vernacular art forms ultimately proved the most effective means of shaping popular sentiment. Audiences who encountered *Journey to the West* principally through film and animation now could enjoy its tales as a diverting work of fantasy, a light-hearted comedy, or an expression of Han Chinese identity. By the 1930s, these readings of the narrative had become so ubiquitous that anyone who performed scenes on ritually charged occasions could be dismissed as hopelessly confused, someone who, in the words of Zheng Zhenduo, "speaks in their sleep in the middle of the day."[76]

In 1942, the same year Waley published *Monkey* in England, Japanese soldiers stationed in the occupied city of Nanjing discovered a long-lost fragment of Xuanzang's skull.[77] The serendipitous find coincided with renewed interest in the historical Xuanzang's life and work both in China and abroad. Several decades earlier, a collection of Yogācāra commentaries, lost in China but preserved in Japan, was returned to the continent. These newly available texts inspired a wave of new publications on Xuanzang and the Yogācāra teachings he championed. After centuries of neglect, Xuanzang was suddenly relevant again.

In Europe, the French scholar Stanislas Julien (1797–1873) produced the first translation of Xuanzang's *Biography* in 1853.[78] His two-volume rendering of the *Record of the Western Regions* followed a few years later—at precisely the same time his compatriot M. Théodore Pavie completed his partial translation of the *Journey to the West* novel.[79] Julien's translations of Xuanzang's *Biography* and *Record* were heralded by European scholars as the keys that would finally unlock the hidden histories of South and Central Asia. They also had the potential to speed the ongoing search for the ruins of Buddhist temples and stupas and the treasures they contained. The British archaeologists Alexander Cunningham (1814–1893) and Aurel Stein (1862–1943) famously relied on translated accounts of Xuanzang's travels to guide their explorations and excavations. As foreign travelers in search of Buddhist paintings, statues, and texts, they felt a particular kinship with the seventh-century monk, whom Stein claimed as his patron saint.

The medieval monk who so impressed European academics and colonial officials bore little resemblance to the fictional character portrayed in *Journey to the West*. That anyone might conflate the two seemed nonsensical. When Aurel Stein encountered murals depicting the Tang Monk and his companions on the walls of cave temples at Dunhuang (see figure 1.2), he was amused that the cave's caretaker—a Daoist priest who Stein dubbed a "credulous cicerone"—had turned Xuanzang into "a sort of saintly Munchausen."[80] Seeing Xuanzang depicted together with animal companions, gods, and demons, Stein concluded that the priest, whose name was Wang Yuanlu 王圓籙 (d. 1931), must be profoundly ignorant of "all that constitutes Chinese learning."[81]

Wang Yuanlu surely saw things differently. The images that adorned the walls of his newly restored temple were standard renditions of a sacred narrative. The Tang Monk and his companions were not literary creations but spirits worthy of veneration. Unbeknownst to Stein, images of the Tang Monk and his attendants had adorned the insides of cave temples throughout China and neighboring territories for more than eight centuries. Wang Yuanlu was thus maintaining a hallowed tradition. It was Stein, not Wang, who was ignorant of Chinese culture. Had he ventured farther afield, he would have seen similar scenes covering the walls of other temples and shrines.[82] He also might have observed the story performed by storytellers, printed in books, recited during rituals, and enacted on and off stage. The Tang Monk and his companions were a familiar presence in the region, and stories of their adventures were known to virtually every man, woman, and child.

Figure 1.2. Wang Yuanlu photographed by Aurel Stein in
front of murals depicting scenes from the Obtaining the
Scriptures narrative. Stein, *Ruins of Desert Cathay,* vol. II,
170b.

With the publication of *Monkey,* Arthur Waley introduced a selection of those
stories to anglophone audiences several decades after Stein left Dunhuang. Following the success of his translation, Waley went on to publish a long and learned essay about the historical figure who had inspired the fictional account. That essay,
titled "The Real Tripitika," drew a clear distinction between Xuanzang and the Tang
Monk. Xuanzang—the author of the *Record;* the subject of the *Biography;* the translator of Buddhist texts—was real. He lived and died during the early Tang dynasty.
The Tang Monk, by contrast, was fictional. He existed only in the imaginations of
readers.

The reality, as we have seen, was more complicated. In China, modern campaigns to establish the entirely fictional, purely secular nature of *Journey to the West*
were reactions against a tenaciously pervasive belief in the historicity and sanctity

of the narrative. For all the efforts to disentangle Xuanzang from the Tang Monk, the two figures remained stubbornly fused in the popular imagination. For many people, Xuanzang was the human progenitor of the deified Tang Monk. Like the bodhisattva Avalokiteśvara, the goddess Mazu, and a host of other deities, the Tang Monk was once an extraordinary historical figure who had shed his mortal frame and become a god. As a spirit who protects and guides his devotees, the Tang Monk was in some ways more accessible and relevant—more *real*—than a long-dead Yogācāra exegete who produced difficult translations of arcane Sanskrit texts.

When the historical Xuanzang's remains were fortuitously unearthed in Nanjing in the 1940s, they caused a minor sensation. Newspapers ran stories. Government dignitaries gave speeches, and huge crowds came to pay their respects. Multiple countries—China, Japan, India, and Taiwan—vied to acquire portions of the relic. The fragment eventually was broken into multiple pieces to be dispersed and enshrined in different cities. When a small shard of Xuanzang's skull was flown by plane from Nanjing to Beijing, a Buddhist monk named Miaoyuan 妙原 took it upon himself to assign roles to other members of the escort. "Great Master Shuangchi 爽痴, you are the special envoy of the Beijing Buddhist Association," Miaoyuan explained, "so you must be in the center [of our group] and carry the reliquary. You will represent Sha Monk."

> Bai Jian 白堅, you are probably the reincarnation of a white horse.[83] You sit in front of Shuangchi, representing the horse that Xuanzang rode. Military attaché Zhang Heng 张恒, since you have the rank of military attaché and are the special envoy of the central government, you will sit by the right side and be in charge of protecting Xuanzang. There will be no doubt that you are Sun Wukong. I am a monk from a small temple and my attainments are few, so I can play only the part of Zhu Bajie."[84]

With Xuanzang's parietal bone traveling in the company of Sun Wukong, Zhu Bajie, Sha Monk, and the white horse, his arrival in the capital was cast as a scene from *Journey to the West*. The flight to Beijing reenacted the moment when, after their long and harrowing journey, the Tang Monk and his divine companions finally return to the imperial palace in Chang'an to present the scriptures to the emperor. Miaoyuan and other members of the escort had been steeped in stories of the Tang Monk's otherworldly pilgrimage their entire lives. When they looked at Xuanzang, they saw the Tang Monk.

2 Apotheosis

The past is never dead. It isn't even past.

—William Faulkner, *Requiem for a Nun*

When Xuanzang walked away from Chang'an in the early years of the Tang dynasty, he was a monk on a covert mission. The court had denied his request to travel and study in India, so for days he had to move under the cover of darkness to avoid being recognized and detained.[1] On returning to the capital nearly seventeen years later, he received a hero's welcome. Laden with treasures from his long and arduous journey, brimming with information about the political, military, and cultural conditions of Central Asia and India, and conversant in the languages and doctrines of contemporary Indian Buddhism, Xuanzang was honored by the emperor and feted by the monastic and lay elite of Chang'an. The elevation from illicit, minor monk to venerable court cleric was remarkable, but it paled in comparison to Xuanzang's subsequent transformations: several centuries after his death, Xuanzang became a god.

Xuanzang's deification was a gradual and fluid process arguably underway in his own lifetime. To many of his contemporaries, he was already a living legend. In the effusive praise showered on a venerable teacher, his extraordinary qualities were extolled and exaggerated. According to Emperor Gaozong, his most prominent patron, Xuanzang "sailed beyond the Milky Way and shook the rings of his staff above the smoke and mist. On the towering swells of the vast ocean, he forged ahead across the frightening waves. Over the heavy frost of the broad earth, he battled the cold and passed alone."[2] Xuanzang's disciple Huili similarly rhapsodized about his master's fearlessness as he brazenly traveled across lands with "dark and frozen mountains, swift and turbulent rivers, black and poisonous winds, and packs of fearsome, predatory beasts."[3] Xuanzang could be so bold in part because heavenly beings, including the bodhisattvas Avalokiteśvara and Mañjuśrī, reportedly watched over him. His advanced spiritual state also endowed Xuanzang with a store of supranormal powers, and readers of his biography learned that he once used the strength of his samādhi to summon up a black wind and repel heretical bandits.[4]

Even while he lived, Xuanzang seemed superhuman to some. After his death, he was accordingly remembered and celebrated as an unusually gifted monk. In biographical accounts and portraits from the Tang dynasty, the Five dynasties (907–960), and the Northern Song dynasty (960–1127), Xuanzang appears as an eminent court cleric and translator. By the early twelfth century, however, more extravagant accounts of his pilgrimage were diffusing across the continent. Paintings and carvings placed him in rarefied company, standing together with a monkey attendant and a horse amid an otherworldly landscape. Xuanzang appeared to be engaging with bodhisattvas and other celestial beings. Written accounts described the strange territories that he and his party passed through and the divine and demonic beings they encountered on their way to the Buddha's realm in the West. The rigorous scholar and accomplished exegete was hardly recognizable; in his place was a magical monk capable of transiting between human and spirit realms.

Picturing Xuanzang

No one really knows what the historical Xuanzang looked like. His disciples described him as standing seven feet tall with pink skin and striking facial features, "solemn as a spirit, handsome as a painting." He apparently "liked to wear clothes from Gandhāra cut of fine cotton cloth and tailored to fit just right."[5] We tend to think of him now as a monk standing with a fly-whisk in his right hand, a scroll in his left, carrying a towering bamboo backpack overloaded with texts (see plate 1), but this iconic image actually derives from thirteenth-century Japan.[6] It was introduced to China and the rest of the world only in the twentieth century.[7] Earlier generations imagined Xuanzang somewhat differently.

Textual references to portraits of Xuanzang made from the seventh through the eleventh centuries describe him not as a lone pilgrim but as one among several prominent historical clerics who made key contributions to the Buddhist tradition, particularly by transmitting and translating Buddhist texts. The first known portrait of Xuanzang was commissioned when he was in his mid-fifties. The year was 656, and the occasion was the ordination of Lady Xue 薛 (fl. 626–656), the tutor to Tang-dynasty emperor Gaozong 高宗 (r. 650–683) and the former concubine of Gaozong's grandfather, the first Tang emperor Gaozu (r. 618–626). After the ordination, Emperor Gaozong had an artist paint Xuanzang, the head preceptor, together with the nine other clerics who participated in the ceremony. This commemorative scene was subsequently displayed at Helin Temple 鶴林寺, the imperial convent

Gaozong had built for Lady Xue, now known as the nun Baosheng 寶乘.[8] It must have been one of the most important—if not one of the only—images made of Xuanzang during his lifetime. Some years later, Gaozong's son and successor Emperor Zhongzong 中宗 (r. 684 and 705–710), who had been close to Xuanzang as a child, had the painting brought from Helin to the great Ci'en Temple 慈恩寺, where he made offerings and composed a verse in praise of his late mentor.[9]

After Xuanzang passed away, other portraits were made and displayed at sites associated with his life. During the Tang dynasty, his image was kept in at least two major monasteries in the imperial capitals. At the Sutra Translation Hall at Ci'en Temple in Chang'an, the former center of Xuanzang's translation activities, his likeness was positioned last in a line of great translators that stretched back to Kāśyapa Mātaṅga 迦葉摩騰 (d. 73), reputed to have been the first Indian monk to translate Sanskrit Buddhist texts into Chinese.[10] At Jing'ai Temple 敬愛寺 in Luoyang, artists placed Xuanzang together with four other great "pilgrim monks" who had traveled to India to study the Buddhist teachings and convey them back to China.[11]

Similar paintings highlighting Xuanzang's travels and translation work (figure 2.1) continued to be commissioned after the fall of the Tang, and these were distributed more broadly to places where Xuanzang had never lived. In recognition of his contributions to the Buddhist canon, several portraits were situated in or near Buddhist libraries. When the Song-dynasty scholar and historian Ouyang Xiu 歐陽脩 (1007–1072) visited Shouning Temple 壽寧寺 in Yangzhou in 1036, for instance, a resident monk explained that several of the temple's murals, which had been painted during the Southern Tang dynasty (937–976), were destroyed when the city was invaded by the Later Zhou army in 975. Only the painting of Xuanzang on the wall of the Sutra Library still survived.[12] A century later, when the Japanese cleric Jōjin 成尋 (1011–1081) traveled through the same region, he saw another portrait of Xuanzang at Puzhao wang si 普照王寺. In this image, Xuanzang held a text in his left hand and the two fingers of his raised right hand were bent to symbolize his scholarly acumen and high spiritual attainment—a pose that later would become popular in drawings, paintings, and sculptures of Xuanzang in Japan.[13] The literatus Dong You 董逌 (fl. 1127) praised the same qualities in an inscription for a portrait that has not survived, acknowledging the debt later generations owed Xuanzang for acquiring, transmitting, and translating the Buddha's teachings.[14]

In this way, Xuanzang was duly remembered as a great patriarch of the Buddhist tradition, and like other esteemed ancestors, he was occasionally the object of veneration and the recipient of offerings. In the twelfth century, the Northern Song scholar-official Li Gang 李綱 (1083–1140) happened upon a shrine while traveling through the mountains of northwestern Fujian. The small structure was located behind a monastic library that housed a complete collection of the Buddhist

Figure 2.1. Xuanzang (left) together with the monks Kumārajīva (center) and Daoxuan (right). Detail from the *Sentoku zuzō* 先德図像. Copied by the Japanese monk Genshō 玄證 (b. 1146). Tokyo National Museum.

canon. On the altar, an image of Xuanzang sat beside a statue of Shanhui 善慧 (497–569), the layman who reportedly oversaw one of the earliest compilations of the canon. Li Gang noted that the resident monks honored these two men as patriarchs, regularly offering them incense, flowers, food, drink, and chants.[15]

Descriptions of images made in centuries after Xuanzang's death thus confirm what we might expect: for hundreds of years, he was extolled as an accomplished monk, a courageous pilgrim, a prolific translator, and a learned exegete. He was grouped together with other historically prominent clerics in murals that commemorated their service to the imperial family and the empire, their transmission of Buddhist traditions from India to China, and their translation of Buddhist texts from Sanskrit into Chinese. Xuanzang was celebrated as a remarkable monk, but he had not yet acquired the divine qualities—the saintly halo, the horse loaded with luminous texts, the animal and demonic attendants, the hovering bodhisattvas and heavenly spirits—that would become ubiquitous features of his later legend and cult.[16]

Early Images of the Tang Monk

The first signs that Xuanzang had shed his mortal shell appear around the beginning of the twelfth century. It is not entirely clear why Xuanzang and his story were reconceived at this time. As Liu Shufen has noted, there was a surge in Xuanzang-related activity during this period. It was toward the close of the Northern Song dynasty, for example, that Xuanzang's skull relic was relocated from a dilapidated reliquary in the remote Zhongnan Mountains to a stupa in the urban center of

Nanjing (where Japanese soldiers would discover it in the mid-twentieth century). Yuhua Monastery 玉華寺, Xuanzang's last residence before his death, also began to attract a steady stream of pilgrims around the same time. In 1115, moreover, the remains of Xuanzang's Korean-born disciple Wŏnch'ŭk 圓測 (613–699) were relocated to Xingjiao Monastery 興教寺, where stupas for Xuanzang and his successor Ji (a.k.a. Kuiji 窺基, 632–682) already stood. Why all this renewed interest in a monk who lived more than four hundred years earlier?

Liu Shufen speculates that these new memorials may have been motivated by Song Buddhists' nostalgia for the Tang dynasty, when prominent monks worked hand-in-hand with Chinese emperors and courtiers to safeguard the empire and promote the Dharma. Early Song emperors looked to Tang emperor Taizong as an exemplar, and Song clerics might have recalled Xuanzang as a not-so-subtle reminder that Taizong and his ministers were famously generous patrons of monks and monasteries.[17]

The Song dynasty also was a time of major social change in China. Beginning in the eleventh century, political unification ended a century of division. Economic integration and increased mobility triggered new waves of migration. The Jurchen invasion of northern China in 1127, moreover, forced the court to relocate to the south and displaced an estimated 500,000 people. Migrants brought their stories, traditions, and cults with them when they resettled.[18] These demographic and cultural shifts help explain why many of the cults that thrived in later eras center on quasi-historical figures who lived prior to the Song dynasty.[19] The veneration of these men and women had previously been limited to their natal regions or spheres of influence; only during the Song did their cults begin to spread and blossom into transregional phenomena.

The same may be true of Xuanzang. Embellished accounts of his extraordinary exploits probably began as local traditions centered in the northern cities where he had lived. By the twelfth century, however, they had diffused—by means of images, written accounts, and oral traditions—across the continent. As the stories traveled, they were inevitably intermingled with other narrative traditions. In this way, Xuanzang's identity and the meaning of his pilgrimage subtly shifted in the process of transmission.

The details of this process—where it began, how it spread, who was involved—are lost to us, but we can be certain that narratives and iconographic forms involving Xuanzang circulated widely at this time. We know this thanks to a series of striking images that have been preserved at multiple sites scattered across a broad swath of China. These images, which are the earliest extant depictions of Xuanzang, appear on the walls of at least fifteen Buddhist cave temples located in northern, northwestern, and western China (see appendix). Some of these are bas relief sculptures carved directly into the rock walls of grottoes. Others are murals painted on the flat surfaces of the caves' interiors. The earliest of these depictions, in cave 3 of the Zhaoan 招安 complex in northern Shaanxi, dates to the late eleventh or early twelfth century. The latest, at Dayun cloister 大雲院 in southeastern Shanxi, was completed in 1293. During this roughly two-hundred-year period, multiple political regimes controlled the regions where these caves were excavated and adorned. Nearly identical representations of Xuanzang were thus made not only in Northern Song (960–1125) territory, but also within the borders of the Jurchen Jin (1115–1234), the Tangut Xixia (1038–1227), and the Mongol Yuan (1279–1368) dynasties. Despite the ethnic, linguistic, and political differences that prevailed in these regions, representations of Xuanzang remained remarkably consistent. Everyone seems to have imagined this seventh-century monk in roughly the same way.[20]

In each rendering, Xuanzang appears, unsurprisingly, as a rather ordinary looking Chinese Buddhist monk. His head, often surrounded by a saintly halo, is shaved and he wears a *kāṣāya* draped over an inner robe. He holds his arms aloft with his palms pressed together in a gesture of supplication. There is nothing particularly novel about these attributes; it is the larger setting that is remarkable. Directly behind Xuanzang stands a smaller attendant dressed in the clothes of a layman. In some of the earliest sculpted images, this figure is clearly human (see figures 2.2 and 2.3). In later murals, however, the attendant sports the head and arms of a monkey (see plate 2 and figure 2.4). A thin headband sometimes serves to hold back his long brown hair. This figure, who appears to be an early progenitor of the famous monkey king Sun Wukong, leads a brown or a white horse. In some images, the horse's saddle is empty. In others, it is loaded with a bundle of scriptures radiating light.

Xuanzang and his peculiar companions always occupy the peripheries of larger scenes centered on a bodhisattva. With one exception, that bodhisattva always is a specific iconographic form of Avalokiteśvara.[21] Known as "Water Moon Avalokiteśvara" (*Shuiyue Guanyin* 水月觀音), this rendering shows the bodhisattva on his island abode of Mount Potalaka in the midst of the South Sea.[22] He sits in the posture of "royal ease," with his left foot resting on a lotus flower and his right foot raised on the platform or rocky outcropping that serves as his seat. His right arm rests on his bent right knee and his left arm extends down to his seat as though supporting his weight. (The name "Water Moon" refers to the surrounding waters and the full moon–like nimbus around the bodhisattva's head.)

In these tableaus, Xuanzang and his entourage are venerating Avalokiteśvara. Other supplicants typically join them. Some of these figures are difficult to identify, but others are more familiar. The young pilgrim Sudhana is sometimes shown approaching Avalokiteśvara on a cloud floating across the sky. The Dragon King and his daughter, the Dragon Princess, often emerge from the sea bearing offerings. Each of these divine beings is connected to the bodhisattva in some way. In

Figure 2.2. Cave 4 of the Mount Zhong cave complex
showing the bodhisattva Avalokiteśvara in the center with
a monk, an attendant, and a horse carrying numinous
scriptures to his lower right. An inscription to the right of
Avalokiteśvara's head reads: "The pure devotee Zhang
created one Avalokiteśvara bodhisattva assembly as an
eternal offering. Recorded on the twentieth day of the
ninth month of the second year of the Zhenghe era
[1112]." Photo courtesy of He Liqun 何利群.

Figure 2.3. Central pillar featuring Avalokiteśvara in cave 2
of the Shihong si complex, mid-twelfth century. The heads
of Xuanzang and his horse, at the lower left, have been
damaged. *Zhongguo shiku diaosu jinghua: Shaanbei shiku,*
plate 8.

Figure 2.4. Detail of Xuanzang, a monkey, and a horse. From the center left section of the Samantabhadra tableau on the south side of the west wall of Yulin cave 3. Xixia era (1038–1227). Dunhuang Yanjiu Yuan, *Zhongguo shiku: Anxi Yulin ku,* plate 160.

the *Gaṇḍavyūha* chapter of the *Avataṃsaka Sūtra,* for example, Sudhana visits Mount Potalaka and receives Avalokiteśvara's teachings.[23] As for the Dragon Princess, according to the *Dhāraṇī of the Great Compassionate Thousand-Handed, Thousand-Eyed Bodhisattva Avalokiteśvara,* when the bodhisattva entered the sea to ease the sufferings of resident dragons, this princess offered him a priceless pearl.[24] From the twelfth century on, Sudhana and the Dragon Princess were regularly depicted together with Avalokiteśvara, making their inclusion in these scenes unremarkable.[25] The presence of Xuanzang and his companions, however, is more enigmatic.

Visually, nothing in any of these images explicitly identifies the monk as Xuanzang or the scene as having been inspired by either his conventional biography or some nascent version of the Obtaining the Scriptures narrative. The monk's attendant in many carvings, to note the most obvious discrepancy, appears to be human rather than simian. It is thus possible that these scenes are just generic renderings of pilgrim-monks in the act of venerating Avalokiteśvara, who is, after all, an avowed protector of pious travelers. Fortunately, an inscription accompanying one early relief removes any ambiguity regarding the monk's identity and his relationship to this bodhisattva. The carving, which dates to 1105, is preserved in the Avalokiteśvara Pavilion 觀音閣, in southern Shandong province. The pavilion is named after an image of Water Moon Avalokiteśvara carved into the back wall of the cave. In a smaller niche on the left wall stand two robed figures and a horse carrying a bundle of scrolls on its back. A cartouche accompanying this trio reads, "The bodhisattva Avalokiteśvara orders Tang Trepiṭaka to obtain the scriptures and return" (觀音菩薩命唐三藏取經回來)."[26]

This sculpture (and presumably others like it) illustrated a pivotal event in Xuanzang's life. It could be the moment when his pilgrimage is first set in motion, not by a desire to correct inconsistencies in existing Chinese translations of Sanskrit texts, as described in Xuanzang's earlier biographies, but because the bodhisattva Avalokiteśvara commanded it. Alternatively, the scene may commemorate the culmination of the divinely ordained pilgrimage when Xuanzang finally receives the scriptures and turns back toward China. In several sculptures and murals, including the one that features this inscription, Xuanzang's horse is loaded with a cache of texts on its back. Given the broader context of these images, viewers would conclude that these sacred scriptures originated not in the monastic libraries of Kashmir or Nālandā but issued directly from the bodhisattva in his heavenly abode.

The prospect that Avalokiteśvara either sent Xuanzang on his mission to India or personally transmitted the scriptures to him is the first of many indications that narratives of Xuanzang's pilgrimage had entered new territory. It is not particularly surprising that accounts of a celebrated Chinese cleric would merge with those of a beloved Mahāyāna bodhisattva. Like most Buddhist monks of his generation, Xuanzang had been a devotee of Avalokiteśvara. During his travels, he prayed to the bodhisattva for protection and sought out Avalokiteśvara's miraculous images in northern India. In one passage in his *Record,* Xuanzang even describes the precipitous cliffs and valleys of Mount Potalaka, evoking a landscape like that later depicted in cave temples: "There is a lake on the summit of this mountain," he wrote. "Its limpid waters issue out in a great river, circling the mountain twenty times before entering the Southern Sea. Beside the lake is a heavenly palace made of stone. This is the dwelling of the bodhisattva Guanzizai [Avalokiteśvara]. Those who wish to see the bodhisattva, without regard for their lives, cross the roiling sea and climb the mountain despite the danger and hardship. Very few can reach this place."[27] In this passage, Xuanzang, one of the few Chinese monks to have traveled to India, was describing what he had *heard* about Mount Potalaka. To many readers, however, it must have seemed as though he himself had stood within sight of Avalokiteśvara's abode. Xuanzang's most famous translation, the *Heart Sūtra,* moreover, was presumed to have been authored by the bodhisattva.

As stories about Xuanzang's life circulated in the centuries after his death, it was a short step for people to imagine that he had received this and other scriptures directly from Avalokiteśvara in India.

Crediting an eminent monk's most extraordinary accomplishments to the will of heavenly beings is a common enough feature of Chinese Buddhist hagiographies. Even Xuanzang's own disciples assumed that the Mañjuśrī—the bodhisattva of wisdom—directed his travels. Divine intervention and instruction are also common tropes in the biographies of other prominent historical clerics.[28] Be that as it may, the sculptures and murals featuring Xuanzang do not appear to be merely fanciful renderings of his conventional biography. The halo encircling his head—a sign of sainthood—and the presence of other non-human figures suggest, instead, that Xuanzang has transcended the mortal world. Not merely a monk aided by celestial beings, Xuanzang himself had crossed over into a heavenly realm.

During the twelfth century, Xuanzang assumed the status of a deity in some regions. In Xixia territory, where all the murals featuring Xuanzang and Avalokiteśvara were made, both figures were treated as spirits who were receptive to the requests of devotees. The divine status of Avalokiteśvara goes without saying, but Xuanzang's place in local pantheons is less intuitive. We can catch a glimpse of the role he played in regional ritual practices through *The Great Tang Trepiṭaka's Book of Trigrams,* a short divination manual written in Tangut script. This text, discovered in 1909 in the ruins of the city of Khara Khoto, describes the process of throwing twelve copper coins to arrive at various prognostications based on the five phases (*wuxing* 五行) or eight trigrams (*bagua* 八卦). Xuanzang, the spirit animating the process, determines how the coins fall, and the results offer revelations about one's health, wealth, marriage prospects, childbirth outcomes, lawsuits, or travel plans.[29] Xuanzang's divination manual was found together with a similar text featuring Avalokiteśvara. These works and the traditions they represented were not anomalies. Divination practices centered on Avalokiteśvara were common in southeastern China, Chosŏn Korea, and Tibet. As for Xuanzang, several other hemerological and astro-calendrical works—preserved at Dunhuang and included in both the *Zhengtong Daoist Canon* and standard Chan liturgies—credit him with establishing the auspicious and inauspicious days for the performance of rituals.[30] *Trepiṭaka's Book of Trigrams* thus belongs to larger, transregional and trans-sectarian traditions of turning to Xuanzang to divine the future—a tradition that continues to this day.[31]

In the earliest sculptures and murals that feature Xuanzang, however, he is not the primary object of veneration. He is, instead, subordinate to the central subject of Avalokiteśvara. This bodhisattva, of course, is an extraordinarily popular, multipurpose deity, endowed with a wide range of powers and depicted in a great variety of forms. In the same Xixia caves that show Avalokiteśvara seated on Mount

Potalaka, for instance, other murals render him with eleven heads and eight arms saving people from drowning, prison, thieves, non-humans, fire, snakes, elephants, and lions. Still other images depict him with a thousand arms or in the form of Amoghapāśa, whose rope of compassion pulls people out of evil realms. Xuanzang and his companions appear only in scenes centered on Water Moon Avalokiteśvara. Why?

The iconography of Water Moon Avalokiteśvara appears to have first developed in China during the tenth century. Once established, it was commissioned by donors for various reasons, ranging from specific requests to more general prayers for protection from harm and the bestowal of blessings. At the time images of Xuanzang began to appear in the presence of this bodhisattva, Water Moon Avalokiteśvara was closely associated with mortuary practices. In a short text describing the proper method for worshipping this form of the bodhisattva, for example, the Japanese monk Shinkaku 心覚 (1116–1180), who introduced this iconography to Japan, quotes the deity's promise to his backsliding devotees: "If you are destined to go to hell because you have broken the precepts, recite [my] mantra three hundred thousand times. All your sins will be dissolved. You will be reborn in the Western Paradise and see the Buddha Amitābha. If all your desires cannot be fulfilled, I vow that I will not attain the unsurpassable Way of the Buddha. You should know that based on my great compassionate vow, I will guide those who break the precepts to the West."[32] Like the bodhisattva Kṣitigarbha, Water Moon Avalokiteśvara pledged to help devotees avoid the punishments of hell and acquire safe passage to *Sukhāvatī*.

In Xixia, this form of the bodhisattva was accordingly venerated as a spirit guide, and images of Water Moon Avalokiteśvara were commissioned to generate merit for the deceased. Inscriptions on some paintings include their donors' stated wish that their ancestors attain rebirth in the Pure Land. At least one such image was dedicated in the middle of the seventh lunar month, the time of the Ghost Festival.[33] (This annual communal rite, centered on offerings for the liberation of the dead, is closely associated with legends concerning Xuanzang and his pilgrimage, a point to which I will return.) By creating images of this bodhisattva, donors hoped to compel him to act on their behalf. Some paintings of Water Moon Avalokiteśvara from Dunhuang and Khara Khoto accordingly show the deceased at the bottom of the painting making offerings to the bodhisattva. In one particularly striking example, Avalokiteśvara receives the spirit of a dead man as musicians accompanied by horses hold a funeral on the far shore beside an open grave.[34] The structural elements of this scene mirror contemporaneous murals featuring Xuanzang and his companions (see plates 3 and 4). In these images, the shore on which the mourners stand appears to represent the boundary of the mortal, human world. Across the water lay the heavenly realm of the bodhisattva, the destination sought by the dead.

Offerings to Water Moon Avalokiteśvara took the form of texts as well as images. A Jurchen Jin copy of the *King Gao Avalokiteśvara Sūtra* (*Gaowang Guanshiyin jing* 高王觀世音經), printed in 1173, for example, bears a frontispiece featuring Water Moon Avalokiteśvara receiving offerings from a devotee. According to its dedicatory prayer, the sutra was copied so that a deceased family member—perhaps the man depicted on the frontispiece—would obtain a favorable rebirth.[35] In mid-tenth century Dunhuang, the same region where the murals featuring Water Moon Avalokiteśvara and Xuanzang were later made, the *Sūtra of the Water Moon Avalokiteśvara* (*Shuiyue Guanyin jing* 水月觀音經) was among ten scriptures copied to aid the spirit of the dead as it navigated the netherworld. Specifically, family members were instructed to copy this sutra on the second week after a person's death so that his or her spirit would "be reborn in the Pure Land and not fall into the three difficult destinies [of hell dwellers, hungry ghosts, and animals]."[36] The second week after death was considered a particularly perilous time. This is when, according to the *Sūtra of the Ten Kings,* the spirit fords the River Nai 奈河, the boundary between the living and the dead.[37] Harsh punishments typically awaited on the other side, but offerings and prayers to Avalokiteśvara could circumvent this unfortunate fate. Rather than crossing into hell, the spirit of the dead, by means of their own accumulated karma and the merit generated by their surviving family members, hoped to pass directly into the pure lands of buddhas and bodhisattvas.

What does any of this have to do with Xuanzang? Some scholars have speculated that Xuanzang's inclusion in these scenes indicates that he, too, played some role in Buddhist mortuary rites.[38] Given the resonant theme of travel across dangerous terrain to arrive in the land of the Buddha, perhaps he and his companions were summoned as sympathetic spirit guides, leading shades safely into the presence of Avalokiteśvara. As will become apparent in chapter 4, there is ample evidence demonstrating that Xuanzang and his fellow pilgrims *did* play this role in later eras. The images in cave temples, however, are simply too ambiguous to draw any definitive conclusions. What we can say for certain is that artists consistently depicted Xuanzang as both a devotee and an emissary of Avalokiteśvara. The texts he obtained and transmitted to China, moreover, appear to derive—directly or indirectly—from the bodhisattva himself. In these images, then, Xuanzang serves as a conduit, conveying the teachings, practices, and powers of the bodhisattva to those in need of protection and salvation.

By the Southern Song dynasty, accounts of the iconic trio of Xuanzang, his monkey attendant, and his horse carrying a bundle of texts radiating light was popular enough to be illustrated on small copper coins (see figure 2.5).[39] Similar

Figure 2.5. Amulet with image of a monkey-like figure holding a
staff, a horse carrying a luminous bundle, and a Buddhist monk,
estimated to date from the Southern Song dynasty. Fang,
Zhongguo huaqian yu chuantong wenhua, 170.

amulets, known as "subjugate-and-achieve-victory coins" (*yasheng qian* 壓勝錢, a.k.a.
"flower coins" 花錢), frequently feature Buddhist or Daoist deities—Avalokiteśvara
was a crowd favorite—and they were worn on the body to ward off evil spirits
and solicit good fortune.[40] It may be that charms featuring Xuanzang and his
companions served the same purpose (later traditions, discussed in the following chapter, would seem to bear this out), but whatever their function, these amulets advertised Xuanzang and his pilgrimage. Durable and portable, they transported his image and associated narratives across China and into neighboring
territories.[41]

The stories people told while squinting at murals in darkened chambers or fin-
gering amulets around their necks have not survived. During roughly the same
time Xuanzang appeared in caves and on amulets, however, related but seemingly
distinct textual accounts of his mythic pilgrimage were circulating along the southeastern coast of China nearly two thousand miles away. These works tell a truly
extraordinary tale.

New Narratives

When Glen Dudbridge published his groundbreaking study of the antecedents to the *Journey to the West* novel in 1970, the sculptures and murals of north and northwestern China were not widely known. At that time, the earliest available evidence pointed to an origin for the narrative in coastal Fujian province sometime during the thirteenth century. We now know that stories and images of Xuanzang's otherworldly pilgrimage had spread across the continent more than a hundred years earlier, but the poems and texts from southeastern China still preserve the most detailed written records of these mythical accounts.

The first textual references to this new vision of Xuanzang, or "Trepiṭaka" as he is often called, are cryptic. In one poem, written sometime prior to 1228, a monk and Fujian native named Zhang Shengzhe 張聖者 (ca. 1194–1264) refers in terse, elliptical succession to several of the plot points of what was presumably an already well-developed narrative:

> The unsurpassed and profound palm-leaf sutras are rare.
> Over several lifetimes, Trepiṭaka traveled to Western Heaven.
> Each line and every character are treasures.
> Every sentence and each word are fields of merit.
> A monkey came and went amidst the waves on the ocean of suffering.
> A horse charged ahead on the river where even feathers sink.[42]
> They crossed the long sands and [endured] the dangers of the golden sands.
> Gazing at the shore, they still knew the way to reach it.
> The *yakṣas* were delighted and answered their questions.
> The bodhisattvas, with palms pressed piously together, transmitted
> over five hundred and sixty cases [of texts].[43]
> Merit beyond measure came to complete fruition.[44]

Zhang Shengzhe's verse, written to commemorate the completion of a new revolving sutra repository, associates Xuanzang, a monkey, and a horse with Buddhist texts obtained from "Western Heaven." The deserts and cities of Xuanzang's historical journey are here reimagined as a liminal landscape occupied by *yakṣas*—nature spirits—and bodhisattvas situated between China and India, or between the human and heavenly realms. Xuanzang had unsuccessfully attempted to pass this way before in previous incarnations. Now, with the help of a monkey and a horse, he can cross a succession of perilous barriers and eventually arrive at the Pure Land. Xuanzang then receives the entire Buddhist canon directly from the bodhisattvas. These are the very books, presumably, that now filled the new library Zhang Shengzhe's verse was meant to memorialize.

Other, contemporaneous accounts affirm that a more fantastical version of Xuanzang's pilgrimage had taken root in the popular imagination in thirteenth-century Fujian. Liu Kezhuang 劉克莊 (1187–1269), a poet and native of Putian, a small city on the central coast of Fujian, alludes to a similar narrative in verse. In one poem, Liu chides Buddhists for needing a "Monkey Novice" (*hou xingzhe* 猴行者) to help retrieve the sutras from India. In another, he mocks himself for being as ugly as the Monkey Novice.[45] Liu, it seems, not only took it for granted that a passing reference to a monkey traveling west to obtain scriptures would resonate with his readers, he also assumed their familiarity with the Monkey Novice's unsightly appearance.

If, as Liu Kezhuang's poems imply, images of Xuanzang's monkey attendant were circulating in Fujian during the thirteenth century, they likely resembled the figure that still adorns a Buddhist stupa in the city of Quanzhou, about sixty miles south of Putian. This stone reliquary, known as the Renshou stupa 仁壽塔, was built on the grounds of Kaiyuan Monastery 開元寺 in 1237, when Liu Kezhuang was fifty years old. Sixteen figures appear on the fourth level of this five-story octagonal tower. Most are identifiable as bodhisattvas and dharma protectors, but three appear to derive from the Obtaining the Scriptures story (see figure 2.6). One of these is a fearsome, muscular monkey-warrior holding a sword or a cudgel. A thin headband holds back his hair and Buddhist prayer beads are draped around his neck. From the monkey's belt hang a gourd and a scroll of the *Sūtra of the Peahen Wisdom Queen* (*Kongque mingwang jing* 孔雀明王經)—a short apotropaic Buddhist text that was a popular panacea for everything from drought to demons, disease, and childbirth. Opposite the monkey stands a figure holding a ball in one hand and a staff in the other. A gourd is suspended from the staff and a horse bearing a bundle on its back rides a cloud that issues from the gourd's mouth. An inscription identifies this figure as the Fire Dragon Prince of the Eastern Sea (Donghai huolong taizi 東海火龍太子)—the name of Xuanzang's horse in the later versions of the Obtaining the Scriptures narrative. On the same level of the stupa, a beatified Xuanzang with palms pressed together stands opposite an image of the famously pro-Buddhist Liang-dynasty emperor Wu (464–549). The emperor is shown reading a copy of the *Heart Sūtra*, presumably (though anachronistically) the version translated by Xuanzang.[46] With the exception of Emperor Wu, the Renshou stupa depicts the main protagonists from the earliest mythical versions of the narrative: Xuanzang, a martial monkey, and a Dragon Horse. On the reliquary, these figures occupy the same position as bodhisattvas, arhats, and guardian deities. Xuanzang and his companions, it would seem, were recognized as members of the Buddhist pantheon, responsible for transmitting and safeguarding the Buddha dharma.[47]

The early visual and poetic evidence from Fujian is intriguing but fragmentary, only hinting at the existence of a more developed and detailed narrative. Fortu-

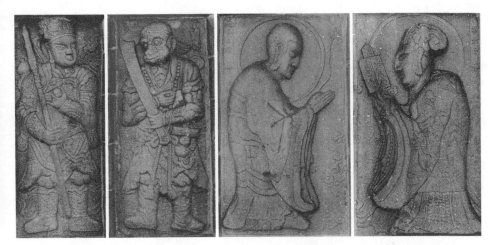

Figure 2.6. Stupa panels showing (from left to right) the Fire Dragon Prince of the Eastern Sea, a monkey warrior, Xuanzang, and Emperor Wu from Renshou stupa in Quanzhou. Ecke and Demieville, *The Twin Pagodas of Zayton*, plates 24 and 26.

nately, a much more elaborate account has been preserved in two texts printed sometime during the Southern Song dynasty (1127–1279), roughly the same period that verses and images from Fujian were produced.[48] The first and probably slightly earlier text was printed in the city of Hangzhou with the title *The Poetic Tale of the Great Tang Trepiṭaka Master's Obtaining the Scriptures* (*Da Tang Sanzang qu jing shihua* 大唐三藏取經詩話). The second printing, titled *The Newly Arranged Record of the Great Tang Trepiṭaka Dharma Master's Obtaining the Scriptures* (*Xin diao da Tang Sanzang fashi qu jing ji* 新調大唐三藏法師取經記), appears to have been made in the city of Fuzhou not long after.[49] Both texts may have originally included illustrations, but these have not survived.[50] On the basis of the first text's title, the two editions are sometimes referred to as the *shihua* 詩話 (poetic tale) versions of the Obtaining the Scriptures legend. Alternatively, they also are known as the Kōzanji 高山寺 editions, named after the temple in Kyoto where they were discovered in the early twentieth century.[51] Although they bear different titles, the two texts are virtually identical in both content and structure.

The Kōzanji narrative appears to flesh out some of the scenes alluded to in Zhang Shengzhe's poem. The story begins abruptly in the second chapter—the title and content of both first chapters have unfortunately been lost—with Xuanzang acquiring the assistance of a white-robed "Monkey Novice," who introduces himself as "none other than the bronze-headed, iron-browed king of the eighty-four thousand monkeys of the Purple Cloud Grotto on the Mountain of Flowers and Fruits." The Monkey King explains that Xuanzang has attempted to travel to India twice before in previous incarnations and each time the Spirit of the Deep Sands murdered him. On this third and final attempt, the Monkey King and five other monks escort Xuanzang. The deity Mahābrahmā Devarāja Vaiśravaṇa (Pishamen dafantianwang 毘沙門大梵天王) also protects him and bestows three magical implements: a cap of invisibility, a golden-ringed staff, and a begging bowl "for quelling demons on the road ahead." Thus equipped, Xuanzang and his companions travel through desolate landscapes devoid of human habitation but crawling with malicious animals, demons, and ghosts. They pass through the country of the tree people and the land of women. Various dangers are endured and overcome for the sake of "sentient beings of the Eastern Lands [who] are still ignorant of the Buddha's Law."[52] Xuanzang's mission, according to this account, is nothing short of introducing the entire Buddhist tradition to China.

Some of the central features of the later, more elaborate legend are present but not fully developed in the Kōzanji texts. The party passes through Avalokiteśvara's kingdom, for instance, but they do not encounter the bodhisattva who becomes Xuanzang's chief protector in later versions of the narrative. (Given the importance of this bodhisattva both in the scenes in cave temples and in later accounts of Xuanzang's mythic pilgrimage, it is possible that he played a part in the lost first chapter.) The pilgrims meet the demon Deep Sands and receive his help, but he does not transform into Sha Monk and join their party. Xuanzang also receives a white horse from the queen of the Land of Women, who is a manifestation of the bodhisattvas Mañjuśrī and Samantabhadra, but the horse is not identified as a transformed dragon, nor does it become a major character in this story as it does is in subsequent accounts.

A major turning point in the Kōzanji texts comes when the party finally arrives on the outskirts of India, or "Western Heaven." Leaving desolation and danger behind, the travelers pass through beautiful, prosperous cities. The Monkey King explains that they have arrived in the celestial realm of the Buddha: "There are no seasons in Buddha's heaven. The red sun sinks not in the west. Children grow not old and there is no sorrow for death. They live twelve hundred years and never lack for food. Those who come to this land return to a hundred good incarnations."[53] The group has thus crossed from a perilous netherworld into a kind of paradise. When they arrive in India proper, described as a "realm of immortals," Xuanzang and the members of his party lodge at a monastery where the resident monks chide them for naively expecting to meet the Buddha. The monks explain that even they have never seen the Buddha, who—like Avalokiteśvara on Mount Potalaka—dwells on the peak of an unscalable mountain on the far side of a roiling sea. Undaunted, Xuanzang fervently prays and, in a flash of lightning and a peal of thunder, all 5,048 volumes of the Buddhist canon miraculously appear beside him. Only the *Heart Sūtra* is missing, and this he obtains on his return journey to China.

When Dīpankara Buddha appears and transmits this final text, he explains that the sutra can still the wind and calm waves, making ghosts weep and spirits howl, and can penetrate both heaven and hell. Dīpankara then commands Xuanzang and his fellow pilgrims to return to heaven three months hence, on the fifteenth day of the seventh month—the day of the Ghost Festival. The pilgrims proceed to Chang'an, offer the *Heart Sūtra* to the emperor, and hold memorial services for the spirits that aided them along their journey.[54] The bizarre beings Xuanzang and his companions encountered during their travels to Western Heaven, it is thus implied, were spirits of the dead who had been condemned to suffer in purgatory. Their liberation is contingent upon the completion of Xuanzang's pilgrimage and the successful transmission of salvific texts and rituals. After these shades have been appeased, the story concludes on the day of the Ghost Festival when, as promised, Dīpankara Buddha descends from the west to lift Xuanzang and his companions up to heaven.

This account, published more than three centuries before the *Journey to the West* novel, contains a rough outline of what would later become a much more intricate and lengthier story. As the earliest instance of the extended narrative, the Kōzanji texts often are read as vernacular fiction, unpolished precursors to the more sophisticated novel. The rough literary quality of the work initially led Dudbridge to conclude that the text was "a collection of related traditions, current perhaps both in oral and written form, strung together by a writer for an audience of humble readers."[55] The tale, he reasoned, was probably part of the repertoires of popular storytellers. Other scholars have since expanded this assessment, pointing out that the Kōzanji texts resemble a genre of popular Buddhist literature known as "sutra telling story scripts" (*shuojing huaben* 說經話本), relatively simple works that present Buddhist teachings to lay audiences through the medium of engaging storytelling.[56] Such scripts, which often were accompanied by images, were crafted to be dramatic and entertaining to better capture the attention of largely illiterate audiences. They were meant to be inviting, but their primary purpose was to proselytize.

Unfortunately, nothing is known about the author(s) of the Kōzanji texts, and the name of only one publisher has been preserved. The Zhang 張 family that printed the earliest known edition of the story was based in Hangzhou, the walled capital of the Southern Song dynasty. No other works published by this family have survived, making it impossible to determine what other kind of material they might have produced. We do know that the Zhangs worked out of Hangzhou's Central Market district (Zhongwazi 中瓦子), a major cultural and business center and a popular location for commercial presses at that time. Other publishers located in the immediate vicinity of the Zhang family's publishing house printed Buddhist and Daoist texts, as well as so-called "paper horses" (*zhima* 紙馬)—single sheets stamped with the images of gods meant to be burned as offerings.[57] The neighborhood where the Kōzanji text was printed was, therefore, home to several presses that specialized in religious texts and icons. It seems likely that this account of Xuanzang's mythical pilgrimage to the land of the Buddha also was sold as an accessible and engaging Buddhist text.

The context and the content of these works offer insight not only into the early development of Xuanzang's legend but also into popular Chinese Buddhist conceptions of death and the afterlife. The Japanese scholar Chūbachi Masakazu (b. 1938) was the first to point out that the Kōzanji narratives mirror two closely related mythic archetypes. The first, derived from ancient Han Chinese traditions, is the journey of the dead to the netherworld. In many accounts of postmortem travels, spirit animals (including but not limited to monkeys) serve as the guides for the dead on their passage through the spirit realm, whether the final destination is the Yellow Springs beneath the earth or Mount Kunlun in the distant west. The other motif, emerging from early Indian Buddhist literature, is the transmigration of the spirit to the Pure Land, which, like Mount Kunlun, was conventionally located somewhere in the west. In Buddhist accounts, animals (again, often but not always monkeys) also serve as escorts for the dead.[58] Chūbachi proposed that these narrative traditions—culturally distinct but thematically and functionally similar— were fused together with the historical account of Xuanzang's journey to India. The Kōzanji texts, according to this reading, represent a complex but organic blending of initially independent narratives. The broad contours of Xuanzang's biography and travelogue were superimposed onto older mythic accounts to provide a new, quasi-historical frame for age-old stories about the transmigrations of the dead.[59]

Viewed from this perspective, Xuanzang was not passing through Central Asia en route to India but, instead, was traversing a hellish purgatory to reach a heavenly pure land. Like a shaman, he departs the human world and enters a dangerous liminal zone. Beset by ghosts and demons, he is guided and protected by powerful spirit animals and Buddhist deities. After enduring extreme hardship, he eventually arrives in an immortal realm populated by spirit monks, immortals, bodhisattvas, and buddhas. From Śākyamuni Buddha, he receives a collection of apotropaic texts with the power to safeguard the living and liberate the dead. Xuanzang then transmits these sacred scriptures back to the human realm before he and his assistants ascend to heaven during the annual ritual for liberating the damned from purgatory. This narrative not only maps the landscape of a postmortem shadow world, it also identifies the scriptures that guard against demonic molestation and ensure a propitious rebirth: the Buddhist canon in general and the *Heart Sūtra* in particular. Those who read, recited, or heard the Kōzanji texts were thus informed of the perils of purgatory and offered the promise of protection and salvation. Xuanzang, they also learned, was the saintly monk responsible for delivering these divine texts and technologies into the hands of humans.

By the end of the thirteenth century, Xuanzang's conventional biography had been transformed into a surreal story of otherworldly travels and divine dispensations. His already extraordinary accomplishments—his quest for more accurate and more efficacious texts, his long, harrowing journey, his visions and accounts of demons and bodhisattvas, his acquisition of sacred scriptures, and his triumphant return—were elevated to the realm of myth. These new narratives not only related the epic travels of an eminent Chinese Buddhist monk in search of authentic Indian Buddhist teachings, they also provided an origin story for the transmission of Buddhist scriptures to China. Over time, Xuanzang, the great master of the Tripiṭaka, became the main conduit for the Buddhist canon and the human embodiment of all its attendant powers.

The texts and images surveyed in this chapter were produced along the perimeter of the Chinese empire, from the coasts of Fujian to the Shandong peninsula, across the borderlands of the north and northwest, and down to southern Sichuan. The location of most of these early images and accounts outside of major population centers may indicate that the narratives they depict developed first in the hinterlands and were introduced to urban areas only later. It is also possible, however, that legends of a divine Xuanzang were even more widespread during the twelfth and thirteenth centuries but have simply been better preserved in lightly populated areas that suffered less destruction over the ensuing centuries. Whatever the case, these new stories, like Xuanzang himself, were intrepid travelers. As they spread, they superseded more historically grounded accounts of Xuanzang's life and work. As far as we know, no images showing Xuanzang at the court of the great seventh-century Indian king Kumara were ever made. There also are no new stories about Xuanzang's years of study in the halls of Nālandā. These and other hugely consequential moments in Xuanzang's life appear to have held scant interest for later generations. Rather than scenes from the *Biography of the Trepiṭaka Master* or the *Record of the Western Regions,* people preferred to picture Xuanzang standing side-by-side with a monkey gazing up at Avalokiteśvara. Crowds gathered in temple courtyards and in village streets not to learn about how Xuanzang labored to translate the *Discourse on the Stages of Yogic Practice* from Sanskrit to Chinese but to hear how he managed to pass safely through the country of tree people on his way to Western Heaven. It was more compelling to imagine that the scriptures he eventually acquired—the very texts that were then housed in local Buddhist monasteries and recited by resident Buddhist clerics—came not from seventh-century south and central Asian monks and laypeople but derived directly from buddhas and bodhisattvas. These scriptures and treatises contained monastic regulations, exegeses on the nature of consciousness, and the doctrinal positions of various Indian Buddhist schools, but they also were, more importantly, endowed with the wisdom, divine presence, and supranormal powers of the Buddhist pantheon. As the monk who conveyed these talismanic texts to the people of China, Xuanzang accrued some of the same divine qualities inherent in the sutras he transmitted.

The historical Xuanzang never claimed to have reached a heavenly realm while he was alive, but he fully intended to go there after his death. He had always been a pious devotee of the future buddha Maitreya and vowed that he would live his next life in the inner cloister of Maitreya's palace in Tuṣita Heaven. In this realm, beings live for hundreds of thousands of years, listening to the teachings of Maitreya and waiting for the time when he will descend to earth to be reborn as the next buddha. When Xuanzang lay dying in the winter of 664, his disciples wondered about his next incarnation, with one asking, "Has the master decided to obtain rebirth in Maitreya's inner cloister or not?"[60] Xuanzang assured them that he had. Shortly thereafter, he passed away.

A series of auspicious signs and visions seemed to confirm that Xuanzang had, indeed, gone to Tuṣita Heaven. In the stories and images that started circulating in the twelfth century, however, Xuanzang seems to have left Maitreya's palace to roam across the realms of demons, ghosts, and gods, and engage with Avalokiteśvara, Mañjuśrī, Śākyamuni, Dīpankara, and a host of other buddhas, bodhisattvas, and dharma guardians. Like these deities, Xuanzang assumed an aura of immortality. His pilgrimage was ongoing, but henceforth he would never travel alone. A monkey attendant and a horse always accompany the Tang Monk. (The pig Zhu Bajie and the demon monk Sha will join the party later.) As we will see, these pilgrims are constantly cycling in and out of the human world, manifesting in various forms to guide others to the Pure Land in the West and to convey the teachings and ritual techniques of buddhas and bodhisattvas back to the people of the east. They work as chaperones, but given the predators lurking on paths they travel, they also serve as shields against demonic attacks.

3 Guardian

We are supplicants to our own fiction.

—Louis Menand, "Karl Marx, Yesterday and Today"

Before Xuanzang set off for India, while he was still a young monk living in Sichuan, he came across a sick man dressed in rags and covered in putrid sores. Xuanzang took the man back to his monastery and gave him food and clothing. Wishing to repay Xuanzang's kindness, the beggar taught him the *Heart Sūtra*. Later, when Xuanzang was traveling alone across the Gobi Desert, he found himself "surrounded by vicious ghosts in all kinds of strange forms." He recited the name of Avalokiteśvara, the patron saint of travelers and protector of people in distress, but the ghosts continued to plague him. Then he remembered the *Heart Sūtra*. On hearing the words of this short text, the spirits scattered. Xuanzang walked deeper into the desert, where "no bird flew above, and no beast roamed below." Having spilled the last of his water, he grew dehydrated and disoriented. The ghosts and demons returned. After five days without water, he lay down on the sand and prayed to Avalokiteśvara for help. That night, a deity, "several tens of feet tall, holding a spear and a flag in his hands," appeared to Xuanzang in a dream and urged him to keep going. After getting up and staggering a few more miles, Xuanzang's horse found an oasis and they were saved.[1]

This was the first of many life-threatening dangers that, according to Huili's biographical account, Xuanzang confronted and overcame on his way to India. The threats Xuanzang faced on his pilgrimage proved much more compelling to later generations than the doctrinal texts he studied at Nālandā and elsewhere. As stories of his epic journey circulated, the path he traversed grew ever more perilous and fantastic. In the Kōzanji texts, for example, the deity Xuanzang encountered in the Gobi Desert is identified as the spirit of Deep Sands (*Shen sha* 深沙). Having murdered and devoured Xuanzang in two previous incarnations, Deep Sands, standing thirty-feet tall and wearing a garland of Xuanzang's past bones, conjures a golden bridge with silver rails so that Xuanzang and his companions can safely cross a particularly treacherous stretch of desert. By the time *Journey to the West* was published in the late sixteenth century, Deep Sands had become a fiend with black and green skin, wild red hair, a mouth "like a butcher's bloody bowl," and teeth "protruding like swords and knives." He now had his own hagiography. Formerly the Jade Emperor's divine general, he had been banished to earth for the crime of breaking a crystal cup. Now, as punishment, he suffers the perpetual stabs of flying swords. He dines on human flesh and wears the skulls of the nine previous pilgrim monks he has killed and consumed. In the novel, after Deep Sands is subdued and converted by Avalokiteśvara, he becomes the monk Sha Wujing 沙悟淨 (Sha Monk) and pledges to accompany and protect Xuanzang on his westward journey.[2]

With the accrual of these kinds of extraordinary embellishments, stories of Xuanzang's pilgrimage grew ever more dramatic and elaborate over time. By the Yuan dynasty (1279–1368), the three figures from earliest narratives and images—Xuanzang, a monkey attendant, and a divine horse—had expanded to the now standard party of five. In addition to Sha Wujing, the group also acquired Zhu Bajie, the cannibalistic human-pig hybrid. As Xuanzang's legend spread, so, too, did his reputation for subjugating demons and dispelling the forces of disorder and death. Later accounts described how a host of bodhisattvas, immortals, and celestial deities watch over him. He also wields several magical implements: the *Heart Sūtra,* a powerful dhāraṇī, a golden robe, and a hell-destroying staff. The appeal of this divinely empowered Xuanzang spread beyond the monasteries, cave temples, and stupas where he was initially memorialized. By at least the fourteenth century, accounts of the five pilgrims' exploits were recited by itinerant storytellers, circulated in print, performed on and off stage, and used to decorate everyday household items. The story, with its bizarre creatures, tense battles, and archetypical themes, captivated audiences throughout China and in neighboring territories.

In the modern era, recitations and dramatic performances of Obtaining the Scriptures narratives typically have been understood as forms of entertainment. While amusement and spectacle were surely features of many performances in the premodern period, the pilgrimage also was reenacted as ritual to address specific kinds of problems. The same crises that afflict Xuanzang in Obtaining the Scriptures narratives—the absence of efficacious ritual texts, the predation of demons, and the obstacles that block access to the buddha realm—also confronted communities of devotees. The performance or oral invocation of Xuanzang's pilgrimage thus drew an equivalence between the events of the myth and the problems of the present. The resolutions of the narrative—the sacred scriptures acquired, the demons converted or destroyed, the pure land obtained—were reproduced and resolved over the course of the rite.

For reasons outlined in the first chapter, most people today are not accustomed to thinking about Xuanzang's story in this way. The ritualization of mythic narratives, however, is a common enough phenomenon, and there are instructive parallels between the enactment of Buddhist legends in medieval China and the ritualistic deployment of biblical stories in medieval Europe. The Dutch historian of religion and Christian theologian Gerard van der Leeuw (1890–1950) referred to ritually invoked narratives as "magical antecedents": brief stories relating an event from the distant past that had acquired a "mythical eternity and typicalness."[3] When spoken aloud, these stories had the effect of conjuring the event in the present. Later scholars, building on van der Leeuw's work, have explored the role of performative utterances in ritually transmitting or replicating the power of the mythic realm in the quotidian world.[4] Throughout the premodern Mediterranean and European worlds, for example, the proper narration or performance of a myth had the potential to rectify the very afflictions that are addressed in the story itself. In the context of many ritual traditions, then, the recitation of mythic narratives does not merely represent or describe an event; it *generates* it.

The principle of *similia . . . similibus* (just as . . . so also) was not limited to speech acts but extended to other kinds of performance as well. In late medieval Europe, elaborate and immersive mystery plays transformed entire cities into ritual arenas for the reenactment of Christ's birth, death, and resurrection. Such dramas were designed to collapse the distance and eradicate the distinction between biblical times and the present.[5] Over the course of such performances, "The dead come to life in the bodies of living."[6]

China, of course, has its own rich tradition of ritual theater and the themes of divine embodiment, audience immersion, and ritual efficacy have been explored by scholars in the context of several dramatic traditions, most notably performances of "Mulian Rescues His Mother" (more on this in chapter 4). Dramas, dances, and recitations of Obtaining the Scriptures narratives, although rarely studied in this context, also aspired to accomplish clearly articulated goals, chief among them the safe transition to a heavenly realm, the acquisition of divine texts and technologies, empowerment, and protection against demonic forces. This chapter and the two that follow examine each of these interrelated roles in turn. Here, I consider instances where Xuanzang is embodied as a guardian figure. Rituals, images, descriptions of dramatic performances, liturgical collections, and references in historical sources all demonstrate that the seventh-century monk who once prayed for protection from ghosts and ghouls in the desert was regularly recalled to exorcise the demons that plagued later generations of his devotees.

Exorcists

The contemporary festival known as the "Dance of the Foreign Monks" (*tiao fan seng* 跳番僧) is a case in point. Every year at the beginning of the sixth lunar month, in the small village of Heyuan 河源 in the mountainous interior of northwestern Fujian province, six young boys and girls put on red head cloths, white shirts, red pants, and wooden masks. The masks are carved with the faces of the Tang Monk, Sun Wukong, Zhu Bajie, Sha Monk, the future buddha Maitreya, and a deity known as the Road Opening Spirit (Kai lu shen 開路神).[7] This six-member troupe walks at the head of a long procession made up of more masked deities, musicians, flag bearers, incense carriers, and villagers, which snakes from village to village over the course of two days before ascending to the peak of Mt. Daofeng 道峰山, the tallest mountain in the region.

The Tang Monk and his companions balance poles across their shoulders with two-sided drums suspended from one end and yellow banners with the single word "scripture" written in red hanging from the other. During the procession, these four figures encircle and protect Maitreya and the Road Opening Spirit, who are portrayed as mirror images of one another. Maitreya crouches and squats, and has a joyful face; the Road Opening Spirit jumps and dances, and wears a mask carved into a fanged scowl. All six deities pause at intersections, bridges, and entrance-ways to perform a choreographed series of steps intended to drive away demons and purify the places they pass through (see plate 5).[8]

This procession, which has been documented in detail by the anthropologist Ye Mingsheng, is the main event of an annual rite known as Welcoming the Three Buddha Ancestors (Ying san fo zushi 迎三佛祖師) or, simply, the Festival for Welcoming the Spirits (Ying shen hui 迎神會).[9] This is the largest communal event held in the rural Heyuan region. The three-day, multipart ritual is structured around two closely related themes: transmission and purification. On the evening of the first day, a ceremony is held at the main temple of the village, Lingxing si 靈興寺, with participants reciting Buddhist scriptures under the guidance of a local Daoist master.[10] (Despite the use of explicitly Buddhist texts and imagery throughout the ceremony, the lead officiants all identify as Daoist.) On the morning of the following day, participants return to the temple to perform the ceremony of "Transmitting the Scriptures." Excerpts from select Buddhist sutras are chanted while the implements to be used during the procession—texts, masks, icons, and offerings—are passed from the ritual master to dozens of older local women, known as "Amitābha Grannies."[11] Each person duly venerates the object before passing it along, thereby enacting the transmission of sacred materials from the deities to ritual masters to members of the community. At the end of the ceremony, talismans reading "Homage to the Great and Vast Buddha's Flower Adornment Scripture" (南無大方廣佛華嚴經) are distributed. These charms are to be brought to the homes of participants and pasted on walls to ward off evil and attract blessings. The procession begins immediately after the ritual of "Transmitting the Scriptures," and the theme of transmission continues as the Tang Monk and his companions carry "scripture" flags from Lingxing Temple through a series of villages and up to the peak of Mt. Daofeng. When they return to the village of Heyuan on the afternoon of the third day, their final dance is performed without the flags, signaling that the scriptures have been delivered and the transmission is complete.[12]

Small statues of the three tutelary spirits of the Heyuan region also are carried in the procession. According to local tradition, sometime in the late ninth or early tenth century, monks named Gong Zhidao 龔志道, Liu Zhida 劉志達, and Yang Zhiyuan 楊志遠 settled in these mountains after training with the renowned Chan master Xuefeng Yicun 雪峰義存 (822–908). These clerics were reportedly all outsiders who had migrated to the region. Gong Zhidao was from Central Asia; Liu Zhida was from Vietnam; and Yang Zhiyuan was from Yunnan.[13] The men thus became known as the Three Foreign Monks or the Three Buddha Ancestors. (The late ninth and early tenth centuries saw a wave of immigration into Fujian province, and these three "ancestors" may, in fact, be the patriarchs of clans that first settled this area. The Gong clan that now lives in the region and is the primary organizer of the festival shares the surname of Gong Zhidao.) The prophylactic powers of these "foreign monks"—preventing drought, warding off pestilence, and repelling demons—remained with their spirits after their deaths. The icons of the Three Buddha Ancestors are enshrined in the village temple and carried in a portable shrine to local settlements during the procession, reinforcing bonds between extended families with common concerns and deeply entwined histories.

While the Dance of the Foreign Monks purifies and protects the community, it also recalls and reestablishes the transmission of Indian Buddhist texts and rituals to northwestern Fujian. Their origins described and their powers extolled, the Buddhist sutras and deities deployed during the rite are welcomed back into the community year after year. Xuanzang and his companions thus serve as both the escorts and the emissaries of the Buddha ancestors. They, too, are "foreign monks." As in other versions of Obtaining the Scriptures narratives, during the festival the pilgrims embark on a mission, traveling from the known world to a distant heavenly realm, in this case Mt. Daofeng. Along the way, they subjugate demons, manifest divine powers, and obtain the sacred scriptures. These talismanic texts then are conveyed to the human realm where they confer the presence and protection of buddhas, bodhisattvas, and ancestors to the village. Most accounts of Xuanzang's mythic pilgrimage end with the arrival of the scriptures in the capital and the apotheosis of the pilgrims, but in the village of Heyuan, the contract between humans and gods must be renewed each year. Divine presence fades over time and demons inevitably return. The pathways connecting the human and the heavenly realms accordingly require regular maintenance.

This particular form of the procession does not appear to be especially old. According to Ye Mingsheng, the first textual reference to a Dance of Foreign Monks in northwestern Fujian comes from a temple inscription dated to 1862. There also are other dances known by this same title, and not all of these feature the Tang Monk and his companions.[14] In the village of Kanxia 坎下 in southern Fujian, for instance, a Dance of the Foreign Monks (held during the eighth lunar month) is performed by a six-member troupe, but in this case the main figures are Maitreya, Maitreya's wife, and their four children. In the village of Daling 大嶺, in northeastern Fujian, a dance by the same name (this one performed in the tenth lunar month) features Maitreya and the Road Opening Spirit. The other four "foreign monks" are not named, but they carry "sutra poles" as in the Heyuan rite.[15] The various Dances of Foreign Monks each have six performers and all feature Maitreya, but only the Heyuan dance identifies four of the monks as the protagonists of the Obtaining the Scriptures narrative. It would thus seem that the Tang Monk and his companions were at some point grafted onto a preexisting rite centered on Maitreya.[16]

The identities of the masked figures in various Dances of Foreign Monks differ according to local tradition, but the ritual itself is a variation on a perennial theme. Purificatory rites of roughly similar structure and content have been performed in China for well over two thousand years. The earliest detailed description of large, communal exorcisms in China comes from the *Rites of Zhou* (*Zhou li* 周禮), an official administrative text issued in the third century BCE. According to the *Rites*, on the last day of the year, demons must be driven from the imperial palace in a ritual known as the Great Exorcism (*da nuo* 大儺). During the ceremony, the chief exorcist, known as the Fangxiang shi 方相氏:

> wears [over his head] a bear skin having four eyes of gold, and is clad in a black upper garment and a red lower garment. Grasping his lance and brandishing his shield, he leads the many officials to perform the seasonal Exorcism, searching through houses and driving out pestilences. When there is a great funeral, he goes in advance of the coffin, and upon its arrival at the tomb, when it is being inserted into the [burial] chamber, he strikes the four corners [of the chamber] with his lance and expels the [demon of pestilence] Fangliang 方良.[17]

A later source, the fifth-century *Book of the Later Han*, provides a more detailed account of official *nuo* rituals, describing palace exorcisms as large-scale, carefully orchestrated affairs performed by casts of hundreds. In these annual events, the chief exorcist in his four-eyed bear-skin mask leads a group of one hundred and twenty eunuchs between the ages of ten and twelve to the front hall of the imperial palace. The boys wear red head cloths and black shirts and hold twirl-drums. Twelve more eunuchs, embodying mythical animals, dress in costumes of fur, feathers, and horns. In the early evening, the entire group gathers at the front hall together with

Plate 1. Xuanzang as pilgrim. Fourteenth century, Japan. Tokyo National Museum.

Plate 2. Detail of Xuanzang, a monkey-like attendant, and a brown horse. From a mural featuring Water Moon Avalokiteśvara on the southern wall of cave 2 of the Eastern Thousand Buddha Caves complex. Gansu. Xixia era (1038–1227). Zhang, *Guazhou dong qian fo dong*, 142.

Plate 3. Water-Moon Avalokiteśvara. At the bottom right, four funeral
performers and two horses stand next to an open grave. The man
approaching the bodhisattva on a cloud may be the spirit of the
deceased. Khara Khoto, Xixia dynasty, twelfth century. State Hermitage
Museum, Saint Petersburg. Piotrovsky, *Lost Empire of the Silk Road,* 199.

Plate 4. Water Moon Avalokiteśvara with a monk, monkey attendant, and horse faintly visible in the bottom right corner. Western wall, north side of Yulin cave 2. Xixia era (1038–1227). Dunhuang Yanjiu Yuan, *Zhongguo shiku: Anxi Yulin ku,* plate 138.

Plate 5. Dance of the Foreign Monks, performed in Heyuan, Fujian in 2003. The masked figures, from left to right, are the Tang Monk, Maitreya, Sun Wukong, the Road Opening Spirit, Zhu Bajie, and Sha Monk. Photo courtesy of Zhaohua Yang.

Plate 6. Funeral procession featuring the figures from the Obtaining the Scriptures narrative, performed by the Taipei Luzhou Sunshine Troupe 台北蘆洲日光陣頭 (Banqiao, Taipei), 2018. Photo courtesy of the Taipei Luzhou Sunshine Troupe.

Plate 7. Universal Salvation Mountain scene with Avalokiteśvara at the upper center and the Tang Monk and his companions at the bottom. Longshan Temple, Taipei, 2014. Photo courtesy of Xie Zongrong 謝宗榮.

Plate 8. Painting of the Potalaka Cliff at the Liwang gong 厲王宮 in Tainan, Taiwan. The Tang Monk and his companions surround Avalokiteśvara at the top. Photo courtesy of Xie Qifeng 謝奇峰.

Plate 9. Funerary scroll dated to 1940, from Qingmei, Taiwan. The inscription reads: "Trepiṭaka went to Western Heaven to obtain the scriptures, traveling thousands of *li* and [visiting] hundreds of thousands of courts. He obtained the *Heart Sūtra* in a single scroll, and this was transmitted in the world for the salvation of the dead." Gift of Stephan Feuchtwang. © The Trustees of the British Museum.

Plate 10. Ritual of Requesting the Scriptures performed by Shijiao masters in Hengshan village 橫山, Xinzhu, Taiwan, 2010. Photo courtesy of Liu Meiling 劉美玲.

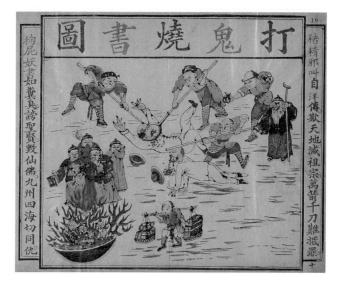

Plate 11. Print titled, "Beat the Ghosts and Burn their Books." The text on the right explains, "The evil pig spirit [Jesus] came from the west. It deceives Heaven and Earth and extinguishes our ancestors. Ten-thousand arrows and a thousand swords are a fitting punishment." The caption on the left reads, "Their dog-fart demonic books stink like shit. They slander the sages and destroy immortals and buddhas. They are the common enemy of [all people of] the nine continents and four seas." *In Accord with the Imperial Edict: Complete Illustrations of the Heretical Religion* (Jinzun shengyu poxie quantu 謹遵聖諭辟邪全圖).

court officials and military officers. When the emperor arrives, the crowd begins chanting, urging the twelve animals to drive out or devour the demons that have infested the imperial precincts over the course of the year. The exorcists threaten any lingering demons with having their bodies roasted, their spines and joints broken, their flesh torn off, and their lungs and entrails ripped out and consumed. As the group chants, the chief exorcist and the twelve animals dance, shout, and wave torches, moving through the buildings and lanes of the palace. The demons are driven out of the southern gate of the walled city where mounted guards take the torches and throw them into the river, extinguishing the danger.[18]

Given the relentless nature of the threats that exorcisms seek to counteract—illness, epidemics, natural disasters, ghosts, malicious spirits, premature death, infertility—the performance of communal exorcisms has remained a vital practice in China for more than two millennia. *Nuo* were conducted in the imperial palace through the Tang dynasty. Presumably, similar, smaller-scale rituals were performed also in cities, villages, and homes, though we know very little about them. The annual communal exorcistic rites that have survived into the modern era, however, preserve certain core elements of earlier *nuo* traditions. These are not precise replicas of earlier rituals, but contemporary adaptations are broadly related to premodern rites in both structure and function.

The Heyuan rite, for example, takes place in mountain villages rather than the imperial palace. It employs an assortment of deities drawn from the popular pantheon instead of the chief exorcist and his twelve animals. It also venerates buddhas and ancestors in addition to destroying demons, but the parallels between imperial *nuo* and the Dance of the Foreign Monks are clear nonetheless.[19] Both are annual purificatory rituals featuring processions of deities, demons, and animal hybrids moving through residential areas while engaging in choreographed battles with invisible malevolent forces. (The sixth lunar month, when the Heyuan festival is held, is when this region historically has suffered outbreaks of bubonic plague, smallpox, malaria, and measles.) As in ancient *nuo* rituals, the exorcists in Heyuan usually are adolescents. They dance, play drums, wear red head cloths, and are masked—a defining feature of many exorcistic rites. Subject to taboos and residing in temples most of the year, such masks are treated as living icons animated by their deities (see figure 3.1). When a person, usually after a period of purification, places one of these masks over their face, they invite the deity to take possession of their body. The performers are thus not portraying or representing the spirits, they *become* them over the course of the ritual.

The Dance of the Foreign Monks is one of many annual *nuo* rituals still performed in mainland China. Other rites feature other deities, but ritual dances involving the figures from the Obtaining the Scriptures narrative were, until very recently, performed throughout the country (see figure 3.2). Examples have been

Figure 3.1. Masks of the Tang Monk, Zhu Bajie, and Sun Wukong used in exorcistic theater performances (*di xi* 地戲) in Anshun region of Guizhou. Gu et al., *Zhongguo Guizhou minzu minjian*, 294.

Figure 3.2. *Nuo* ritual dance with masked figures from the Obtaining the Scriptures performed in Nanfeng county 南豐縣, Jiangsu province. Xue et al., *Zhongguo wunuo mianju yishu*, 66.

documented in Jiangsu, Jiangxi, Fujian, Zhejiang, Hunan, Hubei, Shaanxi, Ningxia, Liaoning, Guizhou, and Guangdong provinces.[20] Several of these traditions were lost after 1949, making the Dance of the Foreign Monks one of the few surviving examples of a once much more prevalent tradition.

Sentinels

When did Xuanzang and his pilgrimage become associated with exorcisms? Most observers assume that modern *nuo* dances involving the Tang Monk derive from the *Journey to the West* novel. That is surely true in some cases, but the prophylactic powers of Xuanzang and his companions were recognized well before the novel's publication in the late sixteenth century. If the apotropaic amulets discussed in the previous chapter are any indication, depictions of Xuanzang's mythic pilgrimage wielded protective powers as early as the Northern Song dynasty. Additional evidence for this quality of Xuanzang's cult comes from the Korean peninsula, where a literary version of the Obtaining the Scriptures narrative, often referred to as the *pinghua* 平話, or vernacular version, had spread by the fifteenth century.

The *Pak t'ongsa ŏnhae* 朴通事諺解, a primer for colloquial Chinese first published in Korea in the late fourteenth century, reproduces one episode of the larger Obtaining the Scriptures story-cycle and alludes to several other scenes.[21] The impression given in this account is that the narrative was read as popular vernacular fiction. In the text, one speaker is called to defend his fondness for the book, which another speaker has derided as inferior to the *Four Books* and *Six Classics*. "What do you want with that sort of vernacular tale (*pinghua*)?" the first asks. "The *Journey to the West* is lively," the other counters. "It's good reading for when you're feeling gloomy." For some readers, then, the narrative was simply a light-hearted, entertaining story, a leisurely diversion to while away the hours.

The *Pak t'ongsa ŏnhae*, together with an entry in the early-fifteenth-century Chinese imperial encyclopedia *Yongle dadian* 永樂大典, constitutes the earliest textual evidence for a more developed version (or versions) of Xuanzang's mythic pilgrimage following the publication of the Kōzanji texts in the thirteenth century. The passages reproduced in these two works are similar in content to the corresponding sections of the later hundred-chapter novel, making it clear that by the late fourteenth or early fifteenth century large portions of the story already were in broad circulation. This was a new phase in the evolution of the narrative, as accounts of Xuanzang's mythical pilgrimage were lifted out of conventional Buddhist contexts and produced for broader consumption. In Yuan-dynasty China, for example, images of Xuanzang and his strange companions adorned mass-produced, common household items such as porcelain pillows and incense braziers (see

Figure 3.3. Yuan-dynasty porcelain pillow featuring the five pilgrims from the Obtaining the Scriptures narrative. Guangdong Provincial Museum.

figure 3.3).[22] The commodification of the narrative would culminate centuries later in the publication of the hundred-chapter novel, but the story as hagiography for a deified Xuanzang continued to inform popular ritual traditions throughout this period. Both strains of the narrative—as sacred history and as mundane entertainment—coexisted and often coalesced, with each informing the content and burnishing the reputation of the other.

On the Korean peninsula, Xuanzang was depicted not only as the protagonist of a "lively" literary tale but also as the divine transmitter of sacred texts and a guardian of palaces and tombs. During roughly the same time some Yuan artisans were painting the five pilgrims on uncomfortable-looking porcelain pillows, other craftsmen from China were carving scenes from Xuanzang's mythic travels on a Buddhist stupa in the capital of the Koryŏ dynasty (918–1392), Songdo 松都 (present-day Kaesong 開城).[23] The ten-level marble stupa was built on the grounds of Kyŏngch'ŏn-sa 敬天寺 in 1348 at the behest of the eunuch Ko Yong-bong 高龍鳳 (d. 1362) and the official Kang Yung 姜融 (d. 1349).[24] The monastery itself was associated with the imperial family and served as the site of memorial rites for the ancestors of the Koryŏ and, later, Chosŏn dynasties (1392–1910).[25] In addition to generating merit for the royal dead, the stupa had a reputation for healing the sick and was popularly known as the Medicine King Stupa (Yakhwangt'ap 藥皇塔).

About one hundred and twenty years after this stupa was erected, Sejo 世祖 (1417–1468), the seventh king of Chosŏn, ordered another marble stupa raised at Wŏngak-sa 圓覺寺 in present-day Seoul (see figure 3.4). The new stupa was an almost exact replica of the one at Kyŏngch'ŏn-sa. It was built to enshrine buddha relics, to preserve Sejo's commentary on the *Sūtra of Perfect Enlightenment*, and,

Figure 3.4. Wŏn'gak-sa pagoda photographed in the early twentieth century. Matsumoto, *Chōsen koseki zufu,* vol. 6, 1901.

one imagines, to alleviate some of the new king's guilt for dethroning and poisoning the former king, his sixteen-year-old nephew.[26]

    The ten main stories of both stupas rise from bases consisting of three levels. Twenty scenes from the Obtaining the Scriptures narrative are depicted on the base's second tier.[27] As the earliest visual depiction of the expanded, five-character version of the narrative, these stupas preserve a rare record of the Obtaining the Scriptures story as it was known in Korèa (and presumably China) during the mid-fourteenth century. While the scenes do not seem to occur in sequential order

Figure 3.5. Line drawing of the southern panel of the Kyŏngch'ŏn-sa stupa showing Xuanzang together with his companions presenting the scriptures to Emperor Taizong. Kungnip Munhwajae Yŏn'guso, *Kyŏngch'ŏnsa sipch'ŭng sŏkt'ap*, III: 494.

and are not all easily identifiable, the narrative appears to begin with the decapitation of the dragon that earns Emperor Taizong a trip to hell. This is followed by the revivified emperor's convening of a great ceremony to succor the dead, the culmination of which is Xuanzang's departure to the West to obtain scriptures. Along the way, he acquires his four companions, although only the conversion of Sha Monk is accorded an image of its own. The group of five pilgrims is then shown encountering various trials: Fire Mountain, the Spider Spirit, the Kingdom of Women, the Lion Monster, and so on. The travelers eventually reach the land of the Buddha and are awarded the scriptures. Finally, the party returns to China, where, in an image that closely resembles the scenes depicted in Chinese cave temples and on amulets, they deliver the luminous scriptures to the emperor (see figure 3.5). The narrative thus matches the basic outline of the *Pak t'ongsa ŏnhae* account, but this display, placed on a Buddhist stupa amid tableaus of buddhas and bodhisattvas, is situated squarely within the context of Buddhist history and cosmology.

On the lowest tier of the stupa's base, below the scenes of Xuanzang's pilgrimage, are motifs of dragons and lotus flowers. Above, on the third tier, are scenes from the Buddha's past lives and his most recent incarnation as Śākyamuni. Each level of the stupa's base thus seems to ascend in sanctity—from the dragons and lotuses of the lower, watery realms to the travails of Xuanzang and other clerics obtaining the scriptures, to the lives of the Buddha himself. Above, on the main body of the stupa, a proliferation of buddha assemblies dwell in their heavenly abodes. In this miniature cosmos, Xuanzang and his companions occupy an intermediate position, bridging the gap between ordinary humans and awakened buddhas.[28]

We can only speculate about why scenes of Xuanzang's pilgrimage were accorded such a prominent place on the Wŏn'gak-sa and Kyŏngch'ŏn-sa stupas. The

Korean scholar Sin So-yŏn has suggested the images were meant to confer protection. Just as they had prevailed over demons on their journey to India, Xuanzang and his companions were appointed to guard the treasures held within these reliquaries.[29] This is only one of many possible interpretations, but the prospect that the pilgrims served as sentinels on stupas during the fourteenth and fifteenth centuries is bolstered by the fact these same figures also were positioned on the roofs of royal temples and palaces in Korea during this same period.

Official buildings in Korea traditionally have a series of ceramic figures called *chapsang* 雜像 (literally "assorted images") adorning their roof hips. These icons serve to protect the structure and its inhabitants against fire and other threats. The custom of stationing guardian figures on roofs was most likely introduced via China, with the earliest examples in Korea dating to the eleventh century.[30] Unlike their counterparts in China, however, in Korea the procession of mythical creatures does not typically follow a man astride a phoenix. Instead, the lead guardian figure is conventionally identified as "The Great Tang Master" 大唐師傅, a.k.a. Xuanzang. He, in turn, is followed by the Sun Wukong, Zhu Bajie, Sha Monk, and—depending on the type of building—up to six other creatures of obscure origin (see figure 3.6).[31]

Figure 3.6. Clay statues (*chapsang*) of the Tang Monk (front) and other figures from the Obtaining the Scriptures narrative on the roof of the recently restored main royal palace of the Chosŏn dynasty, Kyŏngbok kung 景福宮, originally built in 1395. Michelle Gilders/Alamy.

The difficulty of establishing when Xuanzang and his companions were first used as *chapsang* is compounded by the fact that, although they are found on structures that were built in the early fifteenth century, roof tiles are regularly replaced. There is thus no way to know what their original appearance or identities might have been. The earliest explicit textual reference to the placement of these figures on the roofs of official buildings in Korea comes from the miscellaneous writings of the Koryŏ scholar-official Yu Mong-in 柳夢寅 (1559–1623).[32] From Yu's text, we know that the pilgrims from the Obtaining the Scriptures narrative were treated as guardian figures on the peninsula at least as early as 1596, four years after the first known printing of the hundred-chapter novel in China. It is possible, as some scholars have suggested, that the popularity of the novel or earlier versions of the narrative altered the understanding of traditional *chapsang* figures.[33] Unlike Ming-dynasty roof tiles from China, which clearly depict the characters from the Obtaining the Scriptures narrative (see figure 3.7), the forms of Korean *chapsang* bear little resemblance to any known representation of the Tang Monk and his

Figure 3.7. Ming-dynasty roof tiles depicting Zhu Bajie (left) and, possibly, the Tang Monk (right). British Museum.

companions. Without knowing their names, their identities would not be apparent to most viewers. The original names of these figures could have been forgotten as their forms came to be associated with the pilgrims in the popular narrative, which, by 1596, had already been circulating in Korea for nearly two centuries. Whatever the case, by the late sixteenth century, the reputations of Xuanzang and his companions for warding off danger had become so well established that they were appointed to protect some of the dynasty's most precious buildings.

Ritual Theater

The images of Xuanzang cast on amulets, carved on stupas, and perched on rooftops all suggest an association between narratives of defeating demons and real-life efforts to keep threats at bay. The evidence surveyed thus far, however, is largely circumstantial, and interpretations are necessarily speculative. Fortunately, later sources are less ambiguous about how Xuanzang was deployed in Chinese ritual traditions. The strongest evidence in this regard comes from sixteenth-century accounts of ritual theater featuring Xuanzang's mythic pilgrimage. Like the Dance of the Foreign Monks, these dramas were held during communal festivals, and they functioned as both offerings and exorcisms.

Recent decades have seen a surge of scholarship on Chinese ritual theater.[34] Tanaka Issei, a pioneering figure in this field, has argued that theatrical forms were incorporated into exorcistic rituals sometime during the Song dynasty.[35] The contents and themes of these performances resembled those held in commercial urban theaters, but their settings and purposes differed. Unlike productions held before paying audiences, ritual dramas were typically performed either on a temple stage or as street theater in villages, in fields, in homes, or in temporary structures. These plays were staged not by professional actors but by troupes of ritual specialists or specially selected members of the community. In some forms of ritual theater, particularly those in which the performers are masked, the "actors" are akin to mediums, embodying deities and the spirits of the dead, speaking in their voices, and acting with their authority. The ritual space itself functions as an altar onto which deities are invited to descend. Their presence is requested for a variety of reasons: to repay vows, to heal sickness, to protect against disease, to exorcise ghosts and demons, or to pacify the souls of those who died violent or premature deaths. Large-scale dramatic performances were, therefore, usually held during moments of transition or disruption—the end of the year, during seasonal shifts, outbreaks of illness, or after untimely deaths. The gods, the protagonists and primary audience for the plays, were invited to accept the offering, enjoy the show, and, in return, to safeguard the community.

When Glen Dudbridge published his study of the antecedents to *Journey to the West*, only five titles for Obtaining the Scriptures dramas were known to have predated the publication of the novel.[36] The earliest of these titles date to the Yuan dynasty, but nothing is known about the plays' characters, length, structure, or the occasions on which they were performed. (The scripts themselves have not survived.) Most scholars have, nonetheless, presumed they were staged in commercial theaters for the purpose of entertainment. The earliest surviving script for an Obtaining the Scriptures drama, a *zaju* 雜劇 (variety play) in twenty-four scenes, seems to bear this out.[37] Published in 1614, this script features the stock character types, humorous dialogue, and songs typical of the *zaju* genre, which is usually defined as comedy. In a foreword to the published script, a commentator compares the play to Wang Shifu's 王實甫 (1250–1337?) *The Story of the Western Wing* (*Xi xiang ji* 西廂記), a well-known romance with little obvious connection to any ritual tradition. The latest dramatic version of *Journey to the West*, the author of the foreword enthuses, was vastly superior to the "obscene and ridiculous" versions put on by "vulgar performers."[38] The new rendering was thus intended as a more refined interpretation of the narrative, meant to rectify what the author saw as improper and unpolished performances apparently common at that time.

Zaju and other dramas often were held on the occasion of funerals and village festivals, and the author may have been critiquing these kinds of loud, unrefined, and raucous performances. In a description of one contemporaneous festival in the city of Suzhou, for example, a local scholar named Wang Zhideng 王穉登 (1535–1612) expresses his disdain for the backward traditions of the village peasants. "They delight in error and esteem the strange, they make light of human ways and value ghosts and sprits; they abandon medicine and worship male and female shamans; they destroy ancestral halls and build shrines to heterodox deities; and they dismiss the wrath of the ancestors and respect the cruelty of the wilds. Alas!"[39] Wang goes on to describe how the images of deities are paraded through the lanes of villages in procession and venerated by residents as they pass their doorways. "When the spirits alight in homes, they are welcomed with awe-inspiring ceremonies, piping and drumming, and various plays. This is called a 'festival' (*hui* 會). Performers, singers, and musicians put on makeup and fine silk [clothing]. There are wine vessels [in the shape of] fish and dragons in a profusion of colors. Nothing is wasted. The scent of fragrant wildflowers fills the air. Day and night [people] gather and move, crowds forming and dispersing like clouds."[40] Wang notes that several dramas involving "spirits and ghosts" (shen gui ze 神鬼則) were performed during the festival. A piece titled "Obtaining the Scriptures in Western India" (Xizhu qu jing 西竺取經) was among them.[41]

Wang Zhideng's account does not elaborate on the content of the "Obtaining the Scriptures in Western India" dramas performed during the festivals in Suzhou, but the fortuitous discovery of a contemporaneous source offers more insight into ritual reenactments of Xuanzang's pilgrimage. In 1985, a handwritten manuscript, last copied in 1574, was discovered in the home of a family of hereditary musicians living in the village of Nanshe 南舍, in southeastern Shanxi province. The twenty-four-page text, titled *Protocol for the Festival for Welcoming the Spirits, with Forty Musical Pieces* (Ying shen saishe lijie chuanbu sishi qu gongdiao 迎神賽社禮節傳簿四十曲宮調, hereafter *Protocol*), outlines the content and procedures for an annual event centered on dozens of astral deities.[42] The *Protocol* stipulates the requisite offerings to the gods, and it lists the musical and dramatic pieces to be performed on temple stages and at other sites throughout the village. Among the many dramas listed in the text is "The Tang Monk Goes to Western Heaven to Obtain the Scriptures" (Tang seng Xitian qu jing 唐僧西天取经)—the same title as a now lost Yuan-dynasty play attributed to Wu Changling 吳昌齡 (ca. thirteenth–fourteenth century).[43] With more than one hundred and forty participants, it was the largest and most elaborate piece performed during the festival.

The roster of deities and demons given in the cast list loosely parallels Yuan-dynasty versions of the narrative known from the *Pak t'ongsa ŏnhae*, the *Yongle dadian*, and the *Kyŏngch'ŏn-sa* stupa. In addition to outlining the narrative structure of the play, the *Protocol* situates the performance in a very specific context. The manuscript was copied on the thirteenth day of the first lunar month, just before the Lantern Festival, and the three-day event it outlines was presumably the culmination of the village's New Year ceremonies and celebrations.[44] Like the *nuo* exorcisms held at the end of the year in the imperial palace in the past, the festival described in the *Protocol* was a rite of supplication and purification. The event centered on enshrining and making offerings to the twenty-eight deities of the lunar lodges. Seven ceremonial offerings (*zhan* 盞) for each individual deity were required. The first three offerings consisted of musical pieces; the next three were theatrical performances; and the final offerings entailed communal singing and three additional plays. "The Tang Monk Goes to Western Heaven to Obtain the Scriptures" is listed as an offering for the spirit of the eighteenth lunar lodge, Maoriji 昴日雞.[45]

The carnivalesque atmosphere of the festival—the songs, dances, performances, food, family, and friends—must have been fun, but the fact that a performance is dramatic or amusing does not diminish its ceremonial function. On the contrary, elements of comedy, theater, and suspense enhance the appeal and thus the efficacy of rituals. Dramas performed amid New Year festivities brought the community together and reestablished social ties; they also were carefully organized, obligatory rituals for exorcising evil and eliminating pestilence.[46] Other plays performed during the festival enacted the destruction of demons and ghosts by bodhisattvas and spirit generals. The titles of some of these performances, such as "Spirits Kill the Disobedient Child" (Shen sha wunizi 神殺忤逆子) and "Guangong Beheads the Demon" (Guangong zhan yao 關公斬妖), are indicative of their content. Others, including "Zhong Kui [the demon queller] Reveals his Power" (Zhong Kui xiansheng 鍾馗顯聖), "Flogging the Yellow Plague Ghost" (Bianda Huanglao gui 鞭打黃瘄鬼), and "Mulian Rescues his Mother," are well-known ritual dramas traditionally performed during exorcistic and mortuary rites.[47]

In the *Protocol,* dramas featuring the Tang Monk and other exorcistic figures are categorized as "silent processional dramas" (*ya dui xi* 啞隊戲), meaning that they were conducted without dialogue, offstage, at various locations throughout the village. Like ancient *nuo* rituals and the modern Dance of the Foreign Monks, "The Tang Monk Goes to Western Heaven to Obtain the Scriptures" was most likely performed on the streets and lanes of the village. Xuanzang's legendary pilgrimage would thus have been reenacted within the community, and the battles he and his companions engaged in drove out or destroyed the demons that threatened the peace and prosperity of local residents. This dramatic spectacle, performed year after year, reinforced Xuanzang's reputation as a protective deity with the power to purify the places where he appeared.

One other drama listed in the *Protocol* is explicitly linked with the Obtaining the Scriptures narrative. The play is titled "The Bodhisattva Mañjuśrī Subdues the Lion" (Wenshu pusa xiang shizi 文殊菩薩降獅子) and it features the Tang Monk, Sun Wukong, Zhu Bajie, Sha Monk, Mañjuśrī, a lion spirit, a troupe of flower scatterers, a dharma guardian spirit, a prince, and the abbot of a Chan temple.[48] We can only imagine the choreography and content of this play, but it clearly centered on the taming of a lion by Mañjuśrī and must have resembled other lion dances that have been regularly performed during New Year festivals since the Tang dynasty. These dances reenact the pacification of the lion, bringing a potentially dangerous foreign spirit under control and turning its power against outside threats. Given the close association of lions with the Buddha (a "lion of a man") and the bodhisattva Mañjuśrī (who rides a lion mount), one or the other is often responsible for taming and converting the animal in traditional lion dances.[49]

The battle between Mañjuśrī and a lion has featured in ritual dramas and dances since at least the fifteenth century, when the celebrated playwright Zhu Youdun 朱有燉 (1379–1439) composed a play with the same title as that recorded in the *Protocol.*[50] In Zhu's version, Mañjuśrī is accompanied by the Buddha, the mountain god, the earth god, and the child-deity Nezha. It is not clear when the pilgrims from the Obtaining the Scriptures story-cycle were incorporated into the drama, but the *Protocol* makes it clear that the Tang Monk and his companions had taken up the task of bridling the lion by the mid-sixteenth century.[51] This feat was later memorialized in the thirty-ninth chapter of the novel, when Sun Wukong, on the verge of slaughtering a murderous demon that has been plaguing the Black Rooster Kingdom, is stayed by Mañjuśrī. The demon then reverts to his original form as a green-haired lion, and he and Mañjuśrī fly off to Mount Wutai. The conversion, which is of minor consequence in a novel filled with similar transformations, is still recreated in lion dances held throughout southern China, as well as in North Korea and Japan.[52] Importantly, most modern dances do not rotely reproduce the account from the novel but appear, instead, to preserve related but regionally distinct versions of Obtaining the Scriptures narratives.[53] Multiple communities, it seems, recognized the protective capacities of the Tang Monk and his companions, though each explained and enacted those qualities in their own idiosyncratic ways.

Spirit Books

Like many of the ritual dramas and dances involving Xuanzang, Sun Wukong, Zhu Bajie, and Sha Monk performed today, those listed in the *Protocol* were enacted without dialogue. The actions spoke for themselves. In other traditions, however, portions of the narrative were read or sung aloud. By the mid-sixteenth century, the story of Xuanzang's pilgrimage appears to have become a regular part of the repertoires of both itinerant Buddhist monks and Daoist priests. According to the official Li Xu 李詡 (1505–1593), "The sung performances of Daoists include *daoqing* 道情 ("Daoist sentiments"), while the sung performances of monks include *paosong* 拋頌 ("Buddhist hymns").[54] These narratives interspersed with ballad-verse (*cishuo* 詞說), like *Journey to the West* and *Indigo Pass,* have, in fact, the same structure."[55] Such songs, sung to the rhythm of bamboo percussion, were, like the Kōzanji texts, engaging ways to impart basic teachings and drum up donations or sales.[56] As predominantly oral traditions, the ballads reached the broadest possible audience, spreading Obtaining the Scriptures and other narratives to those who could not read. Based on later reports of performances in Jiangsu province, *daoqing* relating Xuanzang's mythic pilgrimage were stirring events, staged in women's quarters, on the street, and in front of temples. The singers, disparaged by one observer as "unemployed vagrants" (*wuye youmin* 無業遊民), would draw large crowds with their spirited singing, drumming, and demonic costumes.[57]

More elaborate and refined recitations of Xuanzang's pilgrimage flourished elsewhere in Jiangsu. Some of these performances still feature in local ritual traditions. One of the best-known examples comes from the Tongzhou 通州 region of southern Jiangsu province, though very similar practices have been documented in neighboring towns and villages.[58] The texts used for recitations in Tongzhou are known as "spirit books" (*shen shu* 神書), several collections of which have recently been published.[59] Accounts of the Tang Monk's pilgrimage make up one portion of these larger compilations. While different ritual specialists maintain their own unique versions of Obtaining the Scriptures narratives, they are all written in simple vernacular Chinese in sections of seven- and ten-character lines, a structure that parallels narrative precious scrolls (*baojuan*) used by sectarian religious groups in Jiangsu and elsewhere (see chapter 5).

The Tongzhou region, situated on the northern reaches of the fertile Yangtze Delta, has a rich history of communal festivals and ritual dramas. An account of a festival for Tongzhou's City God held in 1616, for example, describes a scene very similar to the one Wang Zhideng observed in nearby Suzhou: "people also dressed up as various demons and monsters and paraded through the streets, changing the human realm into the netherworld . . . Paintings of demons and monsters were carried through the city market . . . The sounds of the drums and horns were like thunder; the banners and flags were like the sun and moon. In a place of peace and prosperity, it was like a battleground. There were male and female puppets, masks of horses and oxen, [as though] in the dream-like disorder [we had entered] hell."[60]

The ritual masters who presided over these and other ceremonial events were known by various names—*Xianghuo* 香火 ([Masters of] Incense and Fire), *Duangong* 端工/公 (Upright Masters), or *Tongzi* 童子 (Children)—but they all specialized in exorcism and other rituals that required bridging the human and spirit realms. According to author and playwright Xuan Ding 宣鼎 (1832–1880), unlike the shamans (*wu* 巫) of the past who expelled epidemics and pestilences and prevented droughts and floods, "recent shamans have become more and more deceptive and strange. They hit waist drums, blow horns, and sing with a Qin accent (秦腔). Their disciples sound gongs and dance hysterically. Moreover, some erect stages on which they perform like actors and actresses and practice spirit possession for several days and nights without fatigue. Men and women sit around watching plays about the official Jiulang (九郎官) and the goddess Water Mother (水母娘娘) and then enjoy the sacrificial food. No one returns without being drunk."[61] For Xuan Ding, what should have been a solemn occasion had become a raucous, indecent celebration where the proper boundaries between men and women, actors and mediums, dramas and rituals were breached.

Modern-day ritual masters in the Tongzhou region are descendants of the figures described by Xuan Ding. They are commonly referred to as *tongzi*, a title that preserves a link between prepubescent children and spirit possession that dates to at least the Later Han dynasty. (In modern Taiwan, mediums are known as *jitong* 乩童, "diviner children," and often dress as infants and suck on pacifiers.) Despite their name, contemporary *tongzi* rituals in southern Jiangsu are staged by adult male mediums.[62] These men trace the origins of their tradition to the imperial court of the early Tang dynasty, either during the time of Emperor Taizong (598–649; r. 626–649) or the reign of Empress Wu Zetian (624–705; r. 690–705)—the same period, not incidentally, that the historical Xuanzang lived.[63]

The origin story for *tongzi* rituals is particularly relevant both for understanding the core liturgical texts used during the rites and for appreciating the central place Xuanzang's mythic pilgrimage holds in these traditions. In brief, the account begins when Emperor Taizong's minister, Wei Zheng, beheads the dragon that Taizong has promised to spare. The decapitated dragon then lodges a complaint with the Jade Emperor. Taizong is consequently brought down to the underworld, but the Jade Emperor takes pity on him and asks Yama, the lord of the underworld, to permit Taizong to return to the world of the living for a few more years. Yama at first refuses, but a cousin of Wei Zheng, a man named Cui Xu, happens to be the spirit in charge of the registers of birth and death, which record the allotted life span of every human being. Cui Xu switches Taizong's record with that of an unfortunate man of the same surname. The books thus cooked, ten years are added to Taizong's life and he is able to return to the human realm. To repay Cui Xu's favor, the emperor makes three vows: (1) to dispatch someone to India to obtain Buddhist scriptures, (2) to send melons to the underworld (hell dwellers being particularly fond of this cool, refreshing fruit), and (3) to hold a Yangyuan Hongmen rite 陽元洪門會 (or, in some versions, a Water and Land Dharma Assembly) for the liberation of the dead.[64]

Reestablished on the throne, Taizong can fulfill the first two vows—he sends Xuanzang to India and delivers melons to hell—but not the third. The Yangyuan Hongmen mortuary rite requires the presence of spirits and immortals from the upper (heavenly), middle (earthly), and lower (hell) realms. Although Taizong orders his minister Wei Zheng to summon them, Wei Zheng declines, pleading old age and poor health. Taizong, angered by his refusal, has Wei Zheng thrown in prison to await execution. Wei Zheng's ninth son, Wei Jiulang 魏九郎 (the same official who featured in the nineteenth-century ritual drama criticized by Xuan Ding) then has a premonition that there may soon be a death in his family. Rushing home, he is given three magical implements by the astral deity Taibaijin 太白金: a "heaven-penetrating cap," "cloud-ascending shoes," and a "demon-binding rope." Wei Jiulang subsequently returns to the capital to fulfill his father's charge. Deploying his divine powers, he ascends to heaven and enters the netherworld to summon the spirits and immortals of the three realms. Finally, Wei Jiulang leads a group of *tongzi* to perform the funerary rite. Taizong, pleased, releases Wei Zheng from prison, invests Wei Jiulang as a divine messenger, and designates the *tongzi* as imperial shamans. From that point forward, the story goes, whenever a ritual is required at court, Wei Jiulang again carries petitions to the deities of the three realms requesting their attendance; once they arrive, the *tongzi* commence the ceremony.[65]

Modern-day *tongzi* thus see themselves as members of a guild of ritual specialists empowered by the emperor of the Tang dynasty. Their original task was to perform rites for the liberation of spirits suffering in hell, but they later took on broader ritual responsibilities. According to the sacred history recounted in *tongzi* liturgies, Xuanzang made his pilgrimage to Western Heaven to fulfill Emperor Taizong's vow to send someone to obtain Buddhist texts with the power to protect the living and liberate the dead—the very texts that *tongzi* use during rituals. The liturgies recited during major rites today, however, are not canonical Buddhist scriptures but the very spirit books that recount the history of their tradition. These works fall roughly into four categories: those consisting of spells (*zhou wen* 咒文); those recounting the hagiographies of deities present on the altar (*xiao chan* 小懺); those centered on the affairs of the Tang dynasty (*Tang chan* 唐懺); and those recounting miscellaneous stories (*xian shu* 閒書). Portions of these texts are chanted in front of an altar by the chief officiant, while other *tongzi,* seated on the periphery of the ritual space, provide musical accompaniment.[66] There is a great deal of variability with regard to which sections of larger spirit book collections are recited and how they are performed, but it is the third group of texts, which narrate the hagiographies of figures from the early Tang dynasty, that form the core of most major ritual sequences. These texts are sometimes called the *Thirteen and a Half Shamanic Volumes* (*Shisan benban wushu* 十三本半巫書), and they read something like a novel. In a series of linked stories, they narrate Taizong's tour of the netherworld, Xuanzang's travels to India to acquire scriptures, and Wei Jiulang's journey to the spirit realms, in metered, dramatic detail.[67]

Like the protagonists in the narratives they recite, *tongzi* are intermediaries responsible for summoning and communicating with the deities of the three realms who, it is hoped, will be sympathetic to the needs of the ritual's sponsors. When the spirits are summoned, they manifest in the ritual arena. When Sun Wukong is called, for example, he identifies himself and briefly relates his biography. He then asks, "Why have you requested my spirit to descend to the mortal world?" "To bring good luck and ward off calamities," comes the answer. "To ensure long life and rich harvests, to bring peace to the village." "Ah! My spirit is coming," Sun Wukong responds.[68] After accepting invitations prepared by the *tongzi,* assembled deities assume their place on an inner altar, accept offerings, and hear the requests of their devotees. These spirits, dwelling in cut-out paper images, might number seventy or more.[69] The Tang Monk, Sun Wukong, Zhu Bajie, and Sha Monk often are among them, but the celestial pantheon is vast and nebulous, and different *tongzi* call on different deities depending on the occasion and local custom.

The explicit purposes of specific rites are announced by the lead *tongzi* who, on behalf of the ritual's sponsors, conveys a formal petition to the gathered gods. On the occasion of large-scale, communal ceremonies, which can last between three and seven days, the request might be for bountiful harvests, healthy livestock, timely rains, protection against epidemics, the pacification of the dead, or other matters of collective concern.[70] If it is a shorter, smaller rite, sponsored by an individual family, the *tongzi* might ask for the spirits' help in improving the family's fortune, often by curing an illness.[71] In the local system of traditional pathology, sickness results from the loss of a person's souls, creating a vacancy that a demon can surreptitiously fill, thus infecting the body. The *tongzi* are, consequently, enlisted to identify the demon, expel it, and call back the errant soul.[72]

Obtaining the Scriptures narratives, recited at the inner altar over the course of roughly three hours, recount the origins of the ritual at the same time they enact its primary purposes: to transmit divine texts and to ward off demonic incursions.[73] In the liturgy, the Tang Monk and his companions subdue or destroy spider spirits, nine-headed birds, mouse spirits, and hosts of other monstrosities.[74] As the recitation of the narrative is taking place at the inner, or "civil" (*wen* 文), altar, scenes from Xuanzang's mythic pilgrimage are sometimes also performed outside on a stage near the outer, or "martial" (*wu* 武), altar. In contrast to the relatively subdued ceremonies inside, the activities at the outer altar are more sensational. The *tongzi* who perform there engage in feats of bravado and self-mortification: walking on fire, climbing ladders of swords, cutting their skin, or placing burning embers or heated spades into their mouths.[75] By the end of the performances, the demons have been defeated, and the problems afflicting individuals, families, or communities symbolically resolved. The recounting of the Tang Monk's past accomplishments is, therefore, also an illustration of the *tongzi*'s present power. With the help of the five pilgrims and a vast army of other martial spirits, the *tongzi* drive malevolent spirits out of bodies, homes, businesses, villages, and fields.

The question of which came first, liturgical texts like the spirit books or the hundred-chapter novel, has elicited much conjecture but little consensus. Some scholars have argued that texts used by earlier *tongzi* must have informed the hundred-chapter novel.[76] Wu Cheng'en, the man most often credited with writing the novel, lived in the Jiangsu region. If modern rites preserve some elements of earlier traditions, it is possible that Wu Cheng'en (or whoever wrote the novel) was familiar with hagiographical accounts like those in the *Thirteen and a Half Shamanic Volumes*. He also would have, presumably, seen the dramatic performances held during regional festivals. The prospect that the novel is an elaborate reframing of ritual narratives is intriguing, but these traditions—transmitted orally and by means of manuscripts that are regularly recopied—are fluid. We cannot assume that the rites we see today faithfully replicate earlier practices. Details change, plots develop, and performers improvise. What *is* clear, however, is that contemporary retellings of Xuanzang's mythic pilgrimage in ritual settings are not isolated, modern innovations. Rather, they harken back to an old and pervasive tradition of channeling the prophylactic powers of Xuanzang and his companions for the greater good of communities.

Exorcistic dances, roof guardians, ritual dramas, liturgical texts—the examples gathered here are drawn from different historical eras and disparate regions. Each invocation of the Tang Monk's pilgrimage is embedded in its own particular context. Differences in content and expression reflect the unique circumstances of the times and places where these stories were performed. Focusing on the continuities between various traditions, however, we can see that in regions as far apart as southeastern China and the Korean peninsula, and in eras as distant as the sixteenth and the twenty-first centuries, Xuanzang and his fellow pilgrims were regularly tasked with staving off the forces of death and disorder. Their pilgrimage was reenacted to facilitate the transition from danger and instability to peace and prosperity. Xuanzang was an exemplar, a trailblazer, a guardian, and a guide. He and his entourage were called to forge a path, to safeguard individuals and entire communities from demons, disease, droughts, and fires.

In those places where his image was displayed and his pilgrimage performed, children grew up seeing and hearing narratives about Xuanzang's otherworldly travels. As poet and scholar A. K. Ramanujan observed about the great Indian epics, "no one ever reads the *Ramayana* or the *Mahabharata* for the first time. The stories are there, 'always already.'"[77] Every culture has its underlying narratives, not so much learned as absorbed. In the rural towns and villages of China, outside the walls of major Buddhist monasteries, Daoist abbeys, and Confucian academies (where different kinds of myths were assiduously instilled), knowledge about the seen and unseen world was engendered through story and performance. Narratives about gods, demons, heroes, and villains were entertaining as well as didactic, affecting as well as efficacious. "Always already," they indelibly shaped people's understanding of their past and their perceptions of the present.

Like all effective and enduring myths, Xuanzang's pilgrimage is foreign and remote at the same time that it is personal and immediate. The destinations, dangers, and rewards of his journey invite a range of interpretations, but the themes of transition, protection, and transformation—basic concerns of life and driving anxieties surrounding death—cut across geographic, temporal, and cultural divides. The narratives preserved in modern spirit books describe how Xuanzang and his companions transit between the human and spirit realms to deliver divine texts and destroy malevolent demons. It is significant that those travels were undertaken so that a major mortuary rite could be properly performed. Having considered Xuanzang's role in guarding the living, we can now turn to his related task of delivering the dead.

4 Psychopomp

We tell ourselves stories in order to live.

—Joan Didion, *The White Album*

Mr. Xie's grandfather died in 2007 at the age of ninety-four. When Mr. Xie, who lived in Taiwan's capital Taipei, traveled south to rural Yulin county for the funeral, he found the lengthy series of rituals fascinating but exhausting. In addition to formal ceremonies led by Daoist priests, the family also had hired two processional troupes (*zhentou* 陣頭) to perform throughout the day and into the night. These dramatic ritual performances, common in southern Taiwan, are less familiar to younger generations living in the urban sprawl of the northern capital. Xie was amused by the women hired to cry for hours on end during the day and to sing and play music after dark. At one point, a woman dressed in the red and gold brocade robes of a Buddhist monk arrived astride a white horse led by a man with his face painted like a monkey. They proceeded to act out scenes from *Journey to the West*. Xie was shocked to learn the family paid them 13,000 Taiwanese dollars (roughly $420 US). It was, he felt, an "exceptionally extravagant" event.[1]

In Taiwan, traditional funerals are protracted, elaborate affairs. The family of the deceased, in consultation with professional funerary specialists, usually selects a series of ritual programs to be performed over the course of the event, which can last up to three days. Some rituals are fairly standard and subdued, but the themes and content of other, optional performances span a wide range, from theater to comedy to pole dancing. In addition to their explicit purpose of safely transitioning the dead from the human to the ancestral realm, mortuary rites also provide an opportunity for the family of the deceased to demonstrate their largesse. The quality and quantity of food and drink, the number of prestigious guests, the accumulated offerings of food and flowers, and the caliber of the ritual performances all reflect on the status of the deceased and his or her family. Some rituals are relatively simple, requiring only a small number of amateur performers. Others, including

"Trepiṭaka Obtains the Scriptures" (Sanzang qu jing 三藏取經)—one of the rituals requested by Mr. Xie's family—are more complex and thus more expensive.

Different funerary troupes maintain their own variations of "Trepiṭaka Obtains the Scriptures," but the staging is usually spectacular, often involving highly skilled performers—sometimes on horseback, sometimes on stilts, sometimes on unicycles—as well as music, singing, theater, acrobatics, pyrotechnics, martial arts, and one or more horses. A typical sequence begins on the penultimate day of the funeral, with the Tang Monk's initial subjugation of Sun Wukong. This scene is followed by the acquisition of Zhu Bajie after a dramatic, highly choreographed battle. In some versions of the drama, after Zhu Bajie joins the group, all three figures approach the family of the deceased. Seeing that the children and grandchildren have worked diligently to arrange for the funeral of their ancestor, the Tang Monk (referred to as "Trepiṭaka") announces that he and his companions are on their way to the West to obtain scriptures. They invite the spirit of the newly deceased, also (hopefully) bound for Western Heaven, to join them.[2] On the following day, just prior to the interment of the corpse's remains, the Tang Monk acquires his fourth disciple, the monk Sha, and the entire group puts on a vigorous display of acrobatics and martial arts en route to the burial site or columbarium. As in temple processions and village exorcisms, the pilgrims clear the road of malicious demons and ghosts as they escort the spirit of the dead from the land of the living to the Pure Land in the West (see plate 6).

Performances of "Trepiṭaka Obtains the Scriptures" at funerals in Taiwan, while not uncommon, are staged less frequently than other ritual dramas. Why do some families request this piece instead of or in addition to others? When I put this question to members of the Taipei Luzhou Sunshine Processional Troupe, they explained that the main purpose of the performance is to display the family's respect for the deceased, their generosity toward their family and friends, and, most importantly, their financial status in their community. For this reason, this drama often is requested by people connected to the "brotherhood" (*xiongdi* 兄弟), secret fraternal organizations also known as Triads. These men set great store by their reputation ("face," *mianzi*) and so tend to hold elaborate and expensive public funerals for their associates.

Displays of wealth and status are undoubtedly important aspects of these rituals—as one funerary specialist once put it, "*Mianzi* is worth a lot of money"—but the content of the performance is not incidental.[3] A leader of a Chinese troupe based in Malacca, Malaysia, explained to a reporter that "the Tang Monk is a dharma protector. [The rite] symbolizes that he will escort [the dead] along the journey to reach Western Heaven."[4] A member of another troupe from central Taiwan similarly described the performance as a means of delivering the dead to the Land of Bliss, and the same sentiment has been expressed by those who have attended funerary performances in Singapore.[5] Xuanzang's mythic journey is, in these contexts, not a pilgrimage to India but a passage to heaven.

Like all mortuary rites, "Trepiṭaka Obtains the Scriptures" functions on multiple, interconnected levels—social, economic, aesthetic, symbolic, and soteriological—and there are many equally viable ways to interpret the ritual's meaning and purpose. There also are different explanations for how a popular narrative about a Tang-dynasty monk's pilgrimage to India came to be so closely associated with death and the afterlife. Members of the Sunshine Troupe, for instance, speculate that the performance entered their repertoire relatively recently by way of traditional theater. *Journey to the West* operas in Taiwan, they reasoned, were probably adapted for use in funerary rituals because they were popular, entertaining, and thematically appropriate.

Two anthropologists specializing in modern Taiwanese mortuary rites have come to a similar conclusion, proposing that this drama is most likely a popular conflation of *Journey to the West* operas with other, more conventional funerary rites that enact the journey of the dead through purgatory to a heavenly realm in the West.[6] If these theories are correct, then the incorporation of "Trepiṭaka Obtains the Scriptures" into the routines of funerary troupes in Taiwan is a modern innovation, driven by the tremendous popularity of the novel and its theatrical adaptations rather than by any meaningful link between the narrative and more traditional mortuary rites.

In fact, Obtaining the Scriptures narratives have been associated with death and the afterlife since at least the thirteenth century, hundreds of years before the novel was written. The conviction that Xuanzang's mythical pilgrimage was undertaken to liberate the dead, in other words, has been part of his appeal from the earliest phase of the narrative's development. In the modern period, literary sources, theatrical scripts, liturgical manuscripts, and ethnographies all provide ample evidence that delivering souls to heaven remains a prominent function of Obtaining the Scriptures rituals in China, Taiwan, Malaysia, and Singapore. For many people, both in the past and in the present, Xuanzang's journey to Western Heaven is much more than a diverting fable; it is an established and effective ritual process for liberating the spirits of the dead.

Generally speaking, there appear to be two interrelated traditions that incorporate the Tang Monk's travels into mortuary rites. The first, exemplified by the funeral of Mr. Xie's grandfather, conceives of the pilgrimage as a journey to heaven, where, after a long and dangerous crossing, the spirits of the dead are safely transported into the presence of buddhas and bodhisattvas. The rituals and narratives that replicate this passage predictably emphasize Xuanzang's westward journey (*xi you* 西游) from the human to the heavenly realm. A second set of traditions centers, instead, on Xuanzang's acquisition and transmission of a cache of powerful

Buddhist texts (*qu jing* 取經). In these instances, the narrative functions as a species of *aition* (Greek, "cause"), a story that explains, or in this case reenacts, the origins of a ritual or the founding of a tradition. In funerary rituals that invoke Obtaining the Scriptures narratives as a means of explanation (how the ritual came to be) and authentication (why the ritual works), it is the final portion of Xuanzang's pilgrimage, when he returns from the land of buddhas and bodhisattvas to the human realm laden with redemptive texts, that takes precedence. In both scenarios, caring for the dead remains Xuanzang's constant concern.

The Journey to Heaven

The path to paradise can be perilous, and the role of the Tang Monk and his companions as escorts for the dead is entangled with the exorcistic qualities of the Obtaining the Scriptures rituals and materials discussed in the previous chapter. Exorcists ward off demonic forces and shield the living, but they also serve as guardians for those navigating the dark paths of the netherworld. Recall that accounts of *nuo* rites at the court of the Han dynasty describe how the chief exorcist, the Fangxiang shi, also was responsible for leading the dead to their burial sites and ridding tombs of any loitering demons. Anxieties about the afterlife compelled people to draw up tomb contracts and to commission a range of rituals to protect the dead against molestation by malignant spirits and defend the living against the vendettas of disgruntled ghosts.[7] Mortuary rites therefore enlist benevolent but powerful deities to subjugate demonic forces bent on harming or obstructing the progress of the recently deceased. The safe passage they provide for the dead mirrors the protection exorcisms offered to the living.

In contemporary Taiwan, several deities responsible for delivering the dead join forces on the fifteenth day of the seventh lunar month, the date of the annual Ghost Festival. During rites for the "Release of the Burning Mouths" (Fang yankou 放焰口), a popular ritual with roots reaching back to the Tang dynasty, the head officiant channels Avalokiteśvara bodhisattva as she, recalling the vow of Kṣitigarbha bodhisattva to release all beings suffering in the underworld, opens the gates of hell and feeds hungry ghosts with cool, sweet nectar. Their burning mouths quenched and their sins redeemed, the ghosts are freed from their imprisonment and able to safely transition to a more propitious rebirth.[8] During the Ghost Festival, scenes depicting Avalokiteśvara soothing the Lord of Ghosts (Dashi ye 大士爺) are commonly sculpted out of paper mache or, more rarely, painted on hanging scrolls.[9] While there are regional variations to the iconography—known as Potalaka Cliff (普陀巖), Avalokiteśvara Mountain (觀音山), or Universal Salvation Mountain (普渡山)—a typical arrangement shows Avalokiteśvara seated on the rocky outcropping of Mount Potalaka in the upper center of the tableau. She is immediately flanked by the child Sudhana on one side and the Dragon Girl on the other.[10] In an arrangement that bears some resemblance to the depictions of Water Moon Avalokiteśvara in the cave temples of twelfth- and thirteenth-century China discussed in chapter 2, several other figures flank the main deity or are positioned directly below. These usually include the Mountain Spirit together with his dragon mount, the Earth God and his tiger, and the dragon kings of the four directions. In many versions, the Tang Monk, Sun Wukong, Zhu Bajie, and Sha Monk also appear among the entourage (see plates 7 and 8).[11]

There is no scriptural source for this arrangement, but the association of Xuanzang and his companions with the liberation of hungry ghosts dates to the beginning of the Obtaining the Scriptures story-cycle. As we have seen, in the thirteenth-century Kōzanji accounts, the narrative culminates with a communal rite for the salvation of the dead held on the fifteenth day of the seventh lunar month. Because the first sections of both Kōzanji texts are missing, we do not know what initially inspired Xuanzang to embark on his journey in these early accounts, but later versions of the narrative all highlight his goal of securing texts with the power to release spirits suffering in hell. In the early-fifteenth-century *Yongle dadian*, the late-sixteenth-century novel, and modern spirit books, the pilgrimage to "Western Heaven" is set in motion when Emperor Taizong, who has himself just returned from a harrowing sojourn in hell, prepares to hold a Water and Land Dharma Assembly (Shui lu fahui 水陸法會)—a major mortuary ritual performed during the Ghost Festival and on other occasions—so that those "orphaned souls in the Region of Darkness might find salvation" (see figure 4.1).[12]

The twelfth chapter of the *Journey to the West* novel relates how Xuanzang, the lead officiant of the ritual, is interrupted mid-ceremony by the bodhisattva Avalokiteśvara. Thumping her hands on the platform, she mocks him, shouting, "Hey, Monk! You only know how to talk about the teachings of the Little Vehicle. Don't you know anything about the Great Vehicle?" The texts of the Great Vehicle, she explains, are able to "send the lost to heaven, to deliver the afflicted from their sufferings, to fashion ageless bodies, and to break the cycle of comings and goings."[13] After Avalokiteśvara reveals that the most efficacious mortuary texts can be found in India, Taizong pauses the ritual and provides Xuanzang with an imperial rescript granting permission to travel west to the land of the Buddha to acquire "texts that can save the dead and liberate wandering souls."[14] Finally, in the last chapter of the novel, after Xuanzang and his companions return with the new texts, Taizong reconvenes the Water and Land Dharma Assembly so that, at last, "the damned spirits can be delivered from the nether darkness."[15] This, then, is the basic plot of the novel: the emperor attempts to hold a mass for the dead but, because he lacks the appropriate texts, the ceremony must be postponed until

Figure 4.1. Emperor Taizong announcing the Water Land Assembly. The banner reads: "Convening a Great Assembly of Water and Land to Liberate the Orphaned Souls in the Realm of Darkness." From the Li Zhuoyu 李卓吾 edition of the *Journey to the West* novel. Takimoto, *Chūgoku koten bungaku,* 172.

Xuanzang is able to retrieve them. After he returns with the new texts, the ritual resumes and the spirits imprisoned in hell finally are set free.

Xuanzang and Mulian

Fans of the *Journey to the West* novel are naturally drawn to the perilous threats Xuanzang and his fellow pilgrims face—the ferocious monsters and cunning spirits, the near fatal disasters, the narrow escapes—and it is easy to lose sight of the underlying purpose of the pilgrimage: securing sacred texts with the power to deliver the damned. For those familiar with traditional Chinese culture, stories featuring a Buddhist monk who travels from the human world through a shadowy land haunted by demons and ghosts to a heavenly realm to liberate spirits suffering in hell call to mind not Xuanzang but another popular savior figure, the divine monk Mulian. Although Mulian is a much more familiar figure in this role, he and Xuanzang have long been allies in the effort to empty the subterranean torture chambers of the "earth prisons" (*diyu* 地獄). In many ways, the two deified monks stand together as powerful protagonists in the same mythic metanarrative.

The Mulian story-cycle is traditionally held to have been introduced to China from India during the Western Jin dynasty (265–420) in the form of the *Ullambana Sūtra* 盂蘭盆經. This short text, which Stephen Teiser suggests may have, in fact, been composed in fifth-century China, tells the story of the filial monk Mulian, whose mother dies and is reborn as a hungry ghost because of her "deep and tenacious" sins.[16] Mulian appeals to the Buddha for help, and the Buddha explains that Mulian alone cannot rescue his mother from her fate. He can, however, make offerings of "the sweetest and prettiest things in the world" to monks of the ten directions on the fifteenth day of the seventh lunar month. By giving generously to monastics, the Buddha explains, a person's current parents and seven generations of their ancestors will reap precious rewards. Mulian does as he is told, and, after a difficult journey and a series of trials, his mother eventually is released from her torment and reborn in heaven.[17]

The *Ullambana Sūtra*'s account of a devoted son's single-minded concern for his long-suffering mother extols the virtues of filial piety and provides an origin story for a major communal mortuary rite, the *Yulanpen hui* or Ghost Festival, which has been held annually in China since at least the sixth century. Over time, new, expanded, and revised versions of the Mulian narrative emerged in China. By the Tang dynasty, several *bianwen* 變文, or "transformation text," versions of the tale were in circulation. These stories, which appear to have been accompanied by images and performed orally by Buddhist clerics or itinerant storytellers, describe in gruesome detail the punishments Mulian witnessed as he toured the underworld in search of his mother.[18] Those who read or heard these stories were simultaneously infused with fear and assured that their own loved ones could, like Mulian's mother, be saved from the suffering of hell if the proper offerings were made to Buddhist monasteries during the Ghost Festival.

David Johnson has proposed that early versions of the Mulian story gradually absorbed "material about purification and exorcism that had independent origins and a long prior development."[19] The processes of accretion, conflation, and redundancy are common in Chinese ritual traditions. Deities who perform the same or similar ritual functions frequently are drawn together and, in some cases, merged into a single figure. There are a number of confluences in both the form and the content of narratives featuring Mulian and the Tang Monk. Both monks are intermediaries, crossing the treacherous distances separating the human and the spirit realms, and both selflessly endure adversity for the benefit of others. In the case of Mulian, he overcomes a succession of obstacles for the sake of his mother, and, as a result, the Ghost Festival is established for the benefit of all hungry ghosts. The Tang Monk also accepts hardship to obtain emancipatory sutras for the people of China. These texts have the power to release all souls suffering in the netherworld and are put to use specifically on the occasion of the Ghost Festival. If "Mulian Rescues His Mother" is the *aition* for the Ghost Festival, "Trepiṭaka Obtains the Scriptures" is the origin story for the texts and rituals deployed during the festival itself.

While the Mulian narrative is the older of the two accounts, both story-cycles developed along parallel historical trajectories and appear to have served similar ends. The Mulian legend contained in the original *Ullambana Sūtra* was gradually transformed from a canonical Buddhist scripture into a vernacular "transformation text" during the Tang dynasty, just as Xuanzang's biography was reimagined in prosimetric form for oral recitation during the Northern Song. Scenes from both stories also were staged as ritual theater. Performances of Mulian's journey through hell to save his mother were held annually during the Ghost Festival as well as periodically in response to drought, pestilence, and premature death. As we have seen, Obtaining the Scriptures narratives also were enacted during village festivals to purify and protect communities.

Iconographically, the Tang Monk and Mulian, along with their doppelgänger Kṣitigarbha—the bodhisattva specializing in releasing souls from hell—are virtually identical. All three are conventionally portrayed as monks in brocade robes with shaved heads, often wearing the five-buddha crown, usually seated on a lotus, holding a ringed staff in their right hand and a wish-fulfilling jewel or a bowl in their left (see figure 4.2). Without a label or contextual marker, a devotee would be hard-pressed to distinguish between them. Similarities in appearance correlate with similarities in function. In the thirteenth-century Kōzanji texts, we read that Mahābrahmā Devarāja Vaiśravaṇa gave the Tang Monk the same magical imple-

Figure 4.2. Right to left: Mulian (Xiahai City God Temple 霞海城隍廟, Taipei, Taiwan), Kṣitigarbha (Xiahai City God Temple, Taipei, Taiwan), and Xuanzang (Ziyun Temple 紫雲寺, Yilan, Taiwan). Photos courtesy of the Xiahai City God Temple and the author.

ments that the Buddha bestows on Mulian in tenth-century versions of the Mulian story: an enchanted ringed staff and a begging bowl. In the later hundred-chapter novel, the narrator elaborates that the staff Avalokiteśvara gives to Xuanzang is, in fact, the very same staff that "broke hell's gate where Luo Bo [Mulian] sought his Mother."[20] And when Xuanzang, dressed in his new brocade robe and holding Mulian's staff, visits a temple in the Tang capital before setting off on his journey to India, the resident monks initially mistake him for Kṣitigarbha.[21] The resemblances between these three savior clerics are not coincidental. They were intentionally emphasized by those who maintained and curated these narratives.

The earliest extant description of a ritual performance of Xuanzang's otherworldly pilgrimage, found in the sixteenth-century *Protocol*, is listed alongside a drama of Mulian Rescuing his Mother, suggesting that the two dramas were seen as related and complementary. Over time, these two popular story-cycles, initially independent in origin, merged to form part of a sequence in larger ritual processes involving death and the afterlife. The first unambiguous evidence for the melding of the two narratives comes from the earliest extant script for a Mulian drama, the *New Version of Mulian Rescuing His Mother: A Moralistic Tale (Xinbian Mulian jiu mu quan shan ji* 新編目連救母勸善記; hereafter *Moralistic Tale*). The playwright Zheng Zhizhen 鄭之珍 (1518–1595) wrote this hundred-scene play in 1582, just ten years prior to the first known printing of the hundred-chapter *Journey to the West* novel. The script consists of three scrolls and typically was performed

Figure 4.3. Left: "Generals capturing the white ape" from the earliest Mulian script. Zheng, *Xinbian Mulian jiu mu quanshan xiwen,* 451. Right: The Mind Monkey Returns to Heaven, from the Li Zhuoyu edition of *Journey to the West*. Takimoto, *Chūgoku koten bungaku sōga shūsei,* 178.

over the course of three nights.[22] The first scroll describes the filial devotion of Mulian and the wicked transgressions of his mother. In the second scroll, which begins with Mulian preparing for a long and perilous journey to India to seek the Buddha's help in saving his mother, there are several characters and scenes that also appear in Obtaining the Scriptures narratives. In scene thirty-six, for instance, the bodhisattva Avalokiteśvara sends a pig-demon named Baijie 百介 to ferry Mulian and his companions across the Sand River.[23] This undoubtedly alludes to the figures of Zhu Bajie and Sha Monk. More central to the *Moralistic Tale* is the White Ape, a corollary to Sun Wukong. In the *Moralistic Tale*, Avalokiteśvara orders four generals to subdue the immortal ape and enlists his extraordinary powers to protect Mulian on his westward travels (see figure 4.3). Once captured, Avalokiteśvara instructs the ape to serve Mulian as his master, protecting him against any demons that attempt to obstruct his passage to Western Heaven.

Avalokiteśvara then secures a golden band around the white ape's head, and when he tries to escape by means of a magic somersault, the bodhisattva recites a spell, constricting the band and compelling the ape to submit. Thus tamed, the ape agrees to accompany Mulian on his travels.[24] This, of course, mirrors the account in *Journey to the West,* with Mulian taking the place of the Tang Monk and the white ape standing in for Sun Wukong.

According to the *Moralistic Tale* script, Mulian next takes up a pole with a portrait of his mother hanging from one end and a bundle of Buddhist sutras hanging from the other, and he and his ape companion set off across a haunted landscape. They pass through the same territory the Tang Monk crosses on his own pilgrimage: the Black Pine Forest (scene sixty-one), the Cold Frozen Pond (scene sixty-three), Fire Mountain (scene sixty-four), and the Lansha River (scene sixty-five).[25] Along the way, Mulian and the white ape acquire a third companion, Sha Monk (scenes sixty-five and sixty-six).[26] Finally, after arriving safely in Western Heaven, the overlap with Obtaining the Scriptures narratives comes to an end. The Buddha awards Mulian a pewter staff that can break open the doors to hell and straw sandals that will allow him to fly through the underworld. The third and final scroll narrates Mulian's subsequent travels through the ten courts of hell and his attempts to rescue his mother.

The hundred-scene *Moralistic Tale* and the hundred-chapter *Journey to the West* were published during roughly the same period, and there has been much debate about the direction of influence. Some scholars have asserted that *Journey to the West* must have absorbed elements from an older Mulian story-cycle.[27] This theory presumes the *Moralistic Tale* preserves elements of Mulian dramas that predate the fourteenth century, when the characters and general plot structure of the mature Obtaining the Scriptures narrative were established. The strongest evidence for this claim comes from a thirteenth-century script titled "The Mother of Great Scholar Chen Instructs Her Son" (Zhangyuan tang Chen mu jiao zi 狀元堂陳母教子). In one scene of this play, Scholar Chen's mother remarks that she once heard about a monk who carried a pole with his mother on one end and sutras on the other. Because he did not want to disrespect either his mother or the sutras, he decided to carry the pole horizontally so that neither would be behind the other.[28] Mulian is faced with this same dilemma in the *Moralistic Tale* and settles on the same solution.

It may be that other elements of the *Moralistic Tale,* specifically the figures and scenes that parallel Xuanzang's mythic pilgrimage, also were included in some now-lost early Mulian narrative, but there is no evidence to confirm this. On the contrary, none of the earlier surviving versions or descriptions of the Mulian story—not transformation texts, dramas, or precious scrolls—mention an ape companion or any of the other features of the Obtaining the Scriptures story. The earliest source

for these elements in the plot is the *Moralistic Tale* itself. This has led other scholars to conclude that the *Moralistic Tale* more likely absorbed and assimilated elements of Xuanzang's legend.[29] The five central protagonists and many of the core
scenes of the Obtaining the Scriptures cycle already were in place by the fourteenth
century. These characters and scenes, moreover, are central to accounts of Xuanzang's mythic pilgrimage, whereas they represent an inessential expansion of the
plot known from previous versions of the Mulian story. Without positing some lost
Mulian narrative that included an immortal ape companion, tamed by a golden
headband, who battled demons on the journey to Western Heaven, the evidence
at hand suggests that this and other overlapping narrative elements were part of
the Obtaining the Scriptures narrative *before* their inclusion in Mulian story-cycles.
In the end, however, the direction of influence may be less important than the fact
that both accounts feature the same cast of supporting characters traversing the
same terrain. Both authors and their audiences took it for granted that these figures, particularly the ape/monkey, served as guides and guardians on the road
leading to Western Heaven. Rather than a case of copying, the overlaps in the two
accounts suggest they were conceived as closely related episodes in the same mythic
history.[30]

Recent ethnographic work carried out in the Chinese provinces of Anhui,
Jiangxi, Guangxi, and Fujian and in the country of Taiwan demonstrate that versions
of Mulian's and Xuanzang's narratives continue to be performed as scenes from the
same ritual complex.[31] In some cases, the story of the Tang Monk is staged prior to
the Mulian narrative, implying that the Tang Monk's pilgrimage creates the conditions that make Mulian's journey through hell possible. A manuscript for a Mulian
ritual drama recently discovered in southwestern Fujian province is explicit in this
regard, stating that Mulian follows in the footsteps of the Tang Monk. The script,
titled *Hell Volume,* narrates the familiar story of Mulian's travels to Western Heaven
to meet the Buddha, who bestows sutras, straw sandals, a water pot, and a staff.[32]
In this version, however, the Buddha then instructs Mulian to seek out Avalokiteśvara
and receive from her a golden band with the power to subdue a monkey called the
"novice" (*xingzhe* 杏者).[33] Once subdued, this monkey will protect Mulian on his
journey to hell.[34] When Mulian encounters Avalokiteśvara, he learns that the monkey is the very same Novice Sun that accompanied the Tang Monk on his pilgrimage five hundred years earlier. The monkey's wild nature has not yet been fully
tamed, Avalokiteśvara explains, and he must, therefore, be restrained once again
by the golden headband. Mulian and the Novice Sun then set off together, meet
the pig Bajie (八戒) on the road, and the three begin their descent into hell.[35] The
monkey and the pig take their leave of Mulian when he reaches the gates of hell.
The script concludes with Mulian, presumably channeled by the priest performing

the ritual, chanting the *Hell Scripture* (*Diyu jing* 地獄經), using his staff to smash the gates of hell, and rescuing the spirits of the dead languishing within.[36]

In other rituals performed in other parts of China, the Tang Monk's pilgrimage is enacted *after* the Mulian drama as "a way to finish the entire ritual by 'cleaning up' or 'sweeping up' all the invisible demons left in the air."[37] These sequences, which emphasize the exorcistic qualities of the Obtaining the Scriptures narrative, adhere more closely to the account known from the hundred-chapter novel, where Avalokiteśvara keeps Mulian's demon-subduing staff and conveys it to the Tang Monk for protection along his journey. In still other ritual dramas, the Tang Monk simply assumes the role more conventionally played by Mulian, personally traveling down into hell and using his divine staff to burst open the prison gates and release the orphaned spirits within.[38] The similarity between the two divine clerics prompted the author of one sixteenth-century precious scroll to declare that the Tang Monk was, in fact, a reincarnation of Mulian.[39] By this logic, Xuanzang's mythic pilgrimage simply retraces Mulian's journey through purgatory en route to heaven, achieving the same ends at a later historical moment—a recurring theme that we will return to in the next chapter.

There are many more textual and performative variants involving the Tang Monk and Mulian, all of which demonstrate that people throughout China saw Mulian and the Tang Monk as closely aligned, if not interchangeable. One cleric journeyed through hell, the other traveled to Western Heaven, but both were shamanic figures who passed through the veil to alleviate the suffering of spirits. In their respective hagiographies, places and characters coincided, and brief allusions made in one narrative presume audiences' knowledge of their more detailed treatment in the other.[40] Accounts of Xuanzang's otherworldly pilgrimage were thus not self-contained stories but were, instead, embedded within larger mythic complexes that drew from a common cast of gods, ghosts, and demons who occupied the same liminal landscapes. In all likelihood, formerly independent myths involving the Tang Monk were drawn into this larger web of narratives by the force of their structural and functional complementarity. Only later did people feel compelled to rationalize the relationship between figures like the Tang Monk and Mulian, with different communities developing their own explanations for why these two divine monks so often appeared together.

Mulian and the Tang Monk were not only interchangeable with one another, they were also, and more importantly, idealized representations of the ritual specialists who recited or reenacted their hagiographies. In the context of such rituals, the power of both deified clerics was invoked and channeled by the chief officiant, who, like the Tang Monk and Mulian, typically dressed in a brocade robe, wore a five-pointed crown, and held an apotropaic staff. Over the course of the ceremony, the ritual master embodies these and other deities, bringing their powers to bear on the task at hand. The elaborate, compelling, and familiar narratives of the Tang Monk, Mulian, and other savior figures invested mortuary specialists with the authority and efficacy necessary to successfully execute the rite. For individuals anxious about their own impending death, for families mourning a lost loved one, and for community members concerned about the ill effects of lingering, neglected spirits, it was critical that mortuary rituals be performed properly by people with the requisite abilities to lead the dead away from the living, out of purgatory, and to a place of peace and stability. The presence of the Tang Monk offered the comfort of familiarity, the weight of tradition, and the promise of a story with a predictable and satisfying ending.

Eternal Return

We know more about rituals involving Mulian than we do about parallel performances featuring the Tang Monk. From as early as the thirteenth century, the story of Mulian's passage through hell was performed or recited as part of communal and individual mortuary rites. At what point did Obtaining the Scriptures narratives begin to be deployed in this same way? Prior to the nineteenth century, circumstantial evidence—namely, the narrative's consistent association with Mulian and the Ghost Festival—hints at the existence of funerary traditions involving Xuanzang's mythic pilgrimage, but there are no descriptions of actual rituals. This may be because no such rituals existed, or it may be that the evidence for such rites has not survived. Ethnographic and archival work carried out in mainland China over the past thirty years, however, has documented a rich and widespread tradition of reciting and performing versions of the Tang Monk's journey at funerals. These traditions, which date to at least the late Qing dynasty, bear some resemblance to modern funeral performances like those commissioned for Mr. Xie's grandfather, but there are important structural and thematic differences. In some modern Taiwanese funerals, the Tang Monk and his companions serve as guides and guardians along the route leading from the human to the heavenly realm. For that reason, the first part of the pilgrim's journey, from China to India, or from the mortal realm to Western Heaven, is typically reenacted. Most of the traditions preserved and practiced in mainland China, by contrast, highlight the Tang Monk's acquisition of scriptures from the Buddha and the conveyance of those texts back from heaven to the human world. In these rituals, the Tang Monk still serves as an intermediary between the living and the dead, but his contribution centers less on his passage *to* the Pure Land of the Buddha than on his return *from* heaven bearing newer, more efficacious ritual texts. The emphasis of these rites, therefore, is on the Tang Monk's role as a transmitter of texts and traditions rather than as an exorcist and spirit guide, although the two roles often overlap.

Details about funerary rituals featuring the Tang Monk come from two groups of complementary sources: liturgical manuscripts used throughout China and ethnographic reports from modern scholars working in rural areas. The textual materials first came to light in the late 1980s, when they were discovered by Wang Xiyuan 王熙远, an anthropologist working in Langping Village 浪平鄉 in northwestern Guangxi province.[41] Langping is home to the Zhuang 壮, a Tai-speaking people concentrated in Guangxi but also occupying areas of northwestern Guangdong, southern Guizhou, and eastern Yunnan provinces. In northwestern Guangxi, Zhuang and Han communities both are served by multiple ritual specialists, including native Mogong (Zhuang, *bouxmo* 魔公) priests, Buddhist monks (Zh. *bouxseng;* Ch. *senggong* 僧公), Daoist priests (Zh. *bouxdauh;* Ch. *daogong* 道公), and ritual masters (Zh. *souxsae;* Ch. *shigong* 師公). Despite some division of labor, there is significant overlap among these lay ritualists. David Holm, who has written extensively about Zhuang language, literature, and ritual, describes this fluidity as a cultural code-switching involving complex patterns of "mutual encapsulation."[42]

The manuals discovered by Wang Xiyuan were used by Mogong priests, heirs to a local vernacular tradition that specializes in exorcisms, divinations, healing, and summoning lost souls. Unlike their Buddhist, Daoist, and ritual master counterparts, Mogong priests traditionally recited scriptures written exclusively in Zhuang script, which is a combination of Chinese characters, Chinese-like characters, and other graphs.[43] Over time, the repertoires of indigenous Mogong priests sometimes were assumed by Han Chinese ritual specialists. The Mogong priests that Wang Xiyuan worked with were all Han Chinese, and their manuscripts were written in traditional Chinese characters. Many of their scriptures, moreover, incorporate elements of Buddhist and Daoist traditions that undoubtedly were introduced by the waves of Han migrants that began flowing into this former frontier region in the tenth century.[44]

Three of the texts Wang Xiyuan discovered are based on Obtaining the Scriptures narratives. The first, a short laudatory verse titled "In Praise of the Tang Master," extols the accomplishments and powers of the Tang Monk, referred to here by the honorific "Trepiṭaka."

> Verse in Praise of Trepiṭaka: The great monk who led the white horse bearing scriptures from the Heavenly Library has revealed the truth. Homage to the great bodhisattva Trepiṭaka! Trepiṭaka of the Great Tang went to Western Heaven. The drum and bell towers [of China] were difficult to hear. At Thunderclap monastery, novice Sun's spiritual powers were as great as heaven. He engaged with the Queen Mother and jade immortals

when he attended the Peach Blossom banquet. There was also Zhu Bajie. He was a demon. Monsters [made the road to] Western Heaven difficult to traverse. He subdued them and made them his followers. Praise Trepiṭaka! There is nothing that he does not understand. Our buddha's great compassion delivers us eternally. Homage to the great bodhisattva Trepiṭaka![45]

This invocation celebrates the perilous journey of the Tang Monk, Sun Wukong, and Zhu Bajie from China to Western Heaven, listing some of the hardships they endured so that truth and salvation could be conveyed to the people. These lines are grouped together with four other verses: one for the Bodhisattva Who Saves People from Harm (Jiu ku dashi 救苦大士), one for the *Amitābha Sūtra,* one for the *Heart Sūtra,* and one for Mulian. Among this august company, the Tang Monk is venerated as a prominent bodhisattva who, like other Buddhist saviors and apotropaic texts, has the power to protect the living and deliver the dead.

The two other Mogong manuscripts that feature Obtaining the Scriptures narratives follow directly after this verse in Wang Xiyuan's collection, and they are more revealing of Xuanzang's place in the local pantheon. The first and longer of the two texts, titled the *Ritual Manual for the Buddhist Obtaining Scriptures* (佛門取經道場科書卷, hereafter *Ritual Manual*), consists of ninety-eight lines divided into two discrete sections. The first section recounts the pilgrimage of the Tang Monk and his four companions to Western Heaven where they encounter the Buddha and receive the sutras. This portion of the text is written mainly in ten-character (three-three-four) lines, a form that is common among precious scrolls written after the sixteenth century. The second section recounts a journey through the courts of the Ten Kings of hell. It describes how the spirit of the dead has his or her sins eradicated over the course of several trials, and, with the help of bodhisattvas, eventually ascends to a heavenly realm. This latter section is in prosimetric style; prose passages are interspersed with seven-character couplets, another common feature of precious scrolls.[46] Wang Xiyuan reports that the entire text was recited at the funerals of male members of the community. The purpose of the rite, he explains, is to help the dead "transcend the spectral realm and quickly attain birth in the Pure Land."[47]

The second liturgy is similar to the first but appears to have been recited in a slightly different context. This manuscript, titled the *Ritual of the Compassionate Precious Scroll of the Buddhist's Journey to the West* (佛門西游慈悲寶卷道場, hereafter *Buddhist's Journey*), also begins with an account of the five pilgrims' passage through a purgatory-like realm to Western Heaven, written in alternating prose and couplets of seven-character verse.[48] This narrative is followed not by an account of the Ten Kings of hell, however, but with the opening verse to the *Precious Scroll of*

Rebirth in Heaven (升[生]天寶卷). The main body of this second text, which appears to be a truncated version of the *Precious Scroll of Mulian Rescuing His Mother, Escaping Hell, and [Attaining] Rebirth in Heaven* (目連救母出離地獄生天寶卷), is not included. Presumably, a version of the Mulian story once made up the second half of this liturgy but has since been lost or omitted.[49] Both the *Ritual Manual* and the *Buddhist's Journey* were recited during mortuary rites. The former was a relatively simple affair performed by a small number of priests after the death of a member of the community; the latter was probably a lengthier and more elaborate ceremony staged by a large contingent of ritual specialists as a part of a communal rite for the dead held during the Ghost Festival.[50] In each case, the story of the Tang Monk's pilgrimage centers on his acquisition and deliverance of powerful ritual texts and serves as a prelude to accounts of escaping hell and securing rebirth in heaven.

When the Mogong manuscripts were first published in the mid-1990s, they appeared to be anomalies. Very little was known about the relationship between Obtaining the Scriptures narratives and mortuary rites. Subsequent research has shown, however, that the Mogong rituals are not isolated events but part of a thematically consistent tradition shared throughout the region. We now know, for example, that other Zhuang and Han communities in Guangxi also venerate the Tang Monk as the figure responsible for transmitting the texts and rituals at the core of mortuary rites.

Zhuang ritual texts frequently contain etiological accounts of local funerary traditions. The protagonist in these stories usually is the Han-dynasty filial exemplar Dong Yong 董永 (Zh. Doenving), who is credited with saving his mother by refusing to follow the grisly custom of murdering and butchering the elderly. Instead, tradition holds that Dong Yong allowed his mother to die a natural death and distributed buffalo meat to the community as a substitute for her flesh. This is the conventional origin story for the practice, once common throughout Tai-speaking regions of southwestern China, of sacrificing a buffalo on the occasion of a funeral.[51] There are several variations of this account, however, some of which trace the beginning of newer, more "civilized" mortuary traditions not only to Dong Yong but also to the Tang Monk. The anthropologist Qin Yanjia, observing funeral ceremonies conducted in the 2010s by ritual masters in central Guangxi's Shanglin county 上林縣 (roughly one hundred forty miles southeast of the village where Wang Xiyuan worked), recorded several oral accounts of this mythic history.[52] According to one explanation:

> In ancient times, people did not know about burying the dead. Before a
> person died, they were killed, and their flesh was distributed for the people
> in the village to enjoy. Once, Dong Yong was in the mountains cutting fire-
> wood and saw a ewe in great pain as she gave birth. When he returned

home and told his mother about it, she said that when she gave birth to
Dong Yong she had suffered in the same way. Later, his mother became
gravely ill, but Dong Yong refused to kill her and distribute her flesh. When
his mother died, he sold his body [as a slave to pay for] her burial. This
moved the Heavenly Court, and Heaven sent the Tang Monk to Western
Heaven to obtain the sutras. After [the Tang Monk] returned with the
sutras, the Masters relied on these texts to release the souls of the dead.[53]

For the villagers who upheld this tradition, the ancient practice of cannibalism in
the region was superseded not by animal sacrifice but by new text-based Buddhist
rituals derived from Western Heaven and introduced to China by the Tang Monk.

Another oral tradition from a neighboring community tells the story differently, but the underlying message is the same. Among the repertoire of ceremonial
songs sung by ritual masters (*shigong* 師公) in central Guangxi is a hymn titled
"Song of the Tang Monk Requesting the Scriptures" (唐僧請經唱). The lyrics to this
hymn present a version of the Obtaining the Scriptures narrative that hews more
closely to the account known from the hundred-chapter novel. In the song, Yama,
the lord of the underworld, agrees to send Emperor Taizong back to the land of
the living on the condition that he hold a rite for the liberation of the dragon whose
death he failed to prevent. Taizong then summons Buddhists, Daoists, and ritual
masters to conduct a ceremony (*zhai* 齋) to release the dragon king's spirit. On dis-
covering that none of these specialists possess texts powerful enough to accomplish the task, Taizong dispatches the Tang Monk to Western Heaven to seek out
new ritual manuals. Once the mission is complete, Buddhists, Daoists, and ritual
masters all rely on the newly introduced scriptures for liberating the dead.[54] Additional plays and hymns offer still more variations on more or less the same theme.[55]
As local oral traditions, the details naturally vary, but the overall pattern is consistent; the Tang Monk is revered for introducing new ritual technologies, supplant-
ing those used previously, and less effectively, by competing groups of local ritual
specialists.[56]

Several more liturgical texts involving Obtaining the Scriptures narratives recently have come to light.[57] These manuscripts, many of which were collected and
transcribed by the scholar Hou Chong, were found over a very broad geographic
area. In addition to the two already known from Guangxi, there are eight from
Hubei, three from Hunan, three from Gansu, two from Guizhou, and two from Shandong. None of these texts is identical to any other, but many share the same passages and undoubtedly derive from a common source.[58] In those instances where
the use of these and other liturgies has been documented through fieldwork, certain continuities regarding their position in larger ritual sequences become apparent. As with the Mogong manuscripts, stories centered on the Tang Monk tend to

be recited or performed during the preliminary phases of mortuary rites. In the Dongting Lake 洞庭湖 area in Hunan province, for example, ritual masters of the Pu'an sect 普庵教 recite a text titled "The Tang Monk Goes to Obtain the Scriptures" (Tang Seng qu qu jing 唐僧去取经) on the morning of the second day of a three-day funeral. This is followed by a ritual for opening the five roads to the netherworld and, in the evening, the presentation of a "Memorial to the Bodhisattva Kṣitigarbha" 地藏表. On the third and final day, the coffin is buried, a "Memorial to the Ten Kings" 十王表 is conveyed, and the ceremony is concluded.[59] More than five hundred miles away, in Dushan 独山 county in southern Guizhou province, another funeral performance shares the same structure, though, once again, the details differ. In this case, members of the Buxqyaix (Ch. Buyi 布依) ethnic group recite a prosimetric text titled *The Ritual of Requesting Scriptures in Western Heaven as Spoken by the Buddha* (佛説西天請經道場; this is a slightly modified version of the *Ritual Manual*). This is followed by another liturgy, the *Ritual of the Buddhists Who Compassionately Saves Those in Distress* (佛門慈化氏救苦道場). This latter work describes how Kṣitigarbha and Mulian liberate those suffering in hell and guide them to the Western Pure Land. A third and final text, "The Assembly to Inter in the Earth and Summon the Dragon" (掩土呼龍一宗), details the powers used by ancestral masters to break open the earth and requests the earth dragon protect the one to be buried.[60] In these and related traditions, the pilgrimage of the Tang Monk creates the conditions necessary for figures like Kṣitigarbha and Mulian to successfully carry out the work of liberating the dead.[61]

Six of the liturgies that incorporate aspects of Xuanzang's mythic pilgrimage contain scripted exchanges between the chief officiant and the Tang Monk, here embodied by a ritual performer. These dialogues make explicit what is only implied in other contexts: the primary role of the Tang Monk is to acquire and deliver texts to be used during the ritual itself. A representative example from a manuscript copied in Hubei in 1891 reads:

Question: Why did the Tang Monk obtain the scriptures?

Answer: Because in the past, Emperor Li Shimin [Taizong] traveled to the underworld and saw eighteen levels of hell and limitless hungry ghosts, all in shackles. They were sad and sorrowful, long engulfed in ruin, unable to obtain liberation. If they did not rely on my Buddhist repentance scriptures, there would be no way for them to be redeemed. Therefore, [the emperor] ordered the Tang Monk to venerate the Buddha and seek the scriptures.

Question: Where did the Tang Monk go?

Answer: He and his disciples the Novice Sun, Zhu Bajie, and Sha Monk together went to Western Heaven to obtain the scriptures.

Question: How many years and months was he gone?

Answer: Thirteen winters and summers.

Question: How far did he travel?

Answer: 18,000 *li* in total.

Question: Which sutras did he obtain?

Answer: He obtained the *Mahāyāna Sūtra* (大乘經), *Amitābha Sūtra* (彌陀經), *Prajñā Sūtra* (波惹經), *Avalokiteśvara Sūtra* (觀音經), *Comprehending Ritual Sūtra* (了儀經), *Kṣitigarbha Sūtra* (地藏經), *Blood Bowl Sūtra* (血盆經), *Skeleton Sūtra* (胎骨經), *Obtaining Birth Sūtra* (受生經), *Medicine King Sūtra* (藥師經), *Rescuing from Distress Sūtra* (救苦經), *Saving People Sūtra* (度人經), and the *Birth in Heaven Sūtra* (生天經).

Question: Which repentance texts did he obtain?

Answer: He obtained the *Emperor Liang Repentance* (梁皇懺), *Thousand Buddha Repentance* (千佛懺), *Medicine King Repentance* (藥師懺), *Avalokiteśvara Repentance* (觀音懺), *Six Senses Repentance* (六根懺), and the *Blood Bowl Ten Kings Repentance* (血盆十王懺).

Question: How many texts in total?

Answer: The three storehouses of sutras, the three storehouses of repentance texts, and the three storehouses of dhāraṇī. He obtained these and brought them to the land of the East for the salvation of all beings.[62]

Except for the first four mainstream Mahāyāna sutras, none of the texts listed here were actually brought back from India by the historical Xuanzang.[63] They are all, however, popular Buddhist texts that often are incorporated into mortuary rites. These are, presumably, the very same works that were recited or presented during the funeral ceremony itself. Another manuscript, also from Hubei, appends the following instructions: "When the question and answer is finished, begin the music and welcome the scriptures onto the altar. Have a filial son raise the sutras and repentance texts to his head."[64]

In these ritually charged contexts, Xuanzang's mythical pilgrimage is not merely a play enacted for the entertainment of the audience. It serves to reestablish the transmission of divinely empowered texts. During the funeral, the pilgrimage is repeated in real time as the Tang Monk, taking the form of ritual specialists, crosses over into the realm of buddhas and bodhisattvas to retrieve and deliver the texts necessary for successfully performing the rite. This is a fleeting dispensation; the texts are only on temporary loan. When the next community member passes away, the Tang Monk will be called to undertake the journey once again.

A Note on Dating and Distribution

Obtaining the Scriptures liturgies and the narratives they preserve have been embraced by diverse ethnic and linguistic communities and incorporated into the repertoires of a variety of sectarian traditions. The historical origins of these rites, however, remain unclear. The ephemeral nature of hand-copied manuscripts and oral accounts makes it difficult to trace their development and distribution. At present, the oldest known manuscript of a funeral liturgy featuring the Tang Monk's pilgrimage was copied in Hunan in 1874.[65] Other texts dated slightly later have been found in Shandong (1884) and Hubei (1894). The late nineteenth-century provenance of these manuscripts coincides with the earliest eyewitness account of an actual performance of Obtaining the Scriptures at a funeral. This comes from an ethnographic report on the customs of Hakka 客家 villagers in Taiwan's Xinzhu county 新竹縣, written in 1894.[66] In the report, the author describes the elaborate ceremonies known as Rituals of Merit (*gongguo* 功果) that were popular among the local people.

> Powerful families invite long-haired monks. (These are actually shamans who are called "monks." They are another type of Daoist from Yue 粵 province. When they come on stage, they all dress in monks' clothes, thus the name. They are also called "black hat masters" and they specialize in performing Rituals of Merit during funerals. They do not perform *zhai* 齋 or *jiao* 醮.) They recite sutras and spells and set up wooden boards to make a shelter. They wear the clothing and hats of opera and perform "Tripiṭaka Obtains the Scriptures," "Mulian Rescues his Mother," and various other dramas. Drums, flutes, and stringed [instruments] all play at once. An onlooker who did not know better would think they were watching a play. Many forget that this is a Ritual of Merit.[67]

Two points mentioned in this report are worth highlighting here. The first is the presence of "long-haired monks." As the author notes, these "monks" were not conventionally ordained clerics. They did not shave their heads or, presumably, maintain vegetarian diets and practice celibacy. Instead, they were lay ritual specialists who performed funerary rites for a fee. This tallies with other performances of the Tang Monk's pilgrimage at funerals, nearly all of which are led by lay people. These specialists are known by different names, but they all are non-tonsured and operate independent of mainstream Buddhist or Daoist monastic institutions. Most are the modern-day heirs of what were sometimes called Yoga Monks (Yujia jiao seng 瑜伽教僧) during the Ming dynasty—professional lay priests who supported themselves by performing funerals and other rituals for hire.[68]

The second point to emphasize is that the "monks" performing the ritual were, in fact, a "type of Daoist from Yue." Yue is an alternate name for Guangdong province. Xinzhu, the county in Taiwan where the ritual was observed in 1894, was then, as now, dominated by the Hakka ethnic group, the majority of whom immigrated to Taiwan from Guangdong and southwestern Fujian. In contemporary Taiwan, "Rituals of Merit" involving the Tang Monk and his companions remain part of the funereal programs performed by Shijiao 釋教—Buddhist-oriented lay ritual specialists, also known as Incense and Flower Monks (*Xianghua heshang* 香花和尚) (see plate 10). No one knows precisely when and where the Shijiao tradition originated, but the earliest evidence comes from Mei county 梅縣, a Hakka region of eastern Guangdong province, during the late Ming dynasty. After arriving in Taiwan in the early eighteenth century, the rituals of Shijiao masters continued to evolve, resulting in multiple localized traditions loosely linked through interconnected histories and shared mythologies.[69] It is likely that the "long-haired monks" who performed the Ritual of Merit in 1894 were the predecessors of contemporary Shijiao priests.

The connection with Hakka ritualists from Guangdong is significant because some of the ritual masters that perform mortuary rites involving Obtaining the Scriptures narratives in distant Guangxi province (roughly five hundred miles away) also trace their ancestry back to Meizhou in northern Guangdong and Tingzhou in western Fujian—both major Hakka centers.[70] The Hakka are a famously diasporic people—the name "Hakka" literally means "guest family"—and there were mass migrations of Hakka out of Guangdong to other parts of southern China and Taiwan during the late Ming and early Qing dynasties. These migrations spread Shijiao traditions to other regions of China and this could be how Obtaining the Scriptures mortuary rites were initially distributed. This theory, however, is complicated by the fact that versions of the ritual also are performed in non-Hakka communities—including people of Han, Zhuang, Buyi, and Tujia ethnicities—in areas of China that have no predominant Hakka presence. Whomever first developed and popularized these mortuary rites, their innovations proved so popular that they were eventually adopted by other ethnic groups and sectarian traditions.

In addition to the question of where these rites originated, the issue of when they were first implemented remains unresolved. Some scholars contend that Obtaining the Scriptures funerary liturgies date to the beginning of the sixteenth century or earlier. The strongest evidence for this claim comes from one of the Mogong manuscripts discussed previously. The *Buddhist's Journey* has a colophon stating that it was last copied in 1967. When a Mogong priest dies, it is customary that all his personal belongings, including manuscripts and ritual paraphernalia, be burned. As part of the ordination process, novices are required to copy their own set of the scriptures transmitted to them by their master.[71] There is thus no way to know how many previous generations of Mogong priests had copied the *Buddhist's Journey* prior to 1967, but some scholars maintain that the scriptures recited by Mogong priests show signs of having been standardized sometime during the Ming dynasty.[72]

There is additional evidence suggesting the *Buddhist's Journey* was composed between the late Yuan and the early Ming dynasty. This derives from three markers within the text. The first is its structure. The text, with its seven-character lines, closely resembles the earliest known examples of precious scrolls. Beginning in the sixteenth century, ten-character lines became more common in these works, but precious scrolls from earlier periods typically use seven-character lines.[73] Second, like the *Buddhist's Journey,* the two earliest extant precious scrolls, *The Precious Scroll of Maudgalyāna* (ca. 1234) and *Liturgy Based on the Diamond Sūtra* (ca. 1242), are also adaptations of popular Buddhist narratives.[74] As we will see in the following chapter, later precious scrolls often centered on the lives and teachings of particular sectarian patriarchs rather than conventional Buddhist accounts. In both form and content, then, the *Buddhist's Journey* is like other noncanonical liturgical texts composed prior to the sixteenth century. The specific scenes referenced in the *Buddhist's Journey,* moreover, closely parallel those mentioned in the *Pak t'ongsa ŏnhae,* those depicted on the Kyŏngch'ŏn-sa and Wŏn'gak-sa stupas, and those alluded to in the *Xiaoshi zhenkong baojuan* 銷釋真空寶卷.[75] Based on the structure and content of the *Buddhist's Journey,* Chen Yupi and other scholars in China have argued that the manuscript could have been composed as early as the late fourteenth century, during roughly the same period as the *Precious Scroll of Mulian Rescuing His Mother* that apparently once constituted its second half.[76] A final important piece of corroborating evidence comes from a title used for Confucius in the text. The honorific "Wenxuan wang" 文宣王 (King of Propagating Culture) was bestowed on Confucius in 1307 and discontinued in 1530. Its use in the *Buddhist's Journey* strongly suggests that the original version of the text was written no earlier than the fourteenth century and no later than the early sixteenth century.

The form, content, and language of the *Buddhist's Journey* all point to a *terminus ante quem* of 1530, but it is impossible to know whether and to what extent the received version has been altered in the process of transmission. Most traditions that rely on oral instruction and manuscript copying evolve over time as new passages are added, earlier portions are deleted, or content is edited. We cannot assume, as some scholars have, that the received *Buddhist's Journey* is a perfectly preserved "fossil" from the fifteenth or sixteenth century. Moreover, even if we accept that the Mogong manuscript accurately preserves material from an earlier era, there is no way to know when the Tang Monk's account was first brought together with narratives of Mulian and Ten Kings or when the mythic pilgrimage began to be featured in mortuary rites. In the end, although there remains a strong possibility that funeral ceremonies involving Xuanzang existed during the Ming dynasty or earlier, in the absence of more definitive evidence, we can be certain only that they have been performed since the mid-nineteenth century.

Why did Xuanzang, a monk who was not known for performing funerals during his life, come to be so closely associated with mortuary rites after his death? The contributing factors are, undoubtedly, complex, but one simple explanation has to do with the long-standing association between Buddhism and the afterlife in China. Some of the earliest depictions of buddhas in China, dating to the Eastern Han dynasty (25–220), appear on the walls of tombs, suggesting that buddhas and bodhisattvas initially were understood as deities who could help the dead transition to the ancestral realm. Although Buddhist sutras and treatises contain sophisticated philosophical and soteriological teachings, for many people, the promise of protection during life and rebirth in a heavenly realm after death remained especially appealing aspects of the tradition. Xuanzang was a brilliant translator and a master of arcane Yogācāra doctrine, but he was remembered and celebrated primarily as an extraordinary monk who survived a treacherous journey to a distant land and returned with a collection of powerful Buddhist texts. More than any other cleric, Xuanzang is credited with transmitting Mahāyāna Buddhism to China. Given Xuanzang's identification with Buddhist teachings and those teachings' association with this-worldly protection and postmortem deliverance, it is not surprising that the deified Xuanzang was invoked in the context of exorcisms and mortuary rites (see plate 9). The ritual specialists who officiated at funerals drew on this complex of relations and channeled the spirit of Xuanzang for the benefit of the living and their dead. Like the Tang Monk, these priests were called to retrieve and deploy divine texts to facilitate the dead's transition to the spirit world. By identifying themselves and their traditions with the Tang Monk, ritual specialists situated their work in the context of a narrative that was both easily understood and broadly embraced.

Mortuary rites involving the Tang Monk were not only a means of remembering past events but also a method for recreating and reactivating Xuanzang's pilgrimage in the present. As the Vedic scholar Wade Wheelock once observed, "The 'message' of the ritual is less an idea to be taught and more a reality to be repeatedly experienced."[77] The recitation or reenactment of the Obtaining the Scriptures narrative summons the figures from the myth to manifest in the ritual space and perform the tasks for which they are known. In the context of rituals involving Obtaining the Scriptures narratives, both performers and those in attendance become participants in and witnesses to the pilgrimage. They are immersed in the action, seeing the Tang Monk and his companions—whether as masked performers, images painted on hanging scrolls, icons on the altar, or figurines placed inside the grave—hearing the dialogue spoken, chanted, or sung to the rhythm of percussion instruments and the melody of horns, and smelling the incense wafting from the altar.[78] The effect of this sensory saturation not only is engaging and edifying; it is all-enveloping. The immersive quality of these rituals underscores the critical role of context. Accounts of the Tang Monk's pilgrimage are animated through their application. What these events signify, in other words, is determined in large part by the circumstances in which they are performed. Removed from their settings, liturgies or scripts relating elements of Xuanzang's mythic travels become little more than inert words on a page. Taken out of context, they might appear to be mere stories, folklore, or fairy tales. Performance brings them to life and infuses them with meaning.

The prospect that Xuanzang could, when summoned, return to the human realm to deliver divine texts from Western Heaven surely brought peace of mind to families and communities unsettled by the ever-present specter of death. During the Ming and Qing dynasties, the possibility of Xuanzang's return also offered hope to men and women anxious that the world itself was devolving into chaos and soon would be destroyed. Many of these people longed for more than a disembodied spirit. They sought a flesh-and-blood savior who would descend from heaven to offer immediate instruction and guidance for surviving the impending apocalypse. The Tang Monk heard their prayers.

5 Savior

Things separate from their stories have no meaning.

—Cormac McCarthy, *The Crossing*

In the summer of 1900, the Tang Monk, Sun Wukong, Sha Monk, and Zhu Bajie were among the tens of thousands of young men massing outside the foreign legations in Beijing. Part of the Militia United in Righteousness (Yihetuan 義和團), otherwise known as the Boxers, they had come to drive foreigners out of China. The Boxers relied on spirit possession to invigorate and protect their members. Most had a tutelary deity whom they channeled through a simple ritual of bowing toward the southeast (the direction of Peach Blossom Mountain, an abode of the gods) and reciting an incantation. Their *Spell for Summoning the Spirits* begins with these lines: "Numinous heaven, numinous earth, we respectfully invite the ancestral masters to come and manifest their numen. First, we summon the Tang Monk and Zhu Bajie. Second, we summon Sha Monk and Sun Wukong. Third, we summon Erlang. Come and manifest your sagacity."[1] The spell goes on to call down a contingent of other deities, who, once alerted, were expected to descend, enter the men's bodies, and endow them with enhanced strength and fighting skills.

One witness recalled seeing "a youngster of fifteen or sixteen going through his boxing drills. Facing towards the southeast, he performed the *koutou* and chanted Tang Monk, Sha Monk, [Zhu] Bajie, [Sun] Wukong, and the like. After this, he fell to the ground, scrambled to his feet, and then with greatly increased energy practiced the martial arts."[2] While possessed, Boxers were reportedly capable of extraordinary feats. There were rumors that they could stop bullets, turn invisible, be in two places at once, enlarge their bodies, and resurrect the dead. These magical powers were brought to bear against the Boxers' primary target: Westerners in general and Christians in particular.

Anti-Christian sentiment was running high in China at the end of the nineteenth century. Tens of thousands of Christians—Protestant and Catholic, foreign and Chinese—were attacked and many were killed. Churches and bibles were burned. Foreigners, dehumanized as ghosts, monsters, and demons, were accused of promoting sexual promiscuity, castrating young men, extracting and eating the fetuses of women, and gouging out the eyes of innocent people. Illustrated texts called for missionaries and converts to be bound, force-fed human excrement, and butchered (see plate 11).[3]

The Boxer troops who descended on Beijing meant to put an end to these alleged crimes and reclaim China for the Chinese. Composed mostly of disenfranchised and destitute young male peasants and laborers, they announced their intention to "Annihilate the Qing! Exterminate the foreigners! Reestablish the Han!" They aspired to "Kill all the foreign devils and make their churches burn!"[4] With little more than swords and spears, they stood little chance against the modern firepower of foreign militaries, but they drew courage from their conviction that millions of spirit soldiers fought on their side. The gods described in narratives like *Journey to the West,* with their supranatural powers and magical weapons, were known to be virtually invincible. They had already proven their power over demons far more imposing than foreign troops. When the Boxers and their allies went into battle, they did so not as inexperienced and poorly armed peasants but as immortal, invulnerable deities. Liao Jiumei 廖九妹 (1886–1903), a leader of the Red Lanterns (Hongdeng 紅燈), the predominantly female wing of the broader Boxer movement, concealed an extraordinary identity within her seemingly ordinary body. She was the daughter of a common solider, but she claimed to possess the combined powers of the bodhisattva Avalokiteśvara, Lord Guan (the hero of the *Romance of the Three Kingdoms*), and Sun Wukong.[5] In the hands of these and other incarnated deities, simple staffs and swords could be transformed into divine weapons. Arrayed against the Gatling guns, rifles, and cannons of European and American armies, the Red Lanterns reportedly brandished "Sage Guan's blue dragon sword, [Sun] Wukong's golden rod, Marquis Huan's [Zhang Fei's] whip, Zhen Jiang's ax, and Weituo's demon subduing staff."[6]

The Boxers and Red Lanterns took on the characteristics as well as the attributes of the spirits they channeled. When possessed by Zhu Bajie, for example, they rooted around in the dirt to the astonishment and disgust of foreign onlookers.[7] Those who channeled Sun Wukong moved like monkeys. According to one report, entire battalions marched in formation down city streets, "children in front, adults behind, shorter people at the fore, taller people at the rear. Arranged in this order, they all held short-hilted broadswords. The dharma masters with daggers were at the rear. Shaking their heads and blinking their eyes, they said they were the spirits of Sun Wukong."[8] The Tang Monk's chief protector, the Monkey King, was famous for dividing his body during battle. With an array of Sun Wukong soldiers marshaling for war, it was as though the battles from *Journey to the West* were bleeding over onto the streets of Beijing.

As militants, the Boxers identified mainly with martial deities. Most of these gods were known from vernacular novels and plays. As one incredulous observer remarked: "The spirits [the Boxers] venerate are arbitrarily and absurdly created without any particular system. Most come from the novels *Journey to the West, Investiture of the Gods, Romance of the Three Kingdoms,* and *Water Margin.*"[9] This system, however, was neither arbitrary nor absurd. It reflected the popular religious cultures of northeastern China—the regions of Shandong, Zhili, Shanxi, and Manchuria—where the Boxer movement was strongest. Another critic, after noting that the Boxers tended to be possessed by figures from *Journey to the West* and other popular narratives, remarked that "Country bumpkins probably know these [figures] from the statues they find in common temples."[10] These deities, in other words, were a familiar presence in the local pantheon. Their images were enshrined in temples and their stories were regularly recited and performed. Such stories confirmed that potent spirits support and protect those who fight for a righteous cause. For those living through the difficult final decades of the Qing dynasty, tales of the Tang Monk's heroic pilgrimage and Sun Wukong's victorious battles served simultaneously as sources of entertainment, information, and inspiration. They conferred the courage to fight against more formidable adversaries and promised that good would inevitably prevail over evil.

The Boxers' story, of course, had no fairy tale ending. After allied forces from the United States, France, England, Russia, Germany, Austria-Hungary, Italy, and Japan put an end to the fifty-five-day siege of Beijing's foreign legations in August 1900, tens of thousands of suspected insurgents were massacred during the ensuing punitive campaigns. Some of the surviving Boxers and Red Lanterns fled to the relatively safe haven of Sichuan where they continued to train and stage sporadic attacks over the course of the next decade, but their movement was effectively destroyed.

In the aftermath of the Boxer uprising, Chinese officials cast about for a suitable place to lay the blame. There were obvious candidates: the aggressive proselytizing of Christian missionaries, the economic exploitation of Western nations, the prevarications and perceived weakness of the Qing court, the droughts and floods that had devastated northeastern China, and the endemic poverty of rural areas. For some officials, however, it was vernacular novels that bore responsibility. "Few Chinese novels are not lewd, rebellious, or absurd," according to the minutes of Sichuan's first provincial assembly in 1909. "The worst among them, such as *Journey to the West* and *Canonization of the Gods,* induce superstitious beliefs and resulted in the establishment of the Boxer's Movement and the Red Lantern Sect."[11] The story of the Tang Monk's pilgrimage, some people were convinced, had inspired an insurgency.

The problem, for those who subscribed to this view, was that people in rural areas—the "country bumpkins" who frequented "common" temples—were ignorant. They naively assumed the deities depicted in temples and the stories enacted on stages were real. According to a local gazetteer for Dazu county in Chongqing, for example, one of the Red Lantern leaders who channeled Sun Wukong was nothing but an "extremely dull-witted" laborer. Despite his ridiculous antics—jumping, shaking, swinging around a sword—the "ignorant masses" all worshiped him as the incarnation of the deity.[12] Simple people were susceptible to the outrageous claims and seditious incitements of stories like *Journey to the West*. Better education, conveyed through more decorous narratives, would presumably foster more appropriate behavior.

As we saw in chapter 1, the credulity of the masses disquieted officials in early twentieth-century China, and Obtaining the Scriptures narratives often were accused of invoking dangerous fantasies. This was a long-standing concern. In the mid-sixteenth century, decades before the publication of the *Journey to the West* novel, a playwright named Yang Ti was already declaring that the "wise reject [the story] as false. The ignorant believe it as true."[13] To label the mythical accounts of the Tang Monk's pilgrimage false or fictional, however, was not to dismiss them as meaningless or inconsequential. It was merely to assert that metaphor should not be misconstrued as history. The character of the Tang Monk, according to Yang Ti, was not a real historical figure, but he was an effective allegory for a person's original nature. As for the rest of the pilgrims, they represented components of a person's body and mind. Zhu Bajie was the eyes, Sun Wukong was the mind, the Sha Monk was anger, and the white horse was one's will. Once these mental and physical forces were brought under control, the person—symbolized by the Tang Monk—would be at peace. "If men could with their power of sight first see through the affairs of the world, then suppress the monkey of the mind and bind the horse of the will, and again with wisdom govern their anger and subdue all evil spirits— what difficulty would they have in attaining the Way?"[14] If only they could emulate the ideal of the Tang Monk, in other words, everything would be fine.

This kind of psychologizing of the Tang Monk's pilgrimage was popular among literati committed to salvaging some meaning and value from what harsher critics dismissed as an irredeemable fantasy. When the Shidetang 世德堂 edition of the hundred-chapter novel was published in 1592, it included a preface that lauded the philosophical depth of the narrative while leaving no doubt that the story was allegorical. "Sun is a monkey," the author Chen Yuanzhi 陳元之 explained, but he is also:

> The spirit of the mind. Horse is a horse. He is the galloping of will. Bajie is the eight precepts. He is the wood phase of the liver's *qi*. Sha is flowing sand. He is the water phase of the kidney's *qi*. Trepiṭaka is the three storehouses of spirit, sound, and *qi*. He is the lord of the citadel. Demons are

the mouth, ears, nose, tongue, body, and will when they are obstructed by fear, confusion, and illusion. Therefore, the demons are born of the mind and are also controlled by the mind. To control the mind is to control demons, and to control demons is to return to principle. To return to principle is to return to the beginning of all things where the mind need not be controlled. This is the fulfillment of the Dao. It is what is directly allegorized in this book.[15]

As the lord of the citadel, the Tang Monk represented the reader. The other pilgrims were elements of the reader's body, and their pilgrimage was an exercise in self-control and self-realization.

As the popularity of the novel swelled over the seventeenth century, subsequent prefaces and commentaries repeated and elaborated this point. In a commentary from 1663, the scholar and publisher Wang Xiangxu 汪象旭 (a.k.a. Wang Qi 汪淇, 1604–1668) reminded his readers that *Journey to the West* was only "an analogy for verifying the Dao." Contrary to popular belief, the characters it portrays never really existed and the events it describes never actually took place. These were all merely literary devices employed to illustrate abstract philosophical principles. How could anyone believe that a Chinese Buddhist monk truly traveled in the company of magical talking animals through lands filled with monsters and ghosts to receive sacred scriptures from celestial buddhas? "Who has really seen the Tang Monk obtaining the scriptures?" Wang Xiangxu asked. "Does [Zhu] Bajie actually shoulder the load? Does Sha Monk [really] lead a horse?"[16] Any rational person, Wang implied, would recognize that such stories were merely meant to symbolize the trials and triumphs of ordinary life.

In the eight commentaries on the novel published prior to the Republican period, there was broad agreement that the pilgrimage of the Tang Monk was a metaphor for higher order, psychologically oriented processes of self-cultivation.[17] Exactly what those processes were, however, remained a matter of some debate. Those with Buddhist inclinations interpreted the account as an origin story for the *Heart Sūtra* or the Perfection of Wisdom texts more broadly.[18] Sympathetic Neo-Confucians read the journey as a metaphor for rectifying the mind and cultivating sincerity.[19] For them, the Tang Monk exemplified the learned and courageous *junzi* whose selfless service and unerring discernment earned him a place of honor at court. Perhaps most influentially, those steeped in the teachings of Complete Perfection (Quanzhen 全真) Daoism equated the account of the practice of internal alchemy (*neidan* 內丹) with the pilgrims' progress representing an adept's interior practice.[20] Even Christians, as we already have seen, would later read it as an echo of the New Testament. "We don't see things as they are," according to the old adage,

"We see things as we are."[21] Whatever tradition one ascribed to, *Journey to the West* seemed to illustrate its essential teachings.

Beyond the rarified realm of learned men who wrote commentaries, published texts, and devoted their leisure time to the rigors of self-refinement lay the vast majority of the Chinese population. Many of these men and women dwelled precariously on the economic margins and were preoccupied not with hermeneutics but with survival. They needed a savior more than they needed a symbol. Literati insistence that the Obtaining the Scriptures narrative must be read as metaphor were necessary only because more literal readings remained so pervasive. As the Boxers and other groups made plain, many people *did* believe the spirits of the Tang Monk and his companions existed and occasionally intervened in the affairs of the world. Some of the same scholars who championed allegorical readings of the narrative lamented that *Journey to the West* was so well written that it reoriented a person's sense of reality. Reflecting on the captivating qualities of the novel, Wang Xiangxu observed: "The vividness of the portrayals is so compelling that it causes readers to not dare suspect that it is false on first reading and not to doubt that it is real on subsequent readings."[22] For some people, the novel was so good that it simply had to be true.

Obtaining the Scriptures narratives were both evocative and ubiquitous. During the late Imperial period, they circulated in multiple mass-market literary editions, were performed in commercial theaters and on temple stages, depicted in art, recounted in oral stories and songs, and enacted during communal rituals. People absorbed the stories and their characters as children, and they continued to encounter them in a variety of contexts over the course of their lives. With narratives that are so integral to the identities of communities—with heroes, villains, and plot lines traded among family members, friends, and neighbors—belief is a part of belonging. Over the course of one's life, the Tang Monk's pilgrimage becomes embedded in memory and experience. People enter into the story and make it their own.

Modern anthropologists have studied the processes by which people of faith discern and develop personal relationships with otherwise intangible gods and spirits.[23] The Chinese author Pu Songling 蒲松齡 (1640–1715), writing more than three centuries ago, anticipated some of their conclusions. A short story in his *Strange Tales from a Chinese Studio* nicely captures the influence of belief on perception. The story centers on a traveling merchant who happens upon an icon of Sun Wukong on an altar in Fujian. The merchant is initially incredulous. "Sun Wukong is nothing but a parable invented by old Qiu [Changchun]," he scoffs. "How can people sincerely believe in him?" To demonstrate the foolishness of the temple's devotees, the man invites misfortune to befall him if Sun Wukong is, in fact, an actual god. This, of course, is exactly what happens. The merchant gets sick, and his brother dies. Sun Wukong then appears to him in a dream and promises to resurrect his brother if the man becomes his devotee. This, too, comes to pass, and the story concludes with Pu Songling's insightful observation: "It certainly is not necessary for someone [like Sun Wukong] to actually exist in the world: if people believe someone to be powerful, then he will be powerful for them. Why is this? When the human mind is fixed on something, the spirits will appear."[24] Even fictional parables can be made manifest through the power of belief. When members of the same community collectively share that belief it becomes the consensus reality.

This final chapter considers some of the cases where belief in the Tang Monk and his companions resulted not only in their appearance in the world but in their ability to affect the course of history. Beginning in the mid-sixteenth century and continuing through the early twentieth century, the Tang Monk repeatedly assumed human form to reenact his pilgrimage in real time. Some people claimed to be Xuanzang incarnate, returned to the human realm to transmit new sacred teachings and lead people on a pilgrimage to a heavenly realm in the West. Others asserted that they could transform their ordinary bodies into the extraordinary body of the Tang Monk. When the Boxers and the Red Lanterns channeled the spirits of the Tang Monk, Sun Wukong, and other deities, they were not innovating new practices but were, instead, drawing on centuries-long traditions of interpreting the journey to Western Heaven both as a historical event and as a recurring process. For these and many other people, the Tang Monk's pilgrimage had occurred in the past but could be—indeed, needed to be—repeated in the present.

Prophets

The same spirit that animated Xuanzang in the seventh century was reborn in rural Guangpingfu (present-day Quzhou 曲周 county, Hebei province) in the summer of 1570. The child, initially named Han Taihu 韓太湖 (1570–1598), came from a peasant family of pious Buddhists who had fallen on hard times. At the age of nineteen, Han traveled south to Henan and, after a period of study under a man who claimed to be the reincarnation of Śākyamuni Buddha, he returned home transformed. Han announced that he was no ordinary mortal but the son of a deity named Old Patriarch of Original Chaos (Hunyuan laozu 混元老祖). Patriarch Piaogao 飄高 (Drifting High), as Han now styled himself, explained that he had been dispatched by the Old Patriarch with a message for humankind: the current age was ending and only those who repented and followed the teachings of the new prophet would survive the coming apocalypse. Patriarch Piaogao's mother, elder brother, and ninety fellow villagers, eager to witness the advent of a new era of great peace, were the first to convert.[25] Their new sect, known variously as the Teachings of Vast Yang (Hongyang jiao 弘陽教) or the Teachings of Original Chaos (Hunyuan jiao 混元教), placed Piaogao last in a line of celestial emissaries that had been successively sent from heaven to rescue an elect few on earth. Xuanzang, one of the previous incarnations of this divine force, had performed the same task almost a thousand years earlier.

Patriarch Piaogao was not the first self-proclaimed prophet to trace his lineage through Xuanzang, and he would not be the last. His teachings were part of a growing movement of salvational associations—also known as "sectarian" groups— that flourished during the late Ming and Qing dynasties. Beginning in the early years of the sixteenth century, charismatic lay teachers authored new sets of scriptures and attracted large congregations of devotees. The scriptures used by these groups, usually called "precious scrolls" (*baojuan*), drew liberally from Buddhist sutras, Daoist scriptures, and the mythological narratives of local communities to present new cosmological, soteriological, and eschatological teachings. The Obtaining the Scriptures narratives that suffused the common culture of China in the sixteenth century were inevitably woven into many of these works. Precious scrolls often identified the leaders of salvational associations as human incarnations of divine beings, usually buddhas, bodhisattvas, or other figures from the popular pantheon. Some teachers self-identified as Xuanzang, announcing that they had come to deliver a new cache of sacred scriptures, admonish the wicked, and save the pure. Incorporating elements of the Obtaining the Scriptures narrative into their own biographies, doctrines, and practices, they harnessed the popularity and power of a familiar narrative, claiming the Tang Monk's pilgrimage as a chapter in their own spiritual biography.

Representations of Xuanzang and his mythic travels in precious scrolls are embedded in many of the same cultural and cosmological contexts as those examined in previous chapters. As with the ritual specialists who performed or recited versions of Obtaining the Scriptures narratives during exorcisms and mortuary rites, for example, members of salvational associations were predominantly lay people unaffiliated with mainstream Buddhist or Daoist institutions. The written liturgies used by ritual specialists also parallel, and in some cases replicate, the content and structure of precious scrolls. Despite considerable overlap with related ritual traditions, however, there are several distinguishing features that make it useful to treat the narratives in precious scrolls separately here. To begin with, the authors and audiences of these works tended to be members of exclusive associations or sects. In most cases, they had undergone initiation, made financial commitments, taken vows, and pledged their loyalty to their teachers and their congregations. Active and sustained engagement with the doctrines and practices of their sect set these men and women apart from more casual participants in collective, public rituals. Members of many salvational associations also envisioned a more personal relationship with Xuanzang. Rather than summoning his spirit to descend temporarily into the body of a ritual master or an icon for the duration of a rite, sect leaders asserted a direct and enduring link to the Tang Monk as his successor or reincarnation. Some teachers went even further, instructing their followers that they, too, through devotion, discipline, and self-sacrifice, could transform their vulnerable, flawed human bodies into the immortal form of the Tang Monk.

Salvational associations were hierarchical organizations. Those with significant economic resources occupied influential positions in the sociopolitical landscapes of early modern China, occasionally assuming quasi-governmental functions. Despite the social and economic benefits many groups provided, officials came to see the millenarian beliefs espoused by some associations, with their predictions of societal collapse and visions of a utopian future, as destabilizing or seditious. Government authorities, particularly during the Qing dynasty, were acutely aware that the teachings of certain groups could—and in some cases did—incite unrest or rebellion. The armed insurrections of a relatively small number of salvational associations cast a long shadow over the majority of nonviolent, apolitical congregations. Anxiety over the corrupting influence of precious scrolls and other "heterodox" scriptures eventually culminated in a series of persecutions and reform efforts that would drastically change how later generations related to narratives like Obtaining the Scriptures and their ritual expressions (see chapter 1).

Members of Patriarch Piaogao's Vast Yang sect became targets of government persecution in the eighteenth century, but during Piaogao's brief life, his teachings appear to have elicited little serious concern among officials. If his autobiography, the *Vast Yang Sūtra on Awakening to the Way through Arduous Effort* (*Hongyang kugong wudao jing* 弘陽苦功悟道經), is to be believed, after arriving in the capital of Beijing in 1595, Piaogao quickly secured the support of palace eunuchs and members of the aristocracy.[26] His writings, published by the prestigious imperial printing house, presumably reached a broad audience. He called his written teachings "sutras" or "scriptures" (*jing* 經), but in form and content they belonged to the genre of precious scrolls, which, by the time Piaogao was preaching in Beijing, were an established form of sectarian scripture.[27]

Precious scrolls originated sometime around the thirteenth century as prosimetric works, alternately spoken and sung by Buddhist monks when preaching to laity. The earliest examples convey basic Buddhist teachings, often narrated through the hagiographies of prominent Buddhist saints like Mulian and Avalokiteśvara.[28] Framed as a form of scripture, precious scrolls typically begin with verses for opening the "sutra," incense offerings, and invitations for buddhas and bodhisattvas to descend into the ritual space. After conveying the teachings, these works conclude with verses for sending off the attendant deities. In the early sixteenth century, the founders of new sectarian groups adapted the precious scroll format to present new teachings and auto-hagiographies. As expanding print technologies made large-scale reproductions of texts both more convenient and more affordable, precious scrolls proliferated. The earliest and most influential of these new scriptures were self-consciously Buddhist. Authored by a layman known as Patriarch Luo 羅祖 (trad. 1442–1527), they also were the first precious scrolls to incorporate the Tang Monk and his pilgrimage into the sacred histories of newly emerging lay sectarian movements.

Patriarch Luo is the founding father of these new salvational associations. Despite his prominence, only a few biographical details are known about Luo's life.[29] He was born in Shandong, orphaned at a young age, and eventually served at a military garrison in northern Hebei, the same region where Patriarch Piaogao later lived. The series of scriptures Luo produced for his followers, known as the *Five Books in Six Volumes* (*Wubu liuce* 五部六冊), was first published in 1509 and reprinted no less than twenty-six times during the remainder of the Ming dynasty. These works offer a vision of the world that merges Indian Buddhist views of time and space with native Chinese cosmological traditions. Luo describes the primordial force that created and sustains the world as an ancient buddha, sometimes referred to as the Holy Patriarch of the Limitless (無極聖祖). Śākyamuni Buddha was one of the Holy Patriarch's incarnations, as were Mulian and other figures from the Chinese pantheon.[30] Although Patriarch Luo never explicitly identified himself as a descendant of this divine lineage, later generations of his followers did. One of the earliest biographies of Luo, written nearly seventy years after his death, names him as a manifestation of the Ancient Buddha (老古佛) who had descended to Shandong for the salvation of humankind.[31]

Followers of Luo's Non-Action (Wuwei 無為) sect venerated the *Five Books and Six Volumes* as sacred scriptures, the proclamations of an awakened being. The *Journey to the West* novel later would be conceived in similar terms; one seventeenth-century account likened the *Five Books and Six Volumes* to *Journey to the West* because both works appeared to encapsulate and express the entire cosmos.[32] Luo recorded his teachings more than eighty years before the publication of the *Journey to the West* novel, but he was clearly familiar with Obtaining the Scriptures narratives. In his writings, he does not reference specific episodes, taking for granted that his readers and listeners were familiar with the plot of the story and the identities of its protagonists. Instead, he highlights the parallels between his own life and work and the career of the Tang Monk, emphasizing the difficult and dangerous nature of the Tang Monk's journey, the hardships he endured, and the support and protection he received along the way. In the *Scroll of Non-Action in Sighing for the World,* for instance, Luo raises the example of the Tang Monk's pilgrimage to goad his followers to take his own teachings more seriously. "The old Tang Monk suffered hardship and affliction only for the sake of sentient beings," he wrote.

"I strongly urge you, men and women: stop slandering the Buddha-dharma!"[33] As heir to the Tang Monk's legacy, respect for the Tang Monk's accomplishments, Luo implied, should properly manifest as reverence for Luo and his teachings.

Luo explained that the meritorious work of the Tang Monk and the devotion of his four disciples ultimately resulted in their buddhahood.

> Master Trepiṭaka delivered sentient beings, became a buddha and left.
> Meritorious Buddha, one who has attained the status of a buddha, this is the Tang Monk.
> Novice Sun, protected the Buddha-dharma, became a buddha and left.
> Now he is in the Buddha realm offering the teachings of the World Honored One.
> Zhu Bajie, protected the Buddha-dharma, became a buddha and left.
> Now he is a buddha in the world and presides over heaven and earth.
> Sha Monk engaged the Buddha-dharma, became a buddha and left.
> Now he is in the Buddha realm with a golden body of seven treasures.
> Fire-dragon Horse, protected the Tang Monk, became a buddha and left.
> Now he is in the Buddha realm with an incorruptible golden body.[34]

Like the Tang Monk, Patriarch Luo and his disciples encountered obstacles, surmounted barriers, and sacrificed themselves for the sake of transmitting scriptures and liberating sentient beings. They, too, required the protection and devotion of disciples. They, too, would one day become buddhas and exit the cycle of *samsara*.

In the opening passage of his *Precious Scroll of Deeply Rooted Karmic Fruits, Majestic and Immovable Like Mount Tai,* Luo expresses his indebtedness to those who came before him. "The Sage [Sun Wukong], Zhu Bajie, Sha Monk, and White Horse safeguarded the dharma and liberated all beings," he wrote. "Those who safeguard the dharma all become buddhas and leave. Now is like ancient times, ancient times are like now. It is not because of my abilities [alone], but by the grace of those who have safeguarded and upheld the marvelous dharma, that [these teachings] spread throughout the world."[35] In this way, Luo presented his teachings as part of a tradition that stretched back through the Tang Monk to the ancient buddhas. In the past, in other words, there was the Buddha and the Tang Monk. In the present, there is Patriarch Luo.

As a pioneering lay teacher, Patriarch Luo and his teachings remained relevant long after his death. Subsequent leaders of his Non-Action movement as well as the founding figures of other sects linked themselves with Luo and his legacy, but the tradition he initiated continued to evolve. Descriptions of "returning home" (*gui jia* 歸家) to the "original place" (*ben di* 本地), which Luo had raised as metaphors for awakening, assumed more literal meanings in later precious scrolls. The teachings of Patriarch Piaogao, who was born more than forty years after Luo's death, exemplify this newly emerging theological vision. In broad terms, later salvational associations usually recognize a single, primordial deity known by a variety of names. Patriarch Piaogao called him the Old Patriarch of Original Chaos, but others referred to the Unborn Mother, the Unborn Parents (無生父母), the Ancient Buddha (古佛), or Amitābha. Piaogao's description of the deity's origins and activities was typical. After the Old Patriarch of Original Chaos emerged from the void, Piaogao explained, the world began to differentiate and take shape. Human beings were born to the Old Patriarch but then banished to live in the East—the human realm. Not realizing that they are all members of the same family, these people constantly fight among themselves. Moved by pity and compassion for his orphaned and ignorant children, the Old Patriarch, residing in his Western paradise, periodically dispatches divine messengers to guide and instruct them.

The benighted children in the East are distinct from the Old Patriarch's other divine progeny who remain in the West. These include the buddha Lamp Lighter (Dīpankara 燃燈), who presided over the first of three cosmic eras, or *kalpas*: the period of Blue Yang (*qing yang* 青陽). Lamp Lighter's son, the Sandalwood (Zhantan 栴檀) Buddha, is now caretaker of the present *kalpa*, the period of Vast (or Red) Yang (*hong yang* 弘/紅陽). Piaogao called this buddha "my master" (or "grandfather," *laoye* 老爺) and explained that he already had descended to earth three times.

> The first time he incarnated as the pole-carrying monk [aka Mulian]. He took the five thousand and forty-eight scrolls of the great canon's true scriptures and exhausted himself to carry them up to Thunderclap [Monastery]. The Eastern lands [then] had no scriptures to use for repentance rites for the dead. The second time [the Sandalwood Buddha] incarnated, it was as the Tang Monk. He spent twelve years obtaining the scriptures. When his trials were over, he returned to the Eastern lands, [leaving] Subhūti with nothing to rely on. The third time he incarnated as Patriarch Luo, who left five volumes of true scriptures. After enduring thirteen years of suffering, [Luo] was completely awakened to his true nature. The flower of his heart emitted a luminous [light] and he obtained the true wordless scriptures to [transmit] to the final *kalpa*.[36]

According to Piaogao's mythic history, the Sandalwood Buddha took the form of Mulian and carried the sacred scriptures from east to west. As Xuanzang, he later returned them to China, thus depriving the Buddha's own disciple Subhūti access to the written teachings (see figure 5.1). (Readers of the *Journey to the West* novel

Figure 5.1. The Tang Monk and his four companions carrying texts back to China, as depicted in the twenty-fourth chapter of the *Primordial Chaos-Vast Yang Scripture of the Descent of Piaogao*. Collection of the Kyōto daigaku jinmun kagaku kenkyūjo. Isobe, *Saiyūki shiryō no kenkyū*, 25.

will recall that Xuanzang is identified as a former disciple of the Buddha Golden Cicada. He was banished to earth to atone for the slight of falling asleep while the Buddha was preaching. After he completes the pilgrimage that is his penance, he is apotheosized as the Sandalwood Buddha.) The scriptures Xuanzang delivers to China are reconceived and retransmitted by Patriarch Luo at the beginning of the sixteenth century. Piaogao is thus the most recent dispensation of the primordial buddha's saving grace, and his task is particularly urgent. The current era, he revealed, was on the verge of annihilation, and the vast majority of people were mired in sin and would soon perish. Those who joined his Vast Yang congregation, however, would be reunited with their divine parents in the West and would live to see the dawning of the new White Yang (*baiyang* 白陽) *kalpa*, a time of enduring peace presided over by the future buddha Maitreya.

Based on this extraordinary account, Xuanzang was one of a succession of intermediaries sent by a primordial deity to transmit teachings that will save a select few from annihilation. Those who accepted and implemented these instructions would return to their original home and reunite with their true parents in the West. After Xuanzang, new prophets were periodically dispatched with new collections of texts, a process that culminated with Patriarch Piaogao (or whichever teacher was asserting this otherworldly ancestry). Xuanzang's pilgrimage to Western Heaven, then, was not a singular historical event but part of a repeating cycle. Others had made the journey before him and more would follow. Xuanzang had transmitted the Buddhist canon, Patriarch Luo delivered the *Five Books in Six Volumes,* and Patriarch Piaogao now presented the Vast Yang scriptures. Each collection was a new iteration of the same sacred teaching adapted to suit the capacities of different audiences.

Piaogao's warnings of a looming apocalypse resonated with an audience already accustomed to such prophecies. Both Buddhists and Daoists had long taken it for granted that divine beings periodically descended to earth to deliver new teachings for the salvation of humankind. Whether this was the Dao manifesting in human form or the succession of buddhas that appeared over the course of *kalpas,* a sense of inevitable entropy requiring the intervention of deities pervaded mainstream Chinese religious traditions. Things would eventually get better, the thinking went, but first they were going to get worse. This "eschatological anguish," as Anna Seidel called it, was as political as it was personal.[37] The Heavenly Mandate commanded by emperors, after all, was divinely conferred and subject to revocation. From as early as the Taiping Rebellion of the second century, attempts to overthrow governments perceived as corrupt were framed as heavenly willed restorations of the "Great Peace" (*Taiping* 太平), a utopia free of poverty, famine, epidemics, and war. Early Daoist scriptures foretold the coming of the new messiah, a human incarnation of Laozi or Li Hong, who would guide the chosen few "seed people" to a hidden paradise to wait out the cataclysm and then emerge as the progenitors of a new civilization.[38]

Chinese readers of translated Indian Buddhist texts were similarly informed that the present *kalpa* began decaying as soon as Śākyamuni entered *nirvāṇa.* People's life spans are now gradually decreasing, according to the *nikāyas.* Even their bodies are shrinking. Crime is on the rise, food is losing its flavor, and morality is eroding. Wicked men are rising to positions of power. Floods, droughts, plagues, and famines are growing more severe and frequent. As resources diminish, suspicion and paranoia grow. Communities eventually will be torn apart, and humans will hunt one another like animals. Their desperation and tension will trigger a brutal war, during which most of the population will be slaughtered.[39] Those who survive the massacre will be the first to live during a time when human civilization will once again flourish and the bodhisattva Maitreya, who has been waiting in Tuṣita Heaven, will descend to earth as the first buddha of the new *kalpa.* This was an event that the historical Xuanzang himself fervently hoped to witness, though he expected the wait would be long.[40] The conventional length of time between the death of Śākyamuni and the birth of Maitreya is calculated to be around 5.6 billion years. During the Ming dynasty, however, many people were convinced that the time had come and Maitreya's arrival was imminent.[41]

Every generation harbors some degree of existential anxiety, but Piaogao lived during a time of extraordinary instability. Modern climatologists call the period from the thirteenth through the eighteenth centuries the Little Ice Age. This span of unusually cold temperatures affected different regions in different ways, and northern China during the late sixteenth century was particularly hard hit. The period known as the "Wanli Slough" (1572–1615) suffered a series of erratic fluctuations in weather patterns that precipitated economic and demographic collapse.[42] A devastating drought in 1585 ended with catastrophic floods the following year. In a cruelly recurring cycle, the plagues of locusts that often followed droughts took flight in 1587, decimating crops across the agrarian north. Crop failure led to two years of famine, which coincided with epidemics in the summers of 1587 and 1588. The crowded, unsanitary conditions of densely populated urban centers like Beijing only accelerated the spread of disease. Historians estimate the mortality rate in northern China during this period at somewhere between forty and fifty million people—nearly one-third of the entire population. In the northern provinces where Piaogao and his followers lived, the death toll was probably higher, with one of every two people succumbing to disease or starvation. (Piaogao himself died in the capital in 1598 at the age of twenty-eight.) Amid such dark and desperate times, many people must have found solace in Piaogao's message that the pious would live to see a future free of sickness, starvation, and poverty. Xuanzang had saved the people in the past. Perhaps Piaogao, as Xuanzang's modern heir, could now deliver the people of the present.

Piaogao's Vast Yang sect was far from the only group convinced they were following in the footsteps of Xuanzang. Throughout the late Ming and Qing dynasties, other salvational associations constructed parallel histories based on similar lineages of divine prophets. According to the teachings of these groups, the Tang Monk's acquisition and deliverance of scriptures was one among many inflection points in a cycle of revelation and salvation. Sect members were encouraged to envision themselves as active participants in this ongoing process, receiving sacred scriptures and embarking on a pilgrimage back to their original home in Western Heaven. There were other sects, however, that presented the Tang Monk not only as ancestor and intermediary but as an exemplar and ideal that practitioners should themselves strive to actualize. The pilgrimage to Western Heaven, according to some precious scrolls, could, in fact, be completed during this life within this very body.

Perfected

The *Journey to the West* novel famously frames the Tang Monk's pilgrimage as an internal path of practice. Incorporating the theories and symbolism of both Chan

Buddhism and Complete Perfection Daoism, the narrative reads, in the words of Andrew Plaks, as "a psychomania of the process of the cultivation of mind."[43] The richness of the novel's Daoist imagery convinced one early commentator that it was authored by the Complete Perfection patriarch Qiu Changchun—an attribution so plausible it went virtually uncontested until the early twentieth century.[44] In the modern era, the identity of the novel's author and his or her religious inclinations have been the subjects of a great deal of conjecture. The evidence supporting different candidates remains circumstantial and speculative, and the question may never be resolved. For our purposes, it is enough to note that, whoever wrote the hundred-chapter version of *Journey to the West,* they appear to have inherited rather than invented the trope of the pilgrimage as an allegory for self-cultivation. This interpretation of the Tang Monk's travels already was firmly in place by the mid-sixteenth century, several decades before the novel was published. It is alluded to in some nonsectarian works, but it receives its fullest expression in the teachings of salvational associations.[45] Some of the earliest examples come from a collection of precious scrolls associated with a tradition known as the Teachings of Yellow Heaven (Huangtian jiao 黃天教).

Puming 普明 (a.k.a. Li Bin 李賓, d. 1562), the founding patriarch of the Yellow Heaven sect, was, like Patriarch Luo, a peasant turned soldier who spent most of his life in present-day Hebei province.[46] He and his disciple Pujing 普靜 (d. 1586) both claimed divine provenance. As was common among the leaders of salvational associations, they identified as incarnations of primordial buddhas; Puming was the Ancient Buddha of the August Ultimate (Huangji Gufo 皇極古佛), while Pujing was the Ancient Key Buddha (Yaoshi Gufo 鑰匙古佛). The Tang Monk, they explained, was an incarnation of the Ancient Sandalwood Buddha. In the past, he had descended to earth to transmit teachings with the power to release nine generations of ancestors from hell.[47] Now, he had returned. In the *Precious Scroll of the Tathāgata Pujing and the Key to Heaven,* Pujing revealed his own true identity: "Sentient beings do not know [that having] obtained the three flowers and returned the five breaths, I am the Tang Monk, transformed here in ordinary clothes dwelling in this city. With the three flowers gathered at the summit and the five breaths returned to the origin, the Tang Monk has manifested in the human realm to transmit the Great Way."[48] Like his near contemporary Patriarch Piaogao, Pujing claimed the Tang Monk as an illustrious patriarch of his tradition and insinuated that he was his most current incarnation.[49] For Pujing, however, the Tang Monk's pilgrimage was more than a periodically recurring historical event; it was an ongoing process taking place within his body.[50]

Pujing characterized his teachings as "Complete Perfection," associating his movement with the dominant form of monastic Daoism at that time. The imagery and terminology used throughout Yellow Heaven texts accordingly borrows heavily from the Complete Perfection tradition, specifically the theories and techniques of internal alchemy. Unlike conventional forms of alchemy in China, which seek to transmute physical substances into elixirs of immortality, internal alchemists attempt to revert disparate elements within the human body back to the singular, undifferentiated Dao from which they originally emerged. When Pujing claimed that he became the Tang Monk by obtaining the "three flowers" and returning the "five breaths," he was referring to this process. The three flowers are spirit (*shen* 神), breath (*qi* 氣), and essence (*jing* 精), which the practitioner attempts to channel and merge at the top of the head. The five breaths are the refined pneumas of the five viscera, which, in internal alchemical systems, need to be transmuted back into their state of primal unity.[51] In Pujing's rendering, then, the Tang Monk's pilgrimage is the process of channeling one's internal forces to return to their origins.

The path to Western Heaven, according the Pujing, is traversed within; the five pilgrims are, in fact, aspects of the practitioner's body. Sun Wukong is a person's activity (*xing* 行), Zhu Bajie is their essence (*jing* 精), Sha Monk is their life root (*ming gen* 命根), and the white horse is their will (*yi* 意).[52] The adept thus negotiates an inner landscape, manipulating and refining psychic and physical energies to transmute their ordinary mortal body into an immortal, perfected being. The various places the pilgrims pass through are identified as physical locations within the body, a premise that was elaborated on and illustrated in subsequent commentaries on the *Journey to the West* novel (see figure 5.2). The journey is thus personal transformation that culminates in the generation of a transcendent, divine body. One travels along the path to buddhahood and then, at the end of the journey, becomes a buddha. Pujing, having realized this transformation, might appear to the uninitiated as a common layperson "in ordinary clothes," but he is, in fact, the Tang Monk incarnate.

In subsequent precious scrolls from the Yellow Heaven and other sects, the relatively simple system of associations proposed by Pujing expands to embed the five pilgrims within the broader correlative cosmological system of the five phases (*wuxing* 五行). This ancient theory defines the relationships between phenomena, from numbers to colors, seasons, planets, musical notes, emotions, and bodily organs. All things, according to this system, are associated with one of five phases (or "agents"): wood, fire, metal, soil, or water. Elements belonging to the same phase relate to and resonate with each other. The wood phase, for example, includes the organ of the liver, the emotion of anger, and the planet Jupiter. The motions of Jupiter, therefore, affect the functioning of the liver, which, in turn, influences a person's mood. Each phase also interacts with other phases in predictable ways. Water gives birth to wood but conquers fire, for instance, while wood gives birth to fire

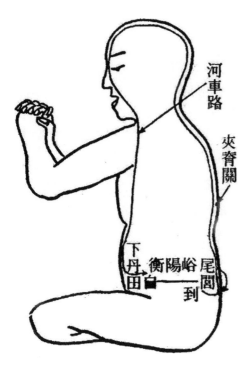

河車路

夾脊關

下丹田 衡陽峪 尾閭 到

Figure 5.2. Diagram of the Tang Monk's pilgrimage as it passes through Hengyang Ravine 衡陽峪, located here in the abdomen between the lower cinnabar field and the sacrum (corresponding to chapters 43–46 of the novel). Chen, *Xiyou ji shiyi* (*Longmen xinzhuan*), 549.

but prevails over soil. When this system is applied to the Obtaining the Scriptures narrative, each of the five pilgrims is correlated with one of the five phases and is thus enmeshed in wider webs of interrelations. According to the *Precious Scroll of the Buddha Preaching the True Meaning of Benefiting Beings*, for example,

> Refining in the east, *jia yi,* wood: Pilgrim [Sun] leads the way.
> Refining in the south, *bing ding,* fire: [Zhu] Bajie goes in front.
> Refining in the north, *ren gui,* water: Sha Monk is dark and mysterious.
> Refining in the west, *geng xin,* metal: White Horse carries the scriptures.
> Refining in the middle, *wu si,* soil: Tang Monk does not move.[53]

In this set of associations, Sun Wukong, characterized by the phase of wood, represents the direction east and the calendrical markers (stems) *jia* and *yi*. By implication, he also is aligned with the organ of the liver and the faculty of the eyes. He has power over fire elements (such as the pig Zhu Bajie) but is vulnerable to water elements. With such an expansive web of relations, the interpretive possibilities become virtually endless. The actions of the pilgrims within the narrative, as they move in different directions throughout various seasons and engage with each other as well as a broad array of gods and demons (each with their own correlations), point to processes playing out at both the macro- and microcosmic levels. Most significantly for members of salvational associations, since each pilgrim is tied to an aspect of the human body, their movements chart a course of interior cultivation. When, at the end of the narrative, all five pilgrims are apotheosized as buddhas and bodhisattvas, it symbolizes the culmination of an internal alchemical practice whereby the practitioner's body is finally transformed and attains immortality.

Not all precious scrolls maintained the same system of correlations. In some texts, Zhu Bajie is north, for example, in others he is south—but most assert the centrality of the Tang Monk. Among the directions, he occupies the unmovable middle. Of the five elements, he is soil (*tu* 土), which, in alchemical systems, is located at the center and is the origin of the four other elements. Among the calendrical markers (*tian gan* 天干), the Tang Monk is *wu* 戊 and *ji* 己. Together, these two stems, comprised of *yin* and *yang,* constitute the totality of all things. The Tang Monk is thus the One that gives rise to the many and the unity to which all things ultimately return. In terms of the physical body, the other pilgrims represent the sense faculties. Typically, Sun Wukong is the eyes or the mind, Zhu Bajie is the ears, Sha Monk is the nose, and the Dragon Horse is the mouth (see figure 5.3). The Tang Monk, by contrast, is the overarching, essential nature of the human being, sometimes called the original person (*benlai ren* 本來人) or the original face (*benlai mianmu* 本來面目).[54] For those who understood the pilgrimage as a psychosomatic process, the Tang Monk was their fundamental identity.

In this way, followers of the Teaching of Yellow Heaven and other sectarian groups read Obtaining the Scriptures narratives not only as descriptions of the Tang Monk's past triumphs but also as methods for realizing human potential. The pilgrim's progress traced the path of practice as the individual inched ever closer to a divine state. During the late Ming and Qing dynasties, such allegorical interpretations of the story resonated with Neo-Confucian scholar-officials engaged in disciplines of mental rectification and bodily control.[55] For the members of the governing class, the premise that the Tang Monk and his companions might be metaphorically present within the body was not necessarily problematic. It sounded alarms, however, when the manifestation of the pilgrims was taken literally rather than symbolically. As some scholars and practitioners sought to decode the esoteric elements of the story, others were attempting to embody the narrative in more concrete ways. Rather than manipulating the Tang Monk and his companions internally to transform the self, these men and women were deploying the pilgrims on the field of battle in an attempt to overthrow the state.

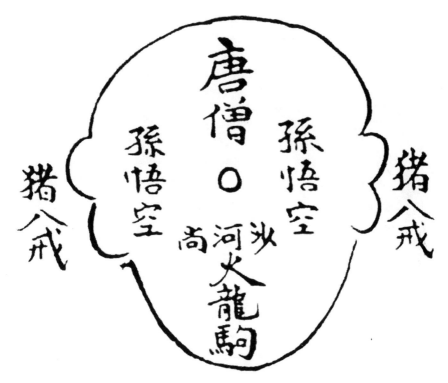

Figure 5.3. Sketch of a human face with Sun Wukong as the eyes, Zhu Bajie as the ears, Sha Monk as the nose, Dragon Horse as the mouth, and the Tang Monk as the mind. *Fozu miaoyi zhizhi xunyuan jiapu*, 300.

Insurgents

In 1622, two men, Xu Hongru 徐鴻儒 (d. 1622) and Wang Haoxian 王好賢 (d.u.), launched a rebellion in southwestern Shandong. Both men were devotees of a teacher named Wang Sen 王森 (d. 1619), the founding patriarch of the sect known as the Incense Smelling Teachings (Wenxiang jiao 聞香教).[56] (Xu Hongru was Wang Sen's disciple, Wang Haoxian was Wang Sen's son.) The aim of their uprising was to overthrow the Ming dynasty and install Xu Hongru as rightful ruler, thereby inaugurating an era of "Great Completion and Renewed Victory" (*dacheng xingsheng* 大成興勝).[57] The men claimed the support of two million followers and a force of fifty thousand troops. According to a government official tasked with defeating the rebels, they precipitated the "most serious crisis in the dynasty's two-hundred and sixty-year history."[58]

The teachings of the Incense Smelling sect derived from earlier salvational associations. Like their predecessors, they recognized a primordial deity—the Unborn Mother—who periodically dispatches emissaries from her heavenly realm in the West to offer guidance to her children in the East. These intermediaries, according to the sect's influential *Precious Scripture of the Dragon Flower, as Verified by the Old Buddha of Heavenly Purity* (*Gufo tianzhen kaozheng Longhua baojing* 古佛天真考證龍華寶經), included Śākyamuni, Nāgārjuna, the Tang Monk, and, of course, the association's founder Wang Sen.[59] Assertions of ancient origins for newly authored precious scrolls were common enough; what set the Incense Smelling sect apart was how these teachings were interpreted and acted upon. Members of the association were instructed that the moral decay of humans was inciting the wrath of gods, who would soon rain down conflagrations, floods, war, famine, and disease. Whereas earlier groups responded to similar warnings by examining and rectifying their own behavior, some of Wang Sen's followers located the source of the corruption within the imperial court. For these people, the teachings conveyed by Śākyamuni, transmitted by Xuanzang, and championed by men like Wang Sen and Xu Hongru, called for nothing short of revolution.

It took three months for the Ming military to put down the Incense Smelling rebellion. The incident was one of the starkest indications that the apocalyptic ideologies of sectarian organizations could pose a serious threat to the state. Membership in some salvational associations was, consequently, criminalized. In an official proclamation issued in 1660, several groups were singled out for censure: "There are heretical doctrines that delude the masses such as the Non-Action [Wuwei], White Lotus [Bailian] or Incense Smelling Teachings [Wenxiang jiao]. They assemble in groups, gathering at night and dispersing at dawn. Minor figures seek wealth and profit and indulge in illicit sex. Major figures recruit desperate men and conspire to commit crimes. Ignorant, common people are fooled by their deceptions. They lose their bearings and grow wild, remaining confused for the rest of their lives."[60] The edict declared these teachings heterodox (*xie* 邪) and called for the arrest of those who joined forbidden sects or failed to report their activities.

Enforcement of this and subsequent proscriptions was lax, however, and salvational associations continued to operate and expand during early Qing dynasty (1644–1912). The precious scrolls central to major groups remained widely available. When Huang Yupian 黃育楩 (fl. 1838), a magistrate serving in the region of Zhili (modern Hebei province), collected precious scrolls in order to repudiate them in his *Detailed Refutation to Destroy Heresies* (*Poxie yang bian* 破邪詳辯), the works of patriarchs Luo, Piaogao, and Puming featured prominently.[61] The problem with these and other sect leaders, according the Qing officials, was not just their unorthodox teachings—which Huang Yupian denounced as "completely unreasonable" and "extremely debased"—but also the growing economic power and social influence of their organizations.[62] Some salvational associations commanded tens of thousands of followers and accumulated significant assets through membership fees and donations. In underdeveloped, economically marginalized areas, they provided aid, assistance, and protection to members, functioning essentially as shadow governments. Of particular concern was the sworn allegiance of sect members, who put loyalty to their congregations before family and empire. According to Huang Yupian, members of these groups believed the directives of their leaders superseded the laws of the court. The followers of Piaogao's Vast Yang teachings, for example, "falsely claim that all men who become believers are incarnated buddhas and that all women who become believers are incarnated buddha mothers . . . Ignorant men and women, after swallowing talismanic water, become convinced that they are buddha incarnates and they fervently desire to ascend to heaven. They therefore sincerely practice their teachings. Even after they have been apprehended by the authorities and sentenced to decapitation and slow slicing, they show no regret."[63] In their devotion to unorthodox gods, members of Vast Yang and other sects proved insufficiently beholden to the authority of the court.

Large-scale persecutions of salvational associations began in earnest during the reign of Emperor Qianlong (r. 1735–1796). In response to concerted efforts to repress and eradicate sectarian networks, some groups disbanded. Others aligned themselves more conspicuously with politically sanctioned "orthodox" traditions. Still others went underground, changing their names and meeting in secret. Among these latter groups, most remained peaceful and apolitical, but some actively sought the overthrow of the Qing dynasty. The armed uprisings of these groups were, in part, a reaction to government harassment and suppression, but they also were an extension of millenarian teachings that prophesized the imminent ascent of a messiah and the beginning of a new world order.

The evolution of Piaogao's Vast Yang sect exemplifies some of the shifting ideologies and tactics of salvational associations during this period. Branches of the Vast Yang sect, which had always maintained a millenarian outlook but never had openly advocated violence, appear to have been radicalized in response to government repression. In the late seventeenth and early eighteenth centuries, the teachings of Piaogao and his successors still were tolerated if not actively supported by government officials. Vast Yang groups established temples throughout northeastern China, with dozens of sites serving the rural areas around the capital at Beijing. The very success of this movement seems to have singled it out for suppression. During a major crackdown in 1746, Vast Yang leaders were arrested and sentenced to death by strangulation. Active members were exiled or enslaved, and even casual affiliates were beaten with one hundred strokes of a heavy stick. The sect's temples, texts, and icons were destroyed.[64] Members who remained loyal to the group were driven underground. By the early nineteenth century, clandestine meetings, anti-Qing sentiments, recruiting, and mobilizing for rebellion—the very activities that compelled the court to preemptively persecute the movement—had become the norm for some branches of the broader association.

When popular discontent with the Qing court, exacerbated by economic disparities and a succession of natural disasters in northern China, culminated in the Eight Trigrams (*bagua* 八卦) rebellion, members of Vast Yang associations assumed leading roles. The Eight Trigrams association was composed of several independent sectarian groups, each with its own hierarchical structure, loosely organized under the leadership of a self-proclaimed incarnation of Maitreya Buddha named Li Wencheng 李文成 (d. 1813). Participants shared an antipathy toward Manchu rule and a conviction that a great war necessarily preceded a great peace.[65] Driven by desperation and buoyed by the promise of a utopian future, over a hundred thousand people attacked the Imperial Palace in Beijing in the autumn of 1813. The siege on the capital held for three months before the Qing military finally reasserted control.

Ensuing efforts to eradicate the affiliates, organizational structure, and ideology of the Eight Trigrams were only partially successful. Those who survived the purge and stayed committed to the cause went into hiding, surfacing later to launch new attacks.[66] One such splinter group was led by Cao Shun 曹順 (d. 1835), a peasant from Shandong province. In 1822, nineteen-year-old Cao joined an association based in northern Shanxi province called the Teachings of Former Heaven (*Xian tian jiao* 先天教), an offshoot of the militant Li Trigram (離卦) branch of the Eight Trigrams. Cao took control of the community in 1834, revealing that he was the reincarnation of Śākyamuni Buddha. Endowed with the power to perceive past lives, he identified core members of his inner circle as the reincarnations of Sun Wukong and other figures from the popular pantheon.[67] In the spring of 1835, the group executed their local county magistrate, set fire to government offices, and opened the prisons. As they moved north and captured a series of towns, Shanxi's provincial governor called in the army. Cao's two thousand troops were vastly outnumbered and outgunned, but he assured his men that their gods would protect them from bullets and cannons. The group was quickly captured and executed, but they left a trail of death and destruction that once again had reached perilously close to the imperial palace. They also established a model the Boxers would later adopt.[68]

Sun Wukong was only one of many deities enlisted in this and other insurgencies. His presence among Cao Shun's troops, however, is indicative of the role Obtaining the Scriptures narratives played in the mythologies of some militant groups. Like the people who identified with them, all five pilgrims were admired as a righteous band of hardscrabble heroes, persevering in the face of seemingly insurmountable obstacles to outwit and overpower formidable enemies. The demons they faced were not psychological constructs but real people—officials, soldiers, foreigners—bent on detaining or murdering the pilgrims and thwarting their divine mission. The survival and ultimate success of the Tang Monk and his companions thus served as a blueprint for salvational associations and secret societies to follow.

In the late nineteenth century, as the Qing dynasty grew increasingly imperiled, Obtaining the Scriptures narratives inspired a host of anti-government movements. Even groups with no direct connection to the Unborn Mother theology of salvational associations cast themselves in the roles of the Tang Monk and his entourage. Heaven and Earth Societies (Tiandi hui 天地會), otherwise known as Triads, looked to the Tang Monk as both illustrious ancestor and aspirational ideal. Originating in Fujian during the mid-eighteenth century as secret mutual-aid brotherhoods of Ming loyalists, the Triads lacked the apocalyptic prophecies typical of sectarian groups, but they venerated many of the same deities and relied on similar ritual traditions to foster group solidarity, convey divine protection, and empower their members.[69] Various Triad groups were implicated in a spate of anti-Qing uprisings in Taiwan and southern China over the course of the nineteenth century, and subsequent raids on Triad strongholds revealed altars centered on Lord Guan and initiation manuals depicting the process of becoming a member as, in part, a ritual reenactment of the Tang Monk's journey to Western Heaven.

During the initiation ritual, which took much the same form throughout China and in diaspora communities as far away as Sumatra and British Columbia, the pledge moved west, entering through an eastern gate and exiting through a western gate. He was then confronted by a symbolic mountain of fire guarded by the Hong Child—one of the better-known demons from the Obtaining the Scriptures narratives. In written versions of the story, the character "hong" 紅 (red) in the demon's name indicates the color of his skin, but in Triad manuals the name is usually written with the homophonous character "hong" 洪, the surname adopted by all members of the brotherhood. When the initiate encounters the Hong Child, he is asked to prove his knowledge of Triad tradition and must respond in verse: "Heaven sent down the Hong Child who devoured men; but, thanks to the Tang Monk, we were saved. When faithful and loyal men pass this place, they shall accompany, in later days, the prince of the Ming."[70] The Hong Child reportedly slays any traitors who attempt to pass the mountain of fire, consigning their spirits to the flames. The pure-hearted, however, can pass, and they emerge as new members of the Hong family.[71] Following the path forged by the Tang Monk and his band of pilgrims, Triad initiates undertook their own metaphorical journey, surmounting obstacles and subjugating enemies in their effort to reestablish the "pure land" of the Ming dynasty.

Despite their righteous rhetoric, the Triads are best known for their criminal activities, which ranged from prostitution to drug trafficking and extortion. By what strange logic could they claim common cause with the Tang Monk, a Buddhist cleric who stringently followed the precepts and was staunchly opposed to violence? In

Triad lore, the Tang Monk is admired as a Han Chinese man who fully committed himself to a noble cause and was willing to sacrifice himself for the greater good. For other groups engaged in violent struggles, however, the Tang Monk made an unlikely hero. Whereas some ritual traditions and precious scrolls valorized Xuanzang either as a deity or the culmination of human potential, in the novel and its many adaptations, he is depicted, instead, as a feeble, skittish, helpless monk. Devout yet credulous, principled yet cripplingly timid, Xuanzang is unable to protect himself against the many threats he encounters and constantly requires rescue. Rather than a fully realized person, he is more akin to an aspirant whose capacities remain latent. Sun Wukong, on the other hand, is cast as an accomplished, prototypical warrior. Fearless and defiant, he does not hesitate to use his formidable powers to vanquish any demons that stand in his or his master's way. Sun Wukong's violent methods were justified by the nobility of his cause: guiding and protecting Xuanzang so the true teachings could be transmitted to China. The *Precious Raft That Returns to the Origin,* a precious scroll written between 1843 and 1846, accordingly exhorted readers to look to Sun Wukong as an exemplar: "I urge you westward travelers grasping the Chan staff, do not study Tang Xuanzang's all-encompassing compassion and humanity. Whenever destructive demons confront you, lock and bind them. You should study the transformative supranatural powers of Sun Wukong."[72] *Journey to the West,* according to the *Precious Raft,* was a guide for cultivating the way and becoming a saint, but it also was a potent talisman for protection against demonic assault. "This work returns to the original sutras. All its words discuss the substance. However, you should know that when spirits come to make mischief, this sutra can subdue them. Rely on this method to reach Western Heaven without suffering demonic attacks. When your efforts are complete and the fruit is cultivated, you will ascend the heights of the nine lotuses [of the Pure Land]."[73] In this reading, a story of demonic subjugation is itself a powerful prophylactic. As for *Journey to the West,* Sun Wukong is the principal demon destroyer. He, rather than the Tang Monk, is the hero worthy of emulation.

The marginal status and martial qualities of Sun Wukong made him a natural ally for insurgents. When the German missionary Georg Maria Stenz (1869–1928) was living in southern Shandong province, he observed rituals of possession involving Sun Wukong that were meant to empower young men to engage in battle. These rites took place during the first lunar month, at which time money was collected from the villagers and four boys were chosen as potential spirit mediums. They were brought to a temple or graveyard and instructed to recite the following verse:

One horse, two horses.
We invite Master Sun to come and perform.

One dragon, two dragons.
We invite Master Sun to descend from Heaven and fight.[74]

Following this invocation, the boys fell face down and lay on the ground until Sun Wukong suddenly possessed one of them. The medium was then carried to a nearby home and roused with incense. Wielding a sword, he proceeded to engage in battle, presumably ridding the house of malevolent forces. Once the incense burned out, the deity left the boy's body and returned to heaven.

In this simple ritual, Sun Wukong descends, performs, and vanishes, but the Tang Monk never appears. This is part of a broader pattern among militant groups in the modern period; Sun Wukong's martial prowess seems to overshadow his master's pilgrimage. It is as though the Tang Monk has been eclipsed by his more charismatic disciple. When the Red Spears (Hongqiang hui 紅槍會) attempted to establish an independent state in western Shandong province in the 1920s, for example, they channeled the spirit of Sun Wukong, not Xuanzang.[75] And when, during the Cultural Revolution, the Red Guards rallied to "sweep away the monsters and demons" that stood in the way of their socialist utopia, they envisioned themselves not as the pious Tang Monk but as an army of Sun Wukongs carrying out the orders of Great Sage Mao. "Revolutionaries are Monkey Kings," they proclaimed. "Their golden rods are powerful, their supernatural powers far-reaching and their magic omnipotent, for they possess Mao Tse-tung's great invincible thought. We wield our golden rods, display our supernatural powers and use our magic to turn the old world upside down, smash it to pieces, pulverize it, create chaos and make a tremendous mess, the bigger the better!"[76]

Does the ascendance of Sun Wukong signal the fading away of the Tang Monk? In some contexts, this does seem to be the case. In others, however, the appearance of the Monkey King implies the presence of his master. The Tang Monk has not become irrelevant; he has become, instead, ubiquitous. When spirit mediums channel Sun Wukong, for example, the devotees who enlist his services as an omnipotent guardian and an infallible guide are assuming the role of the Tang Monk, seeking divine assistance as they navigate challenging passages in their lives. Similarly, if Mao Zedong is the Monkey King and the Red Guards are his body multiplied, the Tang Monk is the Communist Party that they have vowed to safeguard along the perilous passage from revolution to socialist state.[77] Sun Wukong always serves a master. It may be, as Patriarch Pujing and other sectarian teachers were at pains to point out, that we are all the Tang Monk.

Xuanzang's mythic pilgrimage served as a script for real-life dramas that were constantly enacted in the world. People cast themselves in preordained roles and longed for predetermined resolutions. Some sought protection from danger or safe passage to a place of peace and stability. Others hoped for the transmission of more effective teachings or the advent of a heavenly utopia. It was when personal aspiration crossed over into the realm of political action that members of the ruling class took notice. Government officials could appreciate accounts of the Tang Monk's pilgrimage to Western Heaven as imaginative allegories or dismiss them as crude fictions, but they could not accept them as divine revelations or calls for revolution. The prospect of peasants invoking and embodying the Tang Monk, Sun Wukong, and other "fictional" characters in the context of unsanctioned and potentially subversive rituals would not be tolerated. With the Qing court already strained to the breaking point both economically and militarily, if something was not done to quell internal unrest, the survival of the dynasty itself was at risk. For some in positions of power, doing something about these uprisings meant doing something about *Journey to the West.*

Calls to "make a clean sweep" of all religious interpretations of the Tang Monk's pilgrimage (surveyed in chapter 1) belonged to a broader effort to deprive popular ritual traditions of their narrative foundations. For a young nation eager to embrace the promises of science, secularism, and constitutional government, the hide-bound traditions, undereducated citizenry, and superstitious practices of the imperial period were burdens better left behind. The conviction that society was inevitably evolving toward a more perfect state advanced a particular kind of narrative. In the new myths celebrating heroic forces of industry, capital, and globalization, there was little space for heavenly saviors, sacred transmissions, or divine prophesies. For those who survived the many trials of the late nineteenth and early twentieth centuries—wars, natural disasters, persecutions, poverty—tales of inevitable progress might have seemed a hollow sort of story. It is, perhaps, for that reason that, despite efforts to discredit or bowdlerize traditional narratives, they never lost their appeal. On the contrary, accounts of the Tang Monk's triumphs and Sun Wukong's victories only multiplied, telling how marginalized people—those who saw themselves reflected in a courageous cleric or a mischievous monkey—might overcome impossible odds. Obtaining the Scriptures narratives demonstrated that those who appeared most vulnerable were, in fact, invincible. Men and women who were dismissed as inconsequential and derided as ignorant actually were entrusted with a divine mission of paramount importance. Though they may have come from unremarkable beginnings, they were destined to inaugurate a new era of peace and prosperity. The uninitiated were able to see only common people wearing simple clothes and living in humble villages. But others could recognize that the Tang Monk and his companions were manifesting "in the human realm to transmit the Great Way." That was a story to believe in.

Epilogue

Perpetual Pilgrimage

> Without fiction . . . there would be no true faith.
>
> —Joshua Landy, *How to Do Things with Fictions*

There is an extraordinary moment toward the end of the *Journey to the West* novel when Xuanzang at last transcends his mortal body. He, Sun Wukong, Zhu Bajie, Sha Monk, and the Dragon Horse are trying to reach Spirit Mountain, the residence of the Buddha, when a raging river blocks their path. Too frightened to cross a narrow, slippery log bridge, Xuanzang is on the verge of abandoning his quest when he notices a mysterious ferryman approaching in a bottomless boat. Everyone climbs aboard, and the ferryman, who actually is a buddha in disguise, shoves off into the current. In midstream, Xuanzang sees a human corpse floating in the water toward the boat and is frozen with fear. Monkey just laughs at him. "Don't be afraid," he says. "It's actually you." "It's you! It's you!" the rest of the party chime in as they cross the torrent to arrive safely at the other shore.[1] Without realizing it, Xuanzang had shed his body of flesh and bone, the body subject to birth and death. Watching his own corpse drift downstream, he passed from *saṃsāra* to nirvāṇa and became a buddha. Immediately thereafter, he ascends Spirit Mountain, enters Thunderclap Monastery, and receives the scriptures from Śākyamuni.

Crossing the River

During his pilgrimage through Central Asia and India, the historical Xuanzang never did slough off his human shell, but he did acquire a superhuman stature that set him apart from ordinary monks. Having traveled through exotic and unfamiliar lands, braved all manner of discomfort and danger, encountered the traces of buddhas and bodhisattvas, studied with learned South Asian monks and laymen, and gathered a treasure trove of texts, images, and relics, Xuanzang became a living legend in China. That legend, rooted in his reputation, documented in his *Record of the Western Regions,* elaborated in his lengthy biography, and endlessly embellished in the stories people told, took on a life of its own after Xuanzang's death. He may not have forded the river of birth and death in a bottomless boat, but he did cross from history into myth.

The elaboration and expansion of Xuanzang's story necessarily entailed a certain eroding of his personal identity. Later legends elided many of his defining accomplishments, reducing Xuanzang's triumphs to pilgrimage alone. Obtaining the Scriptures narratives say nothing of what he and his disciples surely saw as his most consequential achievements: his mastery of Yogācāra doctrine, his fluent Sanskrit, his voluminous and faithful translations, his service to the Tang court, and his training of a generation of Buddhist clerics in China. Mythical accounts focus, instead, on the dangers he faced on his westward journey and the talismanic qualities of the texts he brought back from India. As a paradigmatic pilgrim, Xuanzang traded the specifics of his biography for the generalities of hagiography. No longer a Yogācāra master, hardly even a Buddhist monk, and, in some of the more recent examples, not necessarily Chinese, Xuanzang is simply the conveyor of truth and wisdom. He is the intrepid hero who ventures into the unknown, surmounts obstacles, obtains treasure, and returns home to enrich his community. The details of the plot are vague—where exactly does he go? Why? What truth does he realize? What does it all mean? Such questions leave spaces for storytellers and their audiences to inhabit.

The story I have told here has neither a neat plot nor a tidy resolution. The chapters have centered on themes rather than strict chronologies. Despite the fragmented nature of the historical record, it is possible to track the progress of Xuanzang's deification and the ritualization of his pilgrimage though a series of loosely defined phases. The first phase, the formative period, lasted from Xuanzang's return to China in the mid-seventh century until the first known depictions of nascent Obtaining the Scriptures narratives around the beginning of the twelfth century. During this time, stories of Xuanzang's life and work circulated widely in predictable ways. Textual accounts and images portray him primarily as an eminent pilgrim, translator, and patriarch. Celebrated for his extraordinary contributions to transmitting and translating Indian Buddhist texts and teachings, Xuanzang was duly revered as a venerable ancestor of the Mahāyāna tradition.

It is during the second, developmental, phase that Xuanzang begins to assume the exalted aura of sainthood. Starting in the early twelfth century and lasting until sometime around the end of the fifteenth century, Xuanzang appears as part of a divine retinue. Most of the earliest images, preserved in paintings and sculptures in over a dozen cave temples, show him together with a monkey-like attendant and a horse in the act of venerating the bodhisattva Avalokiteśvara. By the thirteenth century, the first extended textual accounts of Xuanzang's mythic pilgrimage appear, and these describe a journey with a monkey attendant and a small group of clerics through a dangerous purgatory to a pure land. The goal of their mission is to acquire the entire Buddhist canon from Śākyamuni Buddha. Once secured, these sacred scriptures are delivered to the Chinese emperor on the day of the annual Ghost Festival, a transmission that links Xuanzang's pilgrimage with a major ritual for liberating the spirits of the dead. Sometime in the first half of the fourteenth century, the pig Zhu Bajie and the demon monk Sha join Xuanzang's party, rounding out the group to the five members that have remained standard ever since. Tales of these pilgrims' adventures eventually traveled beyond the confines of the Buddhist temples where they first emerged. Scenes from their pilgrimage soon adorned everyday household items, animated stage performances, and enlivened oral and written stories. While there are hints that Xuanzang and his companions featured in apotropaic and mortuary rites during this period, the first unambiguous evidence for the ritualization of their pilgrimage emerges only in the sixteenth century.

This marks the beginning of what might be called the mature phase of the Tang Monk's cult. From the sixteenth through the twentieth century, ritual reenactments of the pilgrimage proliferate. In precious scrolls, Xuanzang is identified alternately as an emissary for primordial buddhas dwelling in the West, a reincarnated prophet, and an allegory for self-perfection. Ritual dramas recreate the pilgrims' subjugation of demons to purify villages and homes, and mortuary rites summon Xuanzang to guide the spirits of the dead and convey salvific sutras to the land of the living. By the time the hundred-chapter *Journey to the West* was published in 1596, Xuanzang's otherworldly travels were already integrated into a range of regional ritual traditions. With the publication of the novel, a fluid complex of stories became frozen in one form. It was an ingenious account full of poetic allusions, playful innuendo, and open-ended allegories ripe for interpretation and adaptation, but it was only one of many expressions of the narrative. The ensuing popularity of *Journey to the West* inevitably influenced ritual cultures, just as local traditions had informed the content and structure of the novel. In a never ending, always shifting cycle, history inspires narrative and narrative influences history.

The fourth and most recent phase of Xuanzang's postmortem career began in the early decades of the twentieth century. Prompted by concerns over the narrative's potentially subversive influence on the beliefs and behavior of the common people, scholars and officials in China sought to reinterpret and reform the story. Rejecting attempts to identify any "philosophical thesis" or calls for "social reform" in the text, they highlighted, instead, the work's literary qualities and artistic sensibilities. *Journey to the West* thus became an imaginative fantasy fit for entertainment and amusement alone.

At the same time that new versions of the Tang Monk's story saturated Chinese society, *Journey to the West* was translated into European languages and integrated into entirely new cultural contexts. Globalization required radical shifts in meaning as European and American audiences lacked frames of reference for the ritual and cosmological allusions that were so central to the narrative. Western audiences, instead, tended to read the story as an example of "world literature," a window onto exotic cultures and, perhaps, evidence of universal human values. By bringing their own experiences and expectations to bear on the story, they naturally transformed it into a more recognizable and relatable narrative. It may be, as David Damrosch has suggested, that "*All* works cease to be the exclusive products of their original cultures once they are translated."[2] The epic adventures of the Tang Monk, Sun Wukong, Zhu Bajie, Sha Monk, and the white horse have always mirrored the self-conceptions of their authors and audiences. What began as a Buddhist story was later adopted by Daoists, Confucians, Christians, and Communists. It now seems to have entered the hallowed canon of secular humanism.

Receiving the Scriptures

In most modern versions of the Obtaining the Scriptures narratives, Xuanzang is a hapless monk who, protected by an irreverent monkey and a clownish pig, embarks on a journey of self-discovery. As an encapsulation of Xuanzang's life, it is almost the antithesis of hagiography. Rather than elevating an eminent monk to the status of sainthood, recent adaptations of *Journey to the West*, instead, transform an extraordinary cleric into an ineffectual, timid fool. The historical Xuanzang, of course, was anything but incompetent. He left the comfort and familiarity of home to travel vast distances under exceptionally challenging conditions. He studied under demanding teachers and mastered difficult doctrines in newly acquired languages. Back in China, he navigated the responsibilities and risks of life as an elite court cleric. Of the 657 texts he collected in India and carried to China, he labored for nineteen years to translate seventy-four into classical Chinese, a feat that has never been equaled.

Many of the texts Xuanzang translated were Yogācāra treatises, which he held to be the most complete and perfect expressions of the Buddha's teachings. According to these works, the world that appears to ordinary, unawakened people is an illusion generated by the mind. Conventional understandings of individual identity are mere projections of a deluded consciousness. Yogācāra masters like Xuanzang strove to see through those illusions, to purify the mind so the world could be perceived as it truly is: empty, devoid of self, and dependently arisen. Such convictions motivated Xuanzang's work and surely informed his own self-understanding. For him, there could be no "real" person who existed apart from peoples' imaginations. Xuanzang might be surprised to learn how later generations conceived of him, but he, of all people, would appreciate that what a person perceives is entirely dependent on the content of his or her consciousness. In this curious way, the evolution of Xuanzang's identity from conservative cleric to magical monk is a fitting illustration of the very Yogācāra teachings he spent his life championing. Everybody sees the Xuanzang they are conditioned to see.

In the centuries after Xuanzang's death, what many people saw was not an erudite Yogācāra master but a guardian, a guide, or a divine emissary. They imagined a monk who traveled to Western Heaven not to study the *Discourse on the Stages of Yogic Practice* and other sutras and śastras but to receive the "wordless scriptures" from Śākyamuni Buddha. According to later legends, including *Journey to the West*, the texts Xuanzang initially obtains at the culmination of his pilgrimage are literally blank.[3] Their unmarked pages would seem to symbolize the Mahāyāna doctrine of emptiness, the teaching famously expounded in the *Heart Sūtra*, Xuanzang's most influential translation. On his deathbed, Xuanzang reportedly invoked this teaching, reminding his disciples that "Ignorance does not exist [and so on up to] old age and death, which also does not exist. Awakening does not exist. Nonexistence also does not exist."[4] There was no need to grieve, he seemed to be saying. What does not exist can never truly die.

The wordless scriptures Xuanzang receives in later narratives may be an evocative illustration of this principle, but blank pages are also screens onto which anything might be projected. The teachings that Xuanzang transmits have accordingly been associated with everything from the techniques of Daoist internal alchemy to the methods of Confucian mental cultivation, the prophecies of primordial deities, and even the gospel of Jesus Christ. More recently, they have been adapted to the rhythms of American jazz, Japanese gender politics, and South Korean comedy. An empty page is full of potential.

New interpretations and novel associations are forged in the encounter between story and audience. Early accounts of Xuanzang's otherworldly pilgrimage emerged from the fusion of biography, rituals, and narratives from Mahāyāna sutras, Chinese mythology, Daoist scriptures, ghost stories, and local lore. Contemporary retellings of the pilgrimage now betray a bewildering array of new, global influences, from Marxist political theory to the Wizard of Oz. Like Xuanzang himself, stories about his life seem forever drawn across borders and into new territories. These accounts remain relevant by remaining pliable. They reshape readers' sense of the world, just as the stories themselves are constructed and reinvented out of the raw materials of lived experience. Each version of the story reflects the historical contexts of its creation.

Compelling narratives—whether framed as history or fiction—leave impressions that run deeper than distant, disinterested presentations of facts. While we may like to think we use our powers of deduction to dispassionately weigh available evidence and arrive at logical conclusions, the truth is that rationalization often prevails over rationality. As the recent proliferation of conspiracy theories makes plain, people remain irresistibly attracted to stories that confirm their preconceived ideas about the way things are or ought to be. The financial theorist and neurologist William Bernstein, commenting on the erratic behavior of investors, observed that, "however much we flatter ourselves about our individual rationality, a good story, no matter how analytically deficient, lingers in the mind, resonates emotionally, and persuades more than the most dispositive facts or data."[5] Tales of the Tang Monk's travels through demonic lands to a heavenly paradise are good stories. The historical Xuanzang's accounting of the types of crops grown in Samarkand and the number of Mahāyāna temples in Khotan collected dust in monastic libraries, but generations of people eagerly gathered in rural courtyards and urban theaters to hear about how the Monkey King saved the Tang Monk from the clutches of Princess Iron Fan.

Some of those who saw these and other scenes performed on stage or read about them in books appreciated Xuanzang's mythic pilgrimage as metaphor. For them, his journey symbolized the process of self-realization; his companions represented elements of the mind and body; and the demons he encountered were the internal and external obstacles that impede a person's progress. For others, however, the pilgrimage was an event that occurred in the past and continues to reverberate in the present. The Tang Monk was responsible for transmitting divine texts and ritual techniques from the pure land of the Buddha to the human realm. He and his companions were subsequently sanctified, and they continue to incarnate and intervene in the affairs of the world, protecting devotees against demons, guiding the dead through purgatory, and delivering new dispensations of divine teachings. In these and other ways, the Tang Monk is just as "real" as the historical Xuanzang. If anything, he is even more tangible and accessible than his distant forebear.

The same goes for the Tang Monk's closest companions. The pig Zhu Bajie and the monkey Sun Wukong have their own ritual traditions, shrines, and spirit mediums. When asked recently if *Journey to the West* was a faithful account of his past, a medium in Singapore who channels Sun Wukong replied that the novel was about 70 percent accurate.[6] For those who perceive the presence of the Tang Monk, Sun Wukong, and other figures from the narrative, *Journey to the West* is an important but imperfect and incomplete account of the spirit world they inhabit. Unlike characters in a novel, these gods can be approached, questioned, and compelled to act. Their stories are still unfolding.

Blazing the Path

When Xuanzang was returning to China in 644, he had to cross the broad and swift Indus River in what is now northern Pakistan. He waded into the current on the back of his elephant and made it safely to the other shore, but a strong wind upset the boats that were carrying his luggage. Fifty bundles of texts and several packets of seeds fell into the river and were washed away. It was a devastating loss and Xuanzang would spend years trying to replace the lost items.

Xuanzang does not recount the accident in his *Record;* he mentions it only briefly in the letters he later wrote to monks in India requesting copies of the lost texts.[7] The details of the event are provided only in the biography composed by Xuanzang's disciples, who explain that venomous dragons and malicious animals reside in the Indus and often overturn the boats of travelers attempting to carry the seeds of rare flowers and fruits across.[8] In *Journey to the West,* the disastrous crossing is given an even more dramatic treatment. When Xuanzang and his fellow pilgrims were traveling from China to India, the story goes, they crossed the Indus on the back of a giant turtle. In return for this favor, the turtle requested that Xuanzang ask the Buddha when he can finally be reborn as a human. Many years later, as the pilgrims climb aboard the same turtle to recross the Indus on their return trip home, the turtle asks Xuanzang about the Buddha's response to his question. Xuanzang, who forgot to inquire about the turtle's future incarnation, remains silent. The angry turtle then dives under the water, submerging the pilgrims and all their precious cargo. The sodden scriptures are eventually lugged ashore and draped over boulders on the riverbank to dry in the sun. Most of the works survive this laundering, but one text, Aśvaghoṣa's *Life of the Buddha,* sticks to the rock so that only a portion of it can be recovered.[9]

The episode in the novel is a clever blend of historical fact and creative fiction. Xuanzang did, in fact, lose some texts while crossing the Indus River, and his disciples believed strange and spiteful river creatures were likely responsible. The giant, talking turtle of the novel, however, is obviously fictional. As for the *Life of the Buddha,* the received Sanskrit text is, indeed, missing its latter portions, though presumably not because they remain pasted to a rock on the banks of the Indus. In other words, the scene described in the novel is based on a historical event, but it has been transformed into a creative work of fantasy. But as so often happens with sacred narratives, even apparently fictional stories have the power to generate their own realities.

The place where the Tang Monk, Sun Wukong, Zhu Bajie, Sha Monk, and the Dragon Horse emerged from the river and dried the sodden scriptures on the rocks is now located in southern Qinghai province, beside the Batang River. The pavilion that commemorates the spot is festooned with Tibetan prayer flags and white silk scarfs, offerings left by the many Han and Tibetan pilgrims who come to venerate the traces of the great pilgrims. As far as we know, the historical Xuanzang never passed this way. Nor did he stop at any of the other "Scripture Drying Terraces" (*shai jing tai* 曬經台) that can be found throughout Qinghai, Xinjiang, and

Gansu provinces.[10] The landscape of northwestern China turns out to be saturated with sites associated with Obtaining the Scriptures narratives. In addition to multiple Scripture Drying Terraces, the locations of Zhu Bajie's native village, the site of Sha Monk's conversion, and the lairs of the Bull and Black Wind demons all have been located and memorialized.

Nine hundred years ago, in the desert valleys of northwestern China, artists painted images of Xuanzang, a monkey attendant, and a horse bearing a radiant bundle of texts inside caves carved into the cliffsides. Today, freshly painted murals featuring these same figures still adorn the walls of temples in the region. In local villages, stories about the Tang Monk and his companions are recounted through songs, traditional dances, rituals, dramatic performances, puppet shows, and precious scrolls.[11] The memory of the pilgrims' exploits is literally embedded in the landscape and ingrained in the local culture. Xuanzang may have never visited these places, but memories of the Tang Monk remain as strong as ever.

Entering the Temple

According to the author of *Journey to the West,* Xuanzang understood that he had become a god even before he returned to China, delivered the scriptures, and rose up to heaven. After the pilgrims crossed the roiling river in the bottomless boat, encountered the Buddha, and received the scriptures, they started heading for home. At one point, they passed through one of the villages they had visited years earlier on their way to India. Back then, they had saved the lives of two village children who were slated to be sacrificed to a demon who fed on the flesh of young virgins. The villagers, wanting to repay the returning pilgrims for their help in the past, treat them to an elaborate feast. Xuanzang and his companions are then taken to see the temple the villagers built in their honor. Named the "Temple of Saving Life," it was funded by contributions from all the local residents. Inside, Xuanzang, Sun Wukong, Zhu Bajie, and Sha Monk find an altar adorned with four statues carved in their likeness. Sha Monk remarks that they all looked pretty good, but the icon of Xuanzang was especially handsome.[12] "It's just right," Xuanzang agrees. "It's just right."

Appendix

Images of Xuanzang and Water Moon Avalokiteśvara in Cave Temples, 12th–13th Centuries

Date	Dynasty	Modern Province	Site	Images	Form
1094–1102	Northern Song	Shaanxi	Zhaoan 招安, Cave 3	1	Sculpture[1]
1103–1104	Northern Song	Shaanxi	Foye Cave 佛爷洞	1	Sculpture[2]
1105	Northern Song	Shandong	Avalokiteśvara Pavilion 觀音閣	1	Sculpture
1112	Northern Song	Shaanxi	Mt. Zhong 钟山, Cave 4	1	Sculpture[3]
1114–1118	Northern Song	Sichuan	Yanfu si 延福寺, Cave 8	1	Sculpture[4]
1119–1123	Northern Song	Shaanxi	Shisihe 石寺河, Cave 1	1	Sculpture[5]
960–1127	Northern Song	Shaanxi	Shiyao 石窑, Cave 1	1	Sculpture[6]
960–1127	Northern Song	Shaanxi	Shiyao 石窑, Cave 2	1	Sculpture
1141–1154	Jin	Shaanxi	Shihong si 石泓寺, Cave 2	1	Sculpture[7]
1038–1227	Xixia	Gansu	Eastern Thousand Buddhas Caves 東千佛洞, Cave 2	2	Mural[8]
1038–1227	Xixia	Gansu	Eastern Thousand Buddhas Caves, Cave 5	1	Mural
1038–1227	Xixia	Gansu	Ancient Buddha Cave 古佛洞	1	Mural[9]
1038–1227	Xixia	Gansu	Yulin 榆林, Cave 2	1	Mural[10]
1038–1227	Xixia	Gansu	Yulin, Cave 3	1	Mural
1293	Yuan	Shanxi	Dayun yuan 大雲院	1	Sculpture[11]

Notes

Prologue

Epigraph. Elias Khoury, *Broken Mirrors: Sinalcol,* 200.

1. Huili et al., *Da Tang da Ci'en si Sanzang fashi zhuan* (hereafter *Zhuan*), 277a1–6. Unless otherwise noted, all translations are my own.

2. Vauchez and Cusato, *Francis of Assisi,* 336.

3. I discuss Xuanzang's life and work in more detail in *Xuanzang: China's Legendary Pilgrim and Translator.*

4. Other important early biographical sources include Mingxiang's *Datang gu sanzang Xuanzang fashi xingzhuang,* Daoxuan's account in the *Xu gaoseng zhuan,* and the documents collected in the *Si shamen Xuanzang shangbiao ji.*

5. *Zhuan,* 221a8–10. Cf. Huili et al., *A Biography of the Tripiṭaka Master of the Great Ci'en Monastery of the Great Tang Dynasty* (hereafter *Biography*), 7.

6. There is no scholarly consensus regarding the precise date that Xuanzang departed from the capital. Etienne de la Vaissière has argued for 629 ("Note sur la chronologie"), Kuwayama Shōshin believes it was 628 ("How Xuanzang Learned about Nālandā"), and Yoshimura Makoto claims it was 627 ("Genjō no nenji mondai ni tsuite").

7. On the problems with using Xuanzang's *Record* and *Biography* as historical sources, see Deeg, "Has Xuanzang Really Been in Mathurā?" and "Show Me the Land Where the Buddha Dwelled." See also, Kotyk, "Chinese State and Buddhist Historical Sources."

8. Xuanzang's disciple Bianji 辯機 (619?–649) is credited with compiling the work, possibly based on Xuanzang's notes and oral comments.

9. *Zhuan,* 279b24–25; *Biography,* 346.

10. In "The *Heart Sūtra*: A Chinese Apocryphal Text?" Jan Nattier argues that Xuanzang composed rather than translated the *Heart Sūtra.* This theory remains controversial. For one among several counterarguments, see Ishii Kōsei, "Issues Surrounding the *Heart Sūtra.*"

11. Wu Cheng'en and Anthony C. Yu, *The Journey to the West* (hereafter *Journey*).

12. *Xiyou ji*, chap. 29: 337; *Journey*, vol. II: 48.

13. Xuanzang's title of Sanzang is often rendered as "Tripiṭaka." Tripiṭaka refers to the "three baskets" of the Indian Buddhist canon, whereas Trepiṭaka indicates Buddhist teachers who are considered masters of that canon. Other Buddhist monks in China, notably Kumārajīva, Paramārtha, and Amoghavajra, also bear the honorific Trepiṭaka.

14. On the veneration of Zhu Bajie in Taiwan, see Brose, "The Pig and the Prostitute."

15. In addition to the studies discussed here, see also, Cedzich, "The Cult of Wu-t'ung / Wu-hsien in History and Fiction"; Shahar, "Vernacular Fiction"; Clart, "The Relationship of Myth and Cult in Chinese Popular Religion"; Durand-Dastès, "A Late Qing Blossoming of the Seven Lotus"; and, most recently, Ganany, "Origin Narratives: Reading and Reverence in Late-Ming China."

16. Shahar, *Crazy Ji*, xv.

17. Meulenbeld, *Demonic Warfare*, 15.

18. Rawski, *Education and Popular Literacy in Ch'ing China*, 23.

19. Elman, *Civil Examinations and Meritocracy*, 132.

20. Scholarship on the *Journey to the West* novel is far too voluminous to list here, but some landmark studies include Hu, "Xiyouji kaozheng"; Lu, *Zhongguo xiaoshuo shilüe*; Dudbridge, *The Hsi-yu Chi*; Anthony Yu's lengthy introduction to his translation of *The Journey to the West*; Plaks, *The Four Masterworks of the Ming Novel*; Isobe, *Saiyūki shiryō no kenkyū*; and Nakano, *Xiyou ji de mimi*.

21. Palmer, "Folk, Popular, or Minjian Religion?" 157.

22. Sangren, "Great Tradition and Little Traditions Reconsidered," 6.

23. Some of the most recent work is collected in Hou and Wang, Xiyou ji *xinlun ji qita: laizi Fojiao yishi, xisu yu wenben de shijiao.*

24. Lévi-Strauss, *The Naked Man*, 644.

25. Kuusi, *Finnish Folk Poetry*, 40.

26. Duara, "Superscribing Symbols," 791.

27. Katz, *Images of the Immortal*, 92.

28. On Communist readings of the *Xiyou ji*, see Hsia, *Classic Chinese Novel*, 121–128. The second statement comes from Miki Katsumi, *Saiyūki Oboegaki*, quoted in Yu's introduction to *The Journey to the West*, 53.

29. Johnston, *The Story of Myth*, 163.

30. Guattari and Deleuze, *A Thousand Plateaus*, 21.

31. See, for example Yang, *Gifts, Favors, and Banquets*; and Oostveen, "Religious Belonging in the East Asian Context."

32. Rolston, *Traditional Chinese Fiction*, 133.

33. Doniger, *The Implied Spider*, 2.

34. Balazs, *Chinese Civilization and Bureaucracy*, 135.

35. Propp, *Morphology of the Folktale*.

36. Versnel, *Inconsistencies in Greek and Roman Religion,* 86.

37. Jullien, "Naissance de l'imagination," 74.

38. For excellent studies of the processes by which characters from sacred narratives become real to devotees, see Luhrmann, *How God Becomes Real,* and Taves, *Revelatory Events.*

39. Landy, *How to Do Things with Fictions,* 10.

40. See, for example, the sources cited in Hou, "Xuanzang: cong sengren dao xingxiang dashi," 54–56.

41. *Zhuan,* 277b27–c18. Cf. *Biography,* 335–336.

Chapter 1: Fiction

Epigraph. Gopnik, *Angels and Ages,* 4.

1. Portions of this chapter were published previously in Brose, "Taming the Monkey."

2. Waley, *Monkey: Folk Novel of China,* 7–8.

3. Hu Shih's introduction was included in the first American edition of Waley's translation, published in 1943.

4. Lazarus, *The Nation,* 492.

5. See Alan Elliott's pioneering work on Sun Wukong spirit possession in modern Singapore, *Chinese Spirit-Medium Cults in Singapore.*

6. By the turn of the twentieth century, the authorship of Qiu Changchun, first proposed in the Wang Xiangxu 汪象旭 edition of the novel (1663), had been presumed for nearly two hundred and fifty years.

7. Waley, *Monkey,* 9.

8. *Journey,* vol. I: ix.

9. Subsequent scholarship on Daoist elements in the novel include Liu, "Quanzhen jiao he xiaoshuo Xiyou ji," parts 1–5; Plaks, *The Four Masterworks;* Despeaux, "Les lectures alchimiques du *Hsi-yu-chi*"; and Oldstone-Moore, "Alchemy and *Journey to the West.*"

10. On the extraordinary life and work of Pavie, see Crosnier, *Théodore Pavie: Le Voyageur;* and Cordier, "Théodore Pavie: Nécrologie."

11. Pavie published a series of studies on popular Chinese novels, including *Choix de contes et nouvelles;* San-koué-tchy; "Les trois religions de la Chine"; "Yu-Ki le Magicien, Legende Chinoise"; and "La vision de Pao-Ly."

12. Goethe and Eckermann, *Conversations of Goethe,* 212; Pavie, "Étude sur le Sy-Yéou-tchin-tsuén," 357–358.

13. Pavie, "Étude sur le Sy-yéou-tchin-tsuén," 365.

14. Chen, *Xiyou zhenquan.*

15. Doré, *Recherches sur les superstitions en Chine,* vol. VIII, part 2, 562.

16. Taylor, "Chinese Folk Lore," 168. Taylor had spent a decade living in remote areas of southern Taiwan, spoke both Chinese and Paiwan (the language of the aboriginal people of southern Taiwan), and wrote broadly about Taiwanese aboriginal culture. On Taylor and his work in Taiwan, see Taylor and Dudbridge, *Aborigines of South Taiwan.*

17. The first English translation of a story from *Journey to the West* was published three years earlier. In 1884, the Rev. Dyer Ball's translation of chapter ten of the novel—the story of Emperor Taizong and the Dragon King—appeared under the title "Scraps from Chinese Mythology."

18. *The Literary Digest* (Aug. 11, 1900): 167.

19. Candlin, *Chinese Fiction,* 3. For Candlin's largely sympathetic view of Chinese religions, see his "What Should Be Our Attitude towards the False Religions?"

20. Candlin, *Chinese Fiction,* 30.

21. Woodbridge, *The Golden-Horned Dragon King,* 1.

22. Woodbridge, *Fifty Years in China,* 63.

23. Woodbridge, *The Golden-Horned Dragon King,* 1. This statement is also quoted approvingly in the introduction to a summary of *Journey to the West* in Werner, *Myths and Legends of China,* 325.

24. Woodbridge, *The Golden-Horned Dragon King,* 13.

25. McLean, *The History of the Foreign Christian Missionary Society,* 275.

26. Ware, "The Fairyland of China I," 81.

27. For evidence, Ware listed "the death of Tai Tsung, his visit to the prison of the lost, and his resurrection after three days; the crossing of the river of death while the Holy One, sitting on the clouds, stills the winds and the waves; Buddha casting down his rod, which changes into a dragon; the fisherman being told where to let down his net for a good catch of fish, and many other incidents." Ware, "The Fairyland," 81.

28. Ibid.

29. On Timothy Richard and his missionary work in China, see Kaiser, *Encountering China.* Richard's interpretations of Chinese Buddhism are discussed in Scott, "Timothy Richard, World Religion, and Reading Christianity," and Son, "Kindai Bukkyō no tōzai kōshō."

30. The alternative title for the same text is *A Mission to Heaven: A Great Chinese Epic and Allegory by Ch'iu Ch'ang Ch'un, a Taoist Gamaliel Who Became a Nestorian Prophet and Advisor to the Chinese Court.*

31. Richard, *A Journey to Heaven,* xviii. See also, Richard, *Forty-Five Years in China,* 343–344.

32. Richard found his most compelling evidence for the biblical origins of *Journey to the West* in a poem from the eighty-eighth chapter of the novel. In Richard's translation, the poem reads: "The true Illustrious Religion is not human, The great Way, whose origin is in all space, Whose influence pervades the Universe, Has balm to heal

all suffering" (Richard, *A Journey to Heaven,* 309). In a footnote, Richard informs readers that the Chinese word for "Illustrious Religion" is the same name for Christianity used on the Nestorian stele discovered in Xi'an. The Illustrious Religion at the center of *Journey to the West,* in other words, is none other than Christianity. Richard, however, misread the poem. The term he translated as "Illustrious Religion" (*jingxiang* 景象) does not refer to Nestorian Christianity, which is usually written as Jingjiao 景教, but is, instead, a common compound meaning "image." The poem, which plays on Buddhist and Daoist themes, might be more accurately translated as "The image of true Chan is uncommon, the cause of the Great Way fills the vast void. The power of Metal and Wood suffuses the dharma realm, a measure of medicine is equal to omniscience." 真禪景象不凡同, 大道緣由滿太空。金木施威盈法界, 刀圭展轉合圓通。*Xiyou ji,* 2:1054.

33. Richard, *A Journey to Heaven,* xxxii.

34. Ibid., xx.

35. Ibid., xxxvi.

36. Ibid., xxxix.

37. Teaching young princes how to pray, for instance, Sun Wukong instructs them "to close their eyes, concentrate their thoughts on some Scripture truth, and let the breath of Heaven enter their bodies, so that God's spirit might dwell in their heart. After prayer, they would receive renewed power, being born again, their very bones being transformed, and they would become the sons of God." Richard, *A Journey to Heaven,* 310. Other Western interpreters, inspired by Richard, saw Sun Wukong as Christ-like, with his golden headband a modified crown of thorns. See, for example, Gordon, *Symbols of 'The Way'*; and Beck, "The Chinese Pilgrim's Progress."

38. Gordon, *Symbols of 'The Way,'* 1–2. I have not been able to confirm that this translation was, in fact, made.

39. You, *Genzhai zashuo,* 5:2b.

40. Ibid.

41. Tie, *Qinding baqi tongzhi,* 4366.

42. See, for example, the 1928 directive, "Criteria for Keeping or Abolishing Shrines" (Shenci cunfei biaozhun ling 神祠存廢標準令), discussed in Yan, "1930 niandai guomin zhengfu fengsu diaocha," 1163.

43. The veneration of Sun Wukong and other figures from *Journey to the West* in Tibet is mentioned in Li, *Shu shui jing,* 6b–7a. Other references to the cult of the Great Sage Equal to Heaven in China during the Qing dynasty are collected in Miao, "Lun Ming-Qing shiqi de Qitian Dasheng chongbai" and Du, "Gujin zailun zhong de Sun Wukong congsi zhi su."

44. Qian, *Qian yan tang wen ji,* 17:14b. Translation slightly modified from Ropp, *Dissent in Early Modern China,* 53.

45. You, "Xiyou zhenquan xu" 西游真詮序. In Cai, *Xiyou ji ziliao huibian,* 600.

46. Huaiming, *Xiyou ji ji,* 1.

47. *Xiyou yuanzhi dufa* 西遊原旨讀法. In Cai, *Xiyou ji ziliao huibian,* 603–611. Translation slightly modified from Yu, "Liu I-ming on How to Read the *Hsi-yu chi,*" 303. On Liu's commentary, see also Potterf, "Ritualizing the *Journey to the West.*"

48. See Ji, "Ming-Qing xiaoshuo," 62–70. On proscribed novels during this period, see Li, *Zhongguo jinhui xiaoshuo daquan.*

49. Liu, *Zai yuan za zhi,* 84.

50. Shahar, "Vernacular Fiction," 196–198.

51. Liu, *Zai yuan za zhi,* 85

52. Qian, *Qian yan tang wen ji,* 17:15a.

53. On the close relationship between the genres of *xiaoshuo* and *shi* in traditional China, see Rolston, *Traditional Chinese Fiction and Fiction Commentary,* chapters 5 and 6.

54. Zhuo, "Ren de wenxue," 222.

55. Xia, "Xiaoshuo yuanli," 27. See also, Meulenbeld, *Demonic Warfare,* 39.

56. Liang, "Lun xiaoshuo yu qunzhi zhi guanxi," 77.

57. This assessment remained popular in China. In his *Historical Development of Chinese Literature,* the Chinese scholar Liu Dajie (1904–1977) warned that *Journey to the West* incited sex and violence and had become a poisonous influence on society. Its stories were simply too good; they spread quickly among the masses, imperceptibly instilling readers and listeners with irrational ideas about gods and ghosts. These false beliefs, according to Liu, rendered the Chinese people passive and easily manipulated by others. Liu, *Zhongguo wenxue fada shi,* 956.

58. Liang, "Lun xiaoshuo yu qunzhi zhi guanxi," 81.

59. Earlier efforts to revise the *Journey to the West* narrative to better suit the philosophical inclinations of Confucian scholars are reflected in the many sequels and supplements to the novel produced during the Qing dynasty. For an overview of these works, see Li, "Transformations of Monkey," 46–74.

60. Hu Shih argued that China has "a literature richer and more extensive than any modern European language had ever achieved at the time of its establishment as a national language." Hu, "The Literary Renaissance," 48.

61. Ibid.

62. Hu, "Lun huichu shenfo." On the larger context of this and other critiques of religion during the Republican period, see Katz, *Religion in China & Its Modern Fate.*

63. Hu, "The Chinese Novel," 61.

64. Hu, "*Xiyou ji* kaozheng," 390.

65. In the preface to his new version, Hu Shih explained: "Ten years ago I was talking with Lu Xun about the eighty-first trial (ninety-ninth chapter) of the *Journey to the West.* It was really rather shabby and should be rewritten to secure it a place among the great books." Hu, "*Xiyou ji* di jiushijiu hui."

66. Hu Shih's rewrite has been translated with an introduction in Li, "Rewriting of Chapter 99 of *The Journey to the West.*"

67. Nationalistic readings of the *Journey to the West* story were prominent during the Republican era and the early decades of the CCP. For examples, see Sun, *Transforming Monkey,* chapter three.

68. Lu, *Zhongguo xiaoshuo shilüe,* 140.

69. Hayes, who had only introductory-level Chinese, relied heavily on Timothy Richard's English translation and on the help of Japanese assistants when composing her own abridgement. On Hayes and her translation of *Journey to the West,* see Wu, "Duoyuan zongjiao de duihua."

70. Hayes, *The Buddhist Pilgrim's Progress,* 18.

71. Ibid., 19.

72. Ou, *Le Roman Chinois,* 39–40.

73. Zheng, *Xidi shuhua,* 53.

74. Sun, *Transforming Monkey,* 62. The real moral of *Princess Iron Fan,* the directors later admitted, was that "all Chinese people should unite and resist Japanese invaders for the final victory in the anti-Japanese War." Wan, *Wo yu Sun Wukong,* 90. For a detailed discussion of *Princess Iron Fan* and its influence on Chinese and Japanese animation, see Du, *Animated Encounters,* chapter 1.

75. For a vivid description of a dramatic performance of *Journey to the West* at the City God Temple in Xiamen in the 1920s, see Mackenzie-Grieve, *A Race of Green Ginger,* 78–79.

76. Zheng, *Xidi shuhua,* 53.

77. On the history of Xuanzang's relics in China, see Brose, "Resurrecting Xuanzang"; and Sakaida, *Dare mo shiranai* Saiyūki.

78. Julien, *Histoire de la vie de Hiouen-Thsang.*

79. Julien, *Mémoires sur les contrées occidentales.*

80. Stein, *Ruins of Desert Cathay* II, 170. Munchausen, the fictional character Rudolf Erich Raspe (1736–1794) based on a real historical figure, was such an outrageous fabulist that his name later became synonymous with pathological lying.

81. Stein, *Ruins of Desert Cathay* II, 168–169.

82. Some of the extant temple murals depicting scenes from the Obtaining the Scriptures narrative are reproduced in Wei and Zhang, *Xiyou ji bihua.*

83. The "Bai" in Bai Jian's surname means "white."

84. Zhang, "Zai Nanjing faxian de Tang Xuanzang yigu."

Chapter 2: Apotheosis

Epigraph. William Faulkner, *Requiem for a Nun,* 73.

1. Just as there is no consensus regarding the precise date Xuanzang departed from the capital, the conditions under which he began his journey also are unclear.

Huili's biography and Xuanzang's later writings state that he left the capital without the required documentation, thus breaking the law. The biographical account contained in Daoxuan's *Further Biographies of Eminent Monks* (*Xu gaoseng zhuan*), however, states that Xuanzang left the capital after a government directive instructed all monks to disperse because of a grain shortage. On the reliability and textual history of Xuanzang's biography, see Saito, "Features of the Kongō-ji Version;" and Kotyk, "Chinese State and Buddhist Historical Sources on Xuanzang."

2. *Zhuan*, 267a25–27; *Biography*, 269.

3. *Zhuan*, 279a25–26; *Biography*, 344.

4. *Zhuan*, 234a20–29; *Biography*, 77–78.

5. *Zhuan*, 277b18–20; *Biography*, 335.

6. This image is often said to derive from the well-known paintings of itinerant monks from Dunhuang. A lesser-known early example can be seen in cave 2 at Fanzhuang 樊庄, in the Ansai 安塞 district of Shaanxi. The sculpture, created sometime between 1093 and 1113, shows several traveling monks, one of whom wears a large backpack full of scrolls. A photograph of the scene is included in Wei and Zhang, *Xiyou ji bihua*, 9.

7. The history of this image is discussed in Liu, "Gaoseng xingxiang de chuanbo yu huiliu." On the evolution of Xuanzang's image in China and Japan, see Liu, "Tangdai Xuanzang de shenghua"; Isobe, *Saiyūki shiryō no kenkyū*, chap. 1; Wong, "The Making of a Saint"; and Li, "Xuanzang huaxiang." Some of the visual material related to Xuanzang's life and legacy has been collected in Yakushi-ji, *Genjō sanzō shūhōroku*; Nara Kenritsu Bijutsukan, *Saiyūki no shiruku rōdo*; and Nara Kokuritsu Hakubutsukan, *Tenjiku e*.

8. *Zhuan*, 266c8–11; *Biography*, 265–266. On Helin si and Lady Xue, see Chen, "The Tang Buddhist Palace Chapels," 110–113.

9. On the relationship between Xuanzang and the infant Zhongzong, see *Zhuan*, 270c23–272b22; and *Biography* 295–306. A copy of Zhongzong's comments on Xuanzang's image was brought to Japan by Enchin but has not survived. See Enchin, *Nihon biku Enchin nittō guhō mokuroku*, 1101b29.

10. Zhisheng, *Xu gujin yijing tuji*, 367c26–368a2.

11. Zhang, *Lidai minghua ji*, 3:23b.

12. Ouyang, *Yuyi zhi* 于役志, in *Wen zhong ji*, 125:5b–6a.

13. Two of the earliest extant images of Xuanzang in Japan depict him in more generic form, grouped together with other prominent monks of the past. The first image was drawn by Kanyū 觀佑 (1110–1175) in 1163 as a part of a series titled *Kōsō zuzō* 高僧圖像, which depicts thirty Chinese and Japanese clerics venerated by the Tendai and Shingon (Taimistu 台密) sects. Xuanzang is situated between Daoxuan and Jianzhen 鑑真 (688–763), *Taishō shinshū daizōkyō: zuzōbu*, vol. 11, 25.

The original manuscript is held in the collection of the Daitokyu Memorial Library 大東急記念文庫藏 in Tokyo.) A very similar image is included in the *Sentoku zuzō* 先徳図像 (a.k.a. *Sangoku soshiei* 三國祖師影; see fig. 2.1), copies of which date to 1150. This series of forty-six "worthies" includes the patriarchs of the Esoteric, Chan, and Nara schools of Buddhism as well as ancient Chinese heroes such as Confucius and King Wu of the Zhou dynasty. Here Xuanzang appears together with Daoxuan and Kumārajīva (*Taishō shinshū daizōkyō: zuzōbu*, vol. 10, 1420). For a reproduction and study of the oldest edition of this text, see Takahashi, *Kyūan rokunenbon* Sangoku shoshiei *no kenkyū*. A slightly later edition is kept at the Tokyo National Museum and can be viewed online, https://webarchives.tnm.jp/imgsearch /show/E0053427.

14. Dong, "Shu Xuanzang qu jing tu" 書玄奘取經圖, in *Guang chuan hua ba*, 4:4b–5a.

15. The shrine was located on the grounds of Qiyun Chan Cloister 栖雲禪院. Li, *Liang xi ji*, 132:1b–3a. For additional examples of Xuanzang images kept in monastic libraries, see Liu, "Songdai Xuanzang," 188–191.

16. One possible exception to this pattern comes from the report of a Japanese cleric who traveled to India during the ninth century. The monk Kongō Zanmai 金剛 三昧 (d.u.) noted that at least one temple in central India kept an image of Xuanzang, with his hempen sandals, his spoon, and his chopsticks, riding on a multicolored cloud. The image was brought out on feast days and venerated, suggesting that Xuanzang, with his peculiar footwear and eating utensils, may have been memorialized in some parts of India. Duan, *Youyang zazu*, 3:12a.

17. Liu, "Songdai Xuanzang," 172.

18. On the shifting structure of the pantheon during the Song dynasty, see Hansen, *Changing Gods in Medieval China*.

19. See also, the cases of Princess Miaoshan (Dudbridge, *The Legend of Miaoshan*) and Guan Yu (ter Haar, *Guan Yu*).

20. These regions probably had much in common. Kirill Solonin has argued that the Tangut, Jurchen, and Khitan and other cultures of north and northwestern China constituted an interdependent and integrated tradition. "The Glimpses of Tangut Buddhism," 70.

21. The one exception comes from cave 3 of the Yulin cave complex in Gansu province. Here, instead of Avalokiteśvara, Xuanzang and his companions venerate the bodhisattva Samantabhadra. This mural, together with a companion painting depicting Mañjuśrī, flank the entrance passage to the cave. For detailed photographs of this mural, see Dunhuang Yanjiu Yuan, *Zhongguo shiku: Anxi Yulin ku*, plates 158–164. A virtual tour of the entire cave with high-quality digital images is available through the Digital Dunhuang project at http://www.e-dunhuang.com/cave/10.0001/0001.0002.0003.

22. On Water Moon Avalokiteśvara, see Yü, *Kuan-yin*, 233–247; and Rösch, *Chinese Wood Sculptures of the 11th to 13th Centuries*.

23. *Da fanguang Fo huayan jing*, 718a10–c15.

24. *Qian yan qian bi Guanshiyin pusa tuoluoni shenzhou jing*, 88b18–22.

25. On representations of this triad in later precious scrolls, see Idema, *Personal Salvation and Filial Piety*.

26. For images of the site, see Shandong sheng zhongdian wenhua baohu danwei, "Tengzhou shi Guanyin ge."

27. Xuanzang, *Da Tang xiyu ji*, 804a3–6.

28. See, for example, *Zhuan*, 237a8–13 and 244a28–b4; *Biography*, 92 and 127.

29. The original Tangut text is reproduced with Chinese translation in Sun, "Cong liang zhong Xixiawen guashu kan Hexi diqu 'Datang Sanzang.'" My thanks to Michelle McCoy for alerting me to this text.

30. Portions of the Dunhuang texts are reproduced in Hou, "Xuanzang: cong sengren dao xingxiang dashi." The Daoist text *Fashi xuanze ji* (postface 1488) is virtually identical to the work included in the *Chanmen risong*: "Auspicious and Inauspicious Days to Conduct Ceremonies Selected by Dharma Master Trepiṭaka and Promulgated by Tang Emperor Taizong" (Tang Taizong huangdi xuanwen Sanzang fashi xuanze xiuzhai jixiong zhi ri 唐太宗皇帝宣文三藏法師選擇修齋吉凶之日). The historical Xuanzang lamented that monastics in China followed inaccurate ritual calendars and subsequently sought to link the monastic calendar in China to the dates observed in India.

31. In *lingqian* 靈籤 divination systems (including those centered on Avalokiteśvara, Buddhist patriarchs, and the Great Immortal Huang 黄大仙) employed in contemporary Chinese and Taiwanese temples, one of the possible lots that can be drawn is "The Tang Monk Obtains the Scriptures."

32. *Shuiyue Guanzizai gongyang fa* 水月觀自在供養法 (T. *Zuzōbu* 3:209b–c). Translation from Yü, *Kuan-yin*, 244.

33. See Rösch, *Chinese Wood Sculptures*, 40–41; Yü, *Kuan-yin*, 241.

34. Piotrovsky, *Lost Empire of the Silk Road*, 198–201.

35. See Huang, "Reassessing Printed Buddhist Frontispieces from Xi Xia," 151–152 (figures 24 and 25).

36. Ikeda, *Chūgoku kodai shahon shikigo shūroku*, 493–494; and Wang, "Dunhuang xieben *Shuiyue guanyin jing* yanjiu." Rösch also has argued that the Water Moon Avalokiteśvara was linked to Water and Land Dharma Assemblies and the care for the dead at Yanshan temple 岩山寺 in Shanxi. See *Chinese Wood Sculptures*, 77–80.

37. *Fo shuo yuxiu shiwang sheng qi jing*, 409b14–19.

38. See, for example, Zheng, "Guazhou shiku qun Tang Xuanzang qu jing tu yanjiu." Zheng Binglin has likewise concluded that images of Avalokiteśvara and Xuanzang in cave temples like Mount Zhong show the spirit of the dead led by Xuanzang into the presence of the bodhisattva. Zheng, "Huangling xian Shuanglongyu cun Qianfo dong," 642.

39. These amulets lack inscriptions or reign eras and have not been found in any archaeological sites, making them difficult to date. Based largely on their artistic motifs and styles, numismatists estimate that the earliest examples date to the Southern Song. François Thierry notes that the unique design of the horse is like other coins produced during the Southern Song dynasty (personal communication). Alex Fang also explained that the Song date of these coins resulted from over ten years of discussion among numismatists and is based on decorative patterns and iconographic styles (personal communication). On the reverse side of these amulets, a figure dressed in robes stands on a cloud. To its left, occupying the same cloud, stand two smaller figures, one of whom is holding a sword or a staff. At the bottom left is a figure, possibly a monkey, with its arms apparently bound behind its back. Some scholars have identified the robed figure as Sengjia 僧伽 (617–710), a deified Tang-dynasty cleric, and the bound figure as the water-demon Wuzhiqi 無支祈 (a.k.a. Water Mother 水母). Given the apparent repetition of the monkey-like figure on the front and back, it also is possible that these are two scenes from a single narrative: the imprisonment (below) and release (above) of Sun Wukong, presided over by Avalokiteśvara.

40. Fang, *Zhongguo huaqian yu chuantong wenwua*, 170. Coins with nearly identical designs were still being produced throughout the Yuan and Ming dynasties. By the Qing, amulets featuring the individual characters from *Journey to the West* also were in circulation. See Zheng, *Zhongguo huaqian tudian*, 403–404; and Zheng, *Zhongguo huaqian tudian xuji*, 323. For a comprehensive study and catalog of Chinese amulets (not including those associated with Obtaining the Scriptures narratives), see Thierry, *Amulettes De Chine: Catalogue*.

41. A small mural painted in 1289 above a doorway in Qinglong Temple 青龍寺 in Shanxi contains a similar arrangement of a monk with palms together standing at the head of a small procession of figures. He is followed by another slightly smaller monk in the same posture. Behind these clerics is a monkey leading a white horse carrying a chest that is radiating light. On Qinglong Temple and its murals, see Yu, "Shanxi Qinglong si qu jing bihua."

42. The River of Flowing Sand (Liusha he 流沙河) is described in similar terms in the *Journey to the West* novel. Yu's translation reads: "The Flowing-Sand metes, eight hundred wide; these Weak Waters, three thousand deep. A goose feather cannot stay afloat; a rush petal will sink to the bottom." *Xiyou ji*, vol. 1: 248; *Journey*, vol. 1: 421–422.

43. This is most likely a reference to the Chongning edition of the Buddhist canon 崇寧藏, which was printed in Fuzhou in 1112 and comprised of 564 cases with over 5,800 fascicles. The Kaiyuan canon, by contrast, was slightly smaller, at 5,048 fascicles in 480 cases.

44. Zhang, *Youhuan jiwen*, 4:2a–b. See also, Dudbridge, "The Hsi-yu Chi Monkey," 258.

45. Dudbridge, "The Hsi-yu Chi," 45–47. As one of the more original and idio-syncratic characters in premodern Chinese literature, Sun Wukong has attracted a tre-mendous amount of scholarly attention, much of which has attempted to identify his antecedents. The earliest discussions are found in Wilhelm, *Chinesische Volksmärchen*; Hu, "*Xiyou ji* kaozheng"; and Lu, *A Brief History of Chinese Fiction*, 413. A summary of the debate over Sun Wukong's origins and an argument for an Indian provenance is presented in Mair, "Suen Wu-kung = Hanumat?" Hera S. Walker, a student of Mair, argues for Indian as well as Chinese origins in "Indigenous or Foreign?: A Look at the Origins of the Monkey Hero Sun Wukong." On the influence of Chinese Buddhist traditions and hagiographical narratives on the legend of Sun Wukong, see Shahar, "The Lingyin Si Monkey Disciples." In Japanese scholarship, the origins of Sun Wu-kong are typically traced to both Indian and Chinese sources. See, for example, Isobe, *Tabiyuku Son Gokū*, and Nakano, *Son Goku no Tanjo*.

46. The eastern Zhengguo 鎮國 stupa at this same temple also bears an image that Ecke and Demieville identify as Xuanzang with a monkey attendant, but there is no inscription, and its identity remains unclear. See Ecke and Demieville, *The Twin Pago-das of Zayton*, 71, plate 48.

47. There is some evidence that Xuanzang was considered an arhat during this same period. Beginning in the twelfth century, some arhat assemblies include a monk, a horse, and an attendant. In motifs found at two different cave sites at Dazu in Chong-qing, the horse carries a bundle of scriptures on its back (Li and Yao, "Dazu shike Song-dai liang zu qu jing tu"). In the series of five hundred arhats painted at Huian Cloister 惠安院 in Ningbo sometime between 1174 and 1189, moreover, a monk on horseback is led by a demon and followed by an ape-like figure (Nara Kokuritsu Hakubutsukan, *Daitokuji denrai Gohyaku rakanzu*, 86). In still another collection of sixteen arhat por-traits produced in eleventh-century Japan, a monk is shown astride a white horse next to a demonic figure that resembles Sha Monk. The arhat, however, is explicitly identi-fied as "Nakula" 諾矩羅 (Nara Kokuritsu Hakubutsukan, *Tenjiku e*, 182). In some con-temporary Buddhist traditions, the 413th of the 500 arhats is named Mingshijie 明世界 but identified as Xuanzang. See, for example, Liu, *Wubai luohan faxiang*, 18.

48. There has been a great deal of speculation about when these texts were com-posed, with estimates ranging from the late Tang through the Southern Song. For an overview of the evidence regarding the dating of the Kōzanji texts, see Chen, "*Da Tang Sanzang qu jing shihua* shidai xing zaiyi." Here, I follow Isobe Akira (*Saiyūki shiryō no kenkyū*, 57–102) and others who argue for a date sometime in the Southern Song. An argument for an earlier date of composition is made in Li and Cai, "*Da Tang Sanzang qu jing shihua* chengshu shidai kaobian."

49. A facsimile of the original *Newly Arranged Record* was published in Luo, *Jishi an congshu (chu ji)*. For an annotated edition of the text, see Li and Cai, *Da Tang San-zang qu jing shihua jiaozhu*. Charles J. Wivell translated the text into English as "The

Story of How the Monk Tripitaka of the Great Country of T'ang Brought back the Sutras." The publisher of *The Newly Arranged Record* is not identified, but based on the similarity between this text and the Chongning edition of the Buddhist canon printed in Fuzhou in the first years of the twelfth century, Isobe concludes that *The Newly Arranged Record* was printed most likely in Fuzhou around the same time. Isobe, Saiyūki *shiryō no kenkyū*, 79–80.

50. Mair has proposed that the presence of the word "*chu*" 處 in the titles of eleven out of fifteen chapter headings in the Kōzanji manuscripts is evidence that the narrative was either illustrated or enacted through performance. *T'ang Transformation Texts*, 80–84.

51. A catalog for Kōzanji's monastic library, produced in 1633, lists these two volumes as part of the temple's collection of "sacred teachings" (*shōgyō* 聖教). Kōzanji Tenseki Monjo Sōgō Chōsadan, *Kōzanji kyōzō komokuroku*, 30 (section 55, no. 15 in the original). The classification of *shōgyō* refers to noncanonical Buddhist texts fundamental to activities in the monasteries where they are housed. Typical examples include liturgies, ritual manuals, local histories, notes for preaching and oral presentations, and transmission documents. The inclusion of narratives of Xuanzang's mythic pilgrimage in Kōzanji's collection of *shōgyō* suggests that, at least in seventeenth-century Japan, these texts were viewed as part of the Buddhist tradition's sacred history. On *shōgyo*, see Abe, "Koramu 1: shōgyō no sekai," and Sango, "Buddhist Debate and the Production and Transmission of Shōgyō in Medieval Japan."

52. Wivell, "The Story of How the Monk Tripitaka," 1182.

53. Ibid., 1198.

54. Curiously, the emperor is identified as Minghuang 明皇 (a.k.a. Xuanzong 玄宗; r. 712–756), who was born nearly two decades after Xuanzang's death. In the popular imagination, Xuanzang was sometimes confused or conflated with the monk Amoghavajra (705–744), both of whom were known as "Trepiṭaka." Amoghavajra lived during the reign of Emperor Xuanzong.

55. Dudbridge, *The Hsi-yu Chi*, 30. Some confirmation that the text may have been cobbled together from originally independent narratives comes from the final section, which recounts the story of a boy whose evil stepmother attempts to murder him in various terrible ways. The boy is eventually swallowed by a fish. Xuanzang arrives on the scene just as the boy's father returns from a trading mission and schedules a memorial service for his lost son. Xuanzang then cuts open the fish and rescues the still living boy. Mair has shown that this story is an adaptation of an earlier Dunhuang manuscript that narrates the filial feats of Emperor Shun. Mair, "Parallels between Some Tunhuang Manuscripts."

56. See, for example, Zhang, "Beisong de 'shuohua' he huaben" and Cai, "Lun Song Yuan yi lai minjian zongjiao," 134. There also is a Japanese manuscript of Xuanzang's life, the *Genjō Sanzō toten yurai engi* 玄奘三藏渡天由來緣起, which takes the form of a

script for proselytizing in the Shinshū sect. This text, which Tanaka Tomoyuki dates to the nineteenth century, appears to represent an independent tradition. Tanaka, "Ryūkoku daigaku toshokanzō *Genjō Sanzō toten yurai engi.*"

57. See Edgren, *Southern Song Printing at Hangzhou,* 32–33.

58. Monkeys also were venerated inside Buddhist temples as dharma protectors and spirit guides and, in certain regions, as the ancestors of clans. On monkey veneration in Buddhist temples and possible links to the formation of *Journey to the West,* see Shahar, "The Lingyin Si Monkey Disciples."

59. Chūbachi, "*Saiyūki* no seiritsu." Inspired by Chūbachi's work, Dudbridge revised his earlier assessment of the Kōzanji texts as popular entertainment, writing that "already in the Kōzanji version, the clear signs of ritual overtones are there: the use of *khakkara* to ward off evil along the way, the coincidence of Sanzang's [Xuanzang's] final ascension with midday of the fifteenth of the seventh month, the height of the Zhongyuan 中元 season—these echoes ring across seven or eight centuries to our own time. And above all the scriptures themselves, not merely repositories of Buddhist wisdom and learning, but in Chinese society objects of ritual, talismanic power, generators of saving merit, helps [sic] on the road to paradise." Dudbridge, "The Hsi-yu Chi Monkey," 273.

60. *Zhuan,* 277b4–6; *Biography,* 334.

Chapter 3: Guardian

Epigraph. Louis Menand, "Karl Marx, Yesterday and Today"

1. *Zhuan,* 224b8–13; *Biography,* 26–28. The miraculous powers of the *Heart Sūtra* are highlighted in later biographies of Xuanzang, including his entry in the late Yuan/early Ming collection of divine monks, the *Shen seng zhuan,* 985b13–c21.

2. *Journey,* 1:209–210. Some of the long history of Deep Sands is recounted in Strickmann and Faure, *Chinese Magical Medicine,* 312–313 n.47; and Faure, *Protectors and Predators,* 29–31.

3. van der Leeuw and Turner, *Religion in Essence and Manifestation,* 424.

4. Frankfurter, "Narrating Power," 464.

5. Abel, "Ritual Drama and Dramatic Ritual." As Anne Righter describes it, "the action unfolding upon the wooden scaffoldings of the guilds was something more than imitation. In the fourteenth-century streets of Wakefield and Coventry, Chester and York, medieval audiences could achieve actual communion with the events of the Old and New Testaments." The audiences and actors in these dramas, she writes, engaged with these performances as "the reaccomplishment rather than the imitation of an action." Righter, *Shakespeare and the Idea of the Play,* 16–17.

6. Beckwith, *Signifying God,* 72.

7. The Road Opening Spirit has been a central figure in village exorcisms and temple processions since the Song dynasty. Essentially the equivalent of the Fangxiang shi, he clears routes of danger, leading the way around the territory when in procession or pilgrimage, or to the grave in the context of funerals. See Zhang, "Gudai zangli zhong de Kai lu shen."

8. Variant names for the foreign monks include *fan sheng* 番生, *fan seng* 幡僧, and *fan si* 番司.

9. My summary of this festival is based largely on Ye's *Fujian sheng Shaowu shi*. See also, Zhongguo Minzu Minjian Wudao Jicheng Bianjibu, *Zhongguo minzu minjian wudao jicheng: Fujian juan*, 622–630.

10. The recited texts include the *Precious Repentance of the Liang Emperor* 梁皇寶懺, the *Precious Repentance of the Thousand Buddhas* 千佛寶懺, the "Guanshiyin" chapter of the *Lotus Sūtra* 佛説觀世音普門品, the *Diamond Sūtra* 金剛般若波羅密經, and the *Amitabha Sutra* 佛説阿彌陀經. The presiding ritual master at the time of Ye Mingsheng's field work was He Xiaoguang 何小光, who identified as the twenty-fourth-generation ancestor in the Daoist tradition known as "Jiaofa Taishang Laojun zhonghe jingtan" 教法太上老君中和靖壇. Ye, *Fujian sheng Shaowu shi*, 28.

11. The passages read come from the *Avataṃsaka Sūtra* 華嚴經, the *Prajñāpāramitā Sūtra* 般若經, the *Nirvana Sūtra* 涅槃經, and the *Ratnakūṭa Sūtra* 寶積經.

12. Ye, *Fujian sheng shaowu shi*, 76.

13. *Shaowu xian zhi* 邵武縣志, 40:437. Passage reproduced in Ye, *Fujian sheng Shaowu shi*, 59.

14. The records of the Zhongqian Temple 中乾廟, *Zhongqian miao zhong bu* 中乾廟眾簿, give the most detailed historical account of this rite in northwestern Fujian. Originally compiled in the early sixteenth century, this record was regularly revised, but the earliest surviving edition, printed in 1892, preserves an inscription commemorating the reconstruction of the temple following its destruction during the Taiping Rebellion. This inscription, dated to 1862, provides the first mention of the performance of "foreign monks." The relevant portion of the inscription is transcribed in Ye, *Fujian sheng Shaowu shi*, 88.

15. Ye, *Fujian sheng Shaowu shi*, 87–90.

16. The centrality of Maitreya and the Road Opening Spirit to these rites is apparent from a second troupe of masked deities marching and dancing in the Heyuan procession. Following directly behind the "Foreign Monks" are the "Eight Barbarians" (*ba man* 八蠻), consisting of two Maitreyas, two Road Opening Spirits, two green-faced spirits, and two black-faced spirits.

17. *Zhou li zhushu*, 25:5a–b. The translated passages come from Bodde's *Festivals in Classical China*, chap. 4. On the history of *nuo*, see Qu and Fu, *Zhongguo nuo wenhua tonglun*.

18. Fan, *Hou Han shu*, 15:11b–12b.

19. Some scholars have speculated that Sun Wukong, with his fiery eyes, golden pupils, and magic staff, might initially have been modeled on the Fangxiang shi. See, for example, Zhang, "Yuanxing de zaisheng," and Li, "Zai lun Sun Wukong."

20. Many of these dances are described and diagrammed in the multivolume series edited by the Zhongguo Minzu Minjian Wudao Jicheng Bianjibu: *Zhongguo minzu minjian wudao jicheng.*

21. The earliest extant edition of the *Pak t'ongsa ŏnhae* dates to 1677. The section relevant to *Journey to the West* is translated in Dudbridge, *The Hsi-yu chi,* 179–185.

22. The pillow, known as the "Cizhou Ware Pillow Picturing the Tang Monk Obtaining the Scriptures" (磁州窑唐僧取经图枕), is currently in the collection of the Guangdong Museum. It was produced in the workshop of the Zhang 張 family in the Anyang area of present-day Henan province. Other pillows produced in this same workshop also depict scenes from popular literature and drama. Another Cizhou-ware pillow, in the collection of the Hebei Cultural Research Institute 河北文物研究所, also is often identified as depicting a scene from *Journey to the West,* but this is a misidentification. On Cizhou-ware pillows in general, see Zhang, *Cizhou yao ci zhen,* and Mino and Tsiang, *Freedom of Clay and Brush.* The recently discovered incense brazier is the subject of Zhang, "Yuan qinghua *Xi you ji* yuanda xianglu shoucang ji."

23. The Kyŏngch'ŏn-sa stupa, designated National Treasure number 86, was taken to Japan in 1907 but returned to Korea in 1918. It currently resides at the National Museum of Korea in Seoul. For photos of the Wŏn'gak-sa and Kyŏngch'ŏn-sa stupas and a brief account of the latter's recent history, see Brother Anthony, "Bethell, Hulbert, Gale."

24. The definitive study of this stupa is Kungnip Munhwajae Yŏn'guso, *Kyŏngch'ŏnsa sipch'ŭng sŏkt'ap.* Additional historical sources are discussed in Chŏng, "Kyŏngch'ŏn-saji."

25. Kim, "Sabangbul during the Chosŏn Dynasty," 118 n. 58.

26. In South Korea, the Wŏn'gak-sa stupa is designated National Treasure number 2. It is currently encased in glass in Seoul's T'apgol Park. For a detailed study, see Yegŭrin Kŏnch'uksa Samuso, *Wŏn'gaksaji sipch'ŭng sŏkt'ap.* There also may have been a third stone stupa of this same design and iconographic program. According to Ko Yu-sŏp 高裕燮 (1905–1944), a stupa was initially erected at Hŭnggyo-sa 興敎寺, the memorial temple for Chosŏn King Chŏngjong and his wife Queen Chŏngan 定安王后 (1355–1412). Later, this was moved to Yŏn'gyŏng-sa 衍慶寺, the memorial temple for King T'aejong's mother, Queen Sinŭi 神懿王后 (1337–1391). Based on the descriptions of locals and the remaining fragments of the stupa, Ko Yu-sŏp concluded that the Yŏn'gyŏng-sa stupa was very similar Kyŏngch'ŏn-sa stupa, and that both stupas served as models for the Wŏn'gak-sa stupa. See Ko, *Songdo ŭi kojŏk,* and Kim, "Sabangbul during the Chosŏn Dynasty," 118–119.

27. The scenes have no cartouches and are not easily identifiable. For attempts to link the images with episodes known from the hundred-chapter novel and earlier

sources, see Xie, "Hanguo Jingtian si Yuandai shita," and Sin, "Wŏn'gaksaji sipch'ŭng sŏkt'ap."

28. A stele erected at the Thousand Buddha Hall 千佛堂 in Henan's Yanjin County 延津縣 in 1534 suggests that Xuanzang and his mythical companions occupied similar positions in the Buddhist cosmologies of northern China. The nine-foot stele, now kept in the Henan Museum, is covered with hundreds of small images of buddhas framing scenes on the stele's five levels. The uppermost portion depicts a scene centered on Śākyamuni with a garuda perched on his head. Two panels to the left of the Buddha show Sun Wukong and a horse laden with scriptures (below) and Sha Monk (above). The panel to the right of the Buddha shows Xuanzang and another figure, possibly Zhu Bajie, receiving the scriptures at a Buddhist temple. The level below this shows the three bodhisattvas Mañjuśrī, Avalokiteśvara, and Samantabhadra seated on lotus thrones. Further down the stele is a carving of Maitreya as Budai (third level), the bodhisattva Dizang flanked by two attendants (second level), and, finally, on the lowest level, images of the Ten Kings of hell. This arrangement of Buddhist realms appears to depict the origins of the tradition, the transmission of the teachings to China, the bodhisattvas responsible for safeguarding the dharma and those who uphold it, and the consequences awaiting those who transgress. For a description and images, see Tan, "*Qianfo tang bei* yu minsu wenhua."

29. Sin, "Won'gaksaji," 102–106.

30. Cho, "Koryŏ sigi chapsang yŏn'gu," 26.

31. These other figures are Igwibak 二鬼朴, Iguryong 二口龍, Mahwasang 麻和尙, Samsal Posal 三殺菩薩, Ch'ŏnsan'gap 穿山甲, and Nat'odu 羅土頭.

32. Yu, *Ŏu yadam*, 206.

33. Chang, "Chosŏn sidae kunggwŏl changsikki wa chapsang."

34. On the ritual roots of Chinese theater, see Tanaka's classic study *Chūgoku engekishi*. See also, van der Loon, "Les origines rituelles du theatre chinois"; Johnson, "Actions Speak Louder than Words"; Chen, "Ritual Roots of the Theatrical Prohibitions"; Ye, *Zongjiao yu xiju yanjiu conggao;* and Lin, *Mingdai zongjiao xiqu yanjiu.*

35. Tanaka, *Zhongguo xiju shi,* 79–83. Since many ritual dramas center on the hagiographies of cult figures whose historical origins predate the Song, Tanaka has elsewhere argued that the repertoire of exorcistic ritual dramas may have been first standardized during the Song. Tanaka, "Chūgoku shoki engeki shiron," 18.

36. See Dudbridge, *The Hsi-yu chi,* chap. 5.

37. The script is reproduced in Cai, *Xiyou ji ziliao huibian,* vol. 1, 348–426. Dudbridge discusses the script and provides a synopsis of its content in *The Hsi-yu Chi,* 76–89 and 193–200. The play was initially identified as the lost work of Wu Changling then later attributed to Yang Jingxian. In an analysis of the text, Howard Goldblatt concluded that, while the script does contain material from the Yuan dynasty that could plausibly be traced to Yang Jingxian, the received edition also uses theatrical conventions characteristic

of the Ming dynasty. The script thus appears to be a compilation of once independent plays that were edited together into their present form sometime in the early seventeenth century. Goldblatt, "The *Hsi-yu chi* Play."

38. *Yang Donglai xiansheng piping* Xiyou ji, 174a.

39. Wang, *Ding zheng Wu she bian,* 728a.

40. Ibid., 728a.

41. Ibid., 730b.

42. The original handwritten manuscript is reproduced in *Zhonghua xiqu,* vol. 3 (1987). An annotated edition has been made by Han et al. in the same journal issue. The manuscript, copied in 1574, undoubtedly preserves earlier material. Some of the titles of songs and dramas listed in the text are known from the Tang, Song, and Yuan dynasties, and Cai Tieying has speculated that the text preserves traditions dating to the thirteenth century or earlier. More conservative estimates date the festival in its present form to sometime in the early Ming dynasty (1368–1644). See, for example, Cao and Yang, "*Lijie chuanbu* suo zai *Xiyou* xiqu kao." A recent attempt to recreate and revive the festival is discussed in Zavidovskaya, "Celestial and Human Audience of the Traditional Opera."

43. Han et. al., "*Ying shen saishe lijie chuanbu sishi qu gongdiao:* zhushi," 110–112.

44. For a detailed study of New Year festivals in Shanxi province, see Johnson, *Spectacle and Sacrifice.*

45. This and other astral deities are mentioned in passing in the *Journey to the West* novel, but they have no special relationship to the Tang Monk or his pilgrimage. The Mao lunar lodge corresponds with the Pleiades asterism in Western astrology and Kṛttikā in the Indic system. As Jeffrey Kotyk has pointed out (in a personal communication), the date of the historical Xuanzang's death—the fourth day of the second lunar month—is associated with the Mao lunar lodge. This raises the intriguing possibility that ritual performances of Xuanzang's pilgrimage served as offerings to the spirit of the lunar lodge ascendant at the time of his death.

46. Hao, "Cong yishi dao xiju," 222.

47. Several of the other dramas listed in the *Protocol*—"The Bear Spirit Steals Treasure" (Xiongjing daobao 熊精盜寶), "Hariti Uncovers the Bowl" (Guizimu jiebo 鬼子母揭缽), "Queen Mother's Peach Banquet" (Wangmu niangniang pantao hui 王母娘娘蟠桃會), "Dragon King of Jing River Makes Trouble for the Fortune Teller" (Jinghe Longwang nan shenke xiansheng 涇河龍王難神課先生), and "Twenty Eight Lodges Disturb the Heavenly Palace" (Ershiba xiu nao Tiangong 二十八宿鬧天宮)—were part of the larger Obtaining the West narrative by the late sixteenth century. The cast lists for these plays in the *Protocol* do not include any of the main protagonists of the narrative, however, so it is unclear if these dramas were understood as part of the same story-cycle when they were performed during the festival.

48. Han et al., "*Ying shen saishe lijie,*" 115.

49. The *Record of Buddhist Monasteries in Luoyang,* for example, records that one of the monasteries within the city walls had a statue of the Buddha seated atop a six-tusked white elephant. Every year, on the fourth day of the fourth month, this icon would be taken around the city in a raucous procession led by an "evil-dispelling lion." "Sword swallowers and fire-spitters rushed forward together, flagstaff climbers and rope walkers were strange and unusual. Their marvelous skills and peculiar costumes were unmatched in the capital. Wherever the statue stopped, it was encircled by a wall of spectators. With people trampling over one another, there were always casualties," Yang, *Luoyang qielan ji,* 1002c17–20. Translation after Wang, *A Record of Buddhist Monasteries,* 46.

50. On Zhu Youdun's play, see Chen, "Shu 'Wenshu pusa xiang shizi' zaju," and Idema, "The Capture of the Tsou-yü."

51. On the relationship between *nuo* and lion dances, including a discussion of Xuanzang's role in the tradition, see Gao, "Shua shizi yu nuo wenhua guanxi lice."

52. A *gigaku* performance titled Genjō sanzō e taisai 玄奘三蔵会大祭, which features Xuanzang taming a lion, has been held at Yakushiji in Nara every May since 1992. (Traditional *gigaku* performances died out during the Kamakura period and were re-created, on the basis of extant masks and descriptions, only recently.) The Pongsan mask dance, traditionally performed during the Tano Festival in the fifth lunar month in North Korea, reenacts the Black Rooster Kingdom episode known from the hundred-chapter *Journey to the West.* See Wall, "Transformations of *Xiyouji,*" 65–69.

53. One such dance takes place during the Spring Festival, Lantern Festival, and annual temple festivals for local gods in the Dapu 大埔 region of Guangdong province. In this ritual, known as the Golden Lion Dance (金狮舞), Immortal Lion Dance (仙狮舞), or Five Ghosts Tease the Golden Lion (五鬼弄金狮), a buddha tames the wild beast with a fan and a bundle of leaves, while two Sun Wukong, one Zhu Bajie, one Sha Monk, and one hunchbacked monk perform a series of acrobatic leaps over tables set up in the middle of the ritual space. At the end of the performance, after much soothing and cajoling, the lion is leashed and led away. Villagers explain the pairing of characters from the Obtaining the Scriptures narrative with the lion not by reference to the hundred-chapter novel but to events that supposedly took place during Xuanzang's pilgrimage to India. On encountering a poisonous fog, they say, Xuanzang learned there was a powerful lion immortal dwelling on a nearby mountain. He sent Sun Wukong, Zhu Bajie, and Sha Monk to lure the lion spirit out of hiding and enlist him in dispelling the pestilential haze. See Zhu, *Zhonghua wudao zhi: Guangdong juan,* 125–126. Similar exorcistic rites also are performed at lunar New Year celebrations in Yunnan, Guizhou, and Sichuan provinces. These dances go by various names—Lion Lantern (狮灯), Earth Lion (地狮子), Beating the Lion (班打狮子), Dance of the Journey to the West (跳西游)— but they all feature a masked monk and a monkey subduing a lion.

54. The meaning of *paosong* is not entirely clear. It presumably referred to popular Buddhist stories adapted for singing or chanting.

55. Li, *Jie'an laoren manbi*, 173. Translation modified from Idema, "Narrative daoqing," 100.

56. One account from 1930 reports a seller of medicinal candies singing "Journey to the West" *daoqing* to attract customers. See Hou, *Hou Baolin zizhuan*, 26.

57. Wang, *Jiangsu daoqing kaolun*, 99–106.

58. The Tongzhou region includes the counties of Nantong 南通, Rugao 如皋, Rudong 如東, Haimen 海門, and Hai'an 海安, and the city of Qidong 啟東—an area spread over nearly five thousand square miles.

59. Published versions include Zhu and Huang, *Jianghuai shenshu*; Jiang, *Xianghuo xi kao*; and Cao, *Jiangsu Nantong tongzi jisi yishi juben*. For a detailed study of Xianghuo rituals performed in Jiangsu's Liuhe country, see Huang, *Jiangsu Liuhe xian Ma'an xiang*.

60. Shao, *Zhou sheng zi*, 36b–37a.

61. Xuan, "Wu xian," 6:12. Translation slightly modified from Lin, "The Life and Religious Culture of the Freshwater Boat People," 151–152.

62. On the dress and makeup of Tongzi, see Shiga, "Kōsoshō Nantsū no minzoku geinō," 74–75.

63. See Che et al., "Jiangsu Nantong de Tongzi xi he Taiping hui," 174.

64. The "Hongmen" of the title refers to one of the two Tongzi halls established in the Liuhe region of Jiangsu province. The original Hongmen Hall 洪門堂 (or Hongshan tang 洪山堂) was, according to legend, established for *tongzi* by Tang Taizong. The altars used during Tongzi rites are accordingly known as Hongshan altars. Cao, "Jianghai pingyuan shang de gu nuo yufeng," 189–190.

65. The pairing of stories of Taizong's journey to hell and Wei Jiulang's cosmic travels are central to rituals performed by boat people of southwestern Shandong and northern Jiangsu. The narrative of these ritual cycles is similar to those performed in Tongzhou, with Taizong vowing to offer melons, to send a monk to the west, and to petition the gods, though *Journey to the West* is not included among the rituals. See Lin, "The Life and Religious Culture of the Freshwater Boat People."

66. For discussions of the closely related traditions of "scripture-telling" in neighboring areas, see Berëzkin, "Scripture-telling (*jiangjing*) in the Zhangjiagang Area"; Berëzkin, "On the Survival of the Traditional Ritualized Performance Art in Modern China"; and Bender, "A Description of 'Jiangjing' (Telling Scriptures) Services."

67. The entire text is transcribed in Huang, *Jiangsu Liuhe xian*, 133–183. A photograph of one of a set of hanging scrolls featuring the figures from *Journey to the West* displayed on the altar during the ritual is reproduced on page 280.

68. Wang, "Wushu, yishu de jiehe yu fenli," 133.

69. One list, recorded by Cao Lin in 1990 in the village of Si'an 四安 during a festival for averting disasters, provides the names of over seventy deities. Among the first ten are Sha Monk, Zhu Bajie, Sun Wukong, and the Tang Monk. Cao, "Jianghai pingyuan," 196–198.

70. The most detailed account of a large-scale, communal Tongzi ritual comes from Cao Lin's fieldwork in the village of Gongyuan in 1992, *Jiangsu sheng Nantong shi*.

71. According to Jiang Yan, these types of rituals typically are sponsored by farmers and the proprietors of small businesses. The organizer (*jiaoshou* 醮手) invites a guest master (*keshi* 客師) on behalf of the host family (*huizhu* 會主). The guest master is responsible for reciting the repentance texts, summoning the spirits, and performing ritual dramas and other ceremonies. The fees paid by the sponsoring family are usually split evenly between the organizer and the guest master. Jiang, *Xianghuo xi kao*, 17–18. For a detailed report on a private *tongzi* ritual held in the village of Beidian 北店 in 1993, see Cao, *Jiangsu sheng Tongzhou shi*.

72. Che et al., "Jiangsu Nantong de tongzi xi," 179.

73. Bin, *Wuyue minjian xinyang minsu*, 110.

74. Cao, *Jiangsu Nantong tongzi jisi*, 88–123.

75. Cao, "Jianghai pingyuan," 205–206.

76. See, for example, Zhu, "Wu Cheng'en *Xiyou ji* yu nuoge."

77. Ramanujan, "Three Hundred Ramayanas," 46.

Chapter 4: Psychopomp

Epitaph: Didion, *We Tell Ourselves Stories in Order to Live*, 185.

1. http://blog.sina.com.tw/8256/article.php?pbgid=8256&entryid=575214 (accessed 9/20/2021).

2. Yang, *Shenzong zhuiyuan-tushuo Taiwan sangli*, 32–133. See also, Yang, "Kejia Shijiao sangzang yishi 'qu jing' keyi yanjiu," 38.

3. Oxfeld, "When You Drink Water, Think of Its Source," 975.

4. "Huayi bai shan xiao wei xian *Xiyou ji* renwu songbin."

5. "Ling lei songxing!" and Dudbridge, "The *Hsi-yu chi* Monkey," 272.

6. Yang, *Shenzong zhuiyuan*, 132–133; Huang, *Genzhe xiangtouzhen zou*, 104–105.

7. See, for example, Seidel, "Traces of Han Religion in Funeral Texts," and Nickerson, "Opening the Way."

8. On the history and function of this ritual, see Orzech, "Fang Yankou and Pudu."

9. In the *Kāraṇḍavyūha Sūtra* (Ch. *Fo shuo dasheng zhuangyan baowang jing*), translated into Chinese by Tian Xizai 天息災 (d. 1000) in 983, Avalokiteśvara enters the Avīci Hell and extinguishes its flames with water. He then moves on to the realm of hungry ghosts and, emanating water from his fingers, toes, and the pores of his skin, feeds the ghosts so they may be reborn as bodhisattvas in the Pure Land of Sukhāvati. See Studholme, *The Origins of Oṃ Maṇipadme Hūṃ*, 122–123.

10. Liu, *Taibei shi Songshan qi an jian jiao jidian*, 145.

11. Asano, *Hishō tenkai: dōshi no gihō*, 216–219; Yan, "Zhihu Dashiye ji qi yishi de tantao," 28 and 197.

12. *Xiyou ji*, 1:123; *Journey*, 1:273. The "Taizong in Hell" section of the larger narrative circulated as an independent text as early as the eighth century and was appended to the Obtaining the Scriptures story, presumably on the basis of thematic and historical resonance, sometime before the fifteenth century. A partial *bianwen* version of this story, titled *Tang Taizong ru ming ji* 唐太宗入冥記, was found at Dunhuang. It is translated by Arthur Waley with the English title "T'ai Tsung in Hell."

13. *Xiyou ji*, 1:134; *Journey*, 1:287.

14. *Xiyou ji*, 1:337, 2:690; *Journey*, 2:48, 3:99.

15. *Xiyou ji*, 2:1189; *Journey*, 4:381. References to the Ghost Festival run throughout the novel. It is on the fifteenth day of the seventh month, for example, that the Buddha asks Avalokiteśvara to help him find someone to deliver scriptures to the land of the East (chap. 8). When, in chapter 24, an immortal encounters Xuanzang, he recognizes him from a Ghost Festival held five hundred years earlier.

16. Teiser, "The Ritual behind the Opera," 192.

17. The sutra is translated by Teiser in *The Ghost Festival in Medieval China*, 49–54.

18. See, for example, Mair's translation of the "Transformation Text on Mahā-maudgalyāyana Rescuing His Mother from the Underworld."

19. Johnson, "Actions Speak Louder Than Words," 26.

20. *Xiyou ji*, 1:131; *Journey*, 1: 283.

21. *Xiyou ji*, 1:133; *Journey*, 1: 285.

22. See Qitao Guo's excellent study, *Ritual Opera and Mercantile Lineage*.

23. Zheng, *Xinbian Mulian jiu mu quanshan xiwen*, 426b.

24. Ibid., scenes fifty-seven and fifty-eight, 451a–452b.

25. Ibid., 458a, 462a, 463b, 464b.

26. Ibid., 465a. This scene, "Capturing Sha Monk" (擒沙和尚), is missing from the index but included in the script itself, between scenes 65 and 66.

27. Zhu, *Mulian xi yanjiu*; Miao, "Liang tao xiyou gushi de niujie," 108–121; Nakano, *Son Gokū no tanjo*, 78–85.

28. Guan, *Zhuangyuan tang Chen mu jiao zi*, 567 [37a in original script].

29. See, for example, Ota, "A New Study on the Formation of the Hsi-yu chi," 105; Xu, "Mulian xi san ti," 170; and Liu, *Xiyou ji yanjiu ziliao*, 480–481.

30. Another example of narrative overlap occurs in *Journey to the South* (*Nanyou ji* 南遊記), where the protagonist Huaguang transforms himself into the Great Sage Equal to Heaven and steals the peaches of immortality from the garden of the Queen Mother of the West. He then feeds these peaches to his mother, a cannibalistic demon, who is, thereafter, released from hell. See Cedzich, "The Cult of Wu-t'ung," 151.

31. See, for example, Mao, *Anhui Mulian xi ziliao ji,* 67–68; Issei, *Chūgoku chinkon engeki kenkyū,* 332; Dean, "Lei Yu-sheng ("Thunder Is Noisy")," 52; Zhu, "Mulian xi zhong de Sun Wukong gushi xukao"; and Xu, "*Xiyou ji* yanjiu er ti," 123–124.

32. The *Hell Volume* (*Diyu ce* 地獄冊) was last copied in 1948, but Ye Mingsheng speculates that the play may date from as early as the fourteenth century. Ye, "Daojiao Mulian xi Sun Xingzhe xingxiang," 156.

33. The character "*xing*" 杏 is most likely an error for the homophonous "*xing*" 行.

34. The person playing Sun Wukong, who has a prominent speaking role, wears a monkey mask over his face and a red cloth around his head. He is clothed in a white jacket with a red sash around his waist. Ye Mingsheng believes the monkey in this drama originated from monkey worship in Fujian that predated the *Xiyouji* and only later became conflated with that story-cycle. Legends about Sun Wukong, Ye speculates, must have originated in the late Tang/early Song and were later brought from the north to Fujian during the Five Dynasties. Ye, "Daojiao Mulian xi," 166.

35. Zhu Bajie, wearing a pig mask, a black shirt, a red cloth tied around his head, a red sash around his waist, and straw sandals, has no speaking part.

36. Ye, "Daojiao Mulian xi," 159. See also, Ye, "Zhangping daotan posha sai yishi."

37. Wang, "Genre and Empire," 141.

38. See Xie Jian's study of the *Kuangfu xiyou* 枉府西遊, "Difang yishi yu yishi ju." According to field work carried out in Taiwan's Miaoli county by Yu Huiyuan, on the sixth and seventh days after a person's death, a ceremony known as "holding a feast" (作齋) is performed. A ritual space is set up outside the family's home and a series of murals, including images of the Three Purities, the Ten Courts of hell, the Western Pure Land, and the Tang Monk Obtains Scriptures from Western Heaven, are hung along the walls. In the evening, scenes from Xuanzang's pilgrimage are enacted by masked performers. A ritual master then leads the family of the deceased around a makeshift bridge several times, singing songs about Mulian rescuing his mother and the Tang Monk obtaining scriptures. The family then burns a "bridge fee" to bribe malicious ghosts so they do not harass the spirit of the dead. Yu, "Kejia Shijiao sangzang yishi ji qi yinyue zhi yanjiu," 42. A recording of this performance at a funeral in 2001 was made by Li Maoshun: "Miaoli Kejia zhuang zuo gongde yishi."

39. *Hunyuan hongyang linfan Piaogao jing,* 718–719. Dizang bodhisattva also was sometimes identified as a reincarnation of Mulian, and for some modern devotees all three monks are understood as distinct emanations of the same divine cleric. Dizang bodhisattva's former life as Mulian is recounted in *Huitu Sanjiao yuanliu soushen daquan,* 308. Xie Jian, in her study of ritual dramas in southwestern Guangxi, notes that Xuanzang, Dizang, and the Pole Bearing monk (何擔和尚) all are considered incarnations of Mulian. Xie, "Difang yishi yu yishi ju," 146–147.

40. The same phenomenon is known from Greek mythology, where inter-textual allusions evoke "the history of not only a single character but also an entire dynasty or a complex of companions who are associated with that character." According to Sarah Johnston, "a well-known character may be 'crossed over' into a new myth that a poet is creating and used to endorse the new myth by his or her mere presence." Johnston, *The Story of Myth*, 25–26.

41. On Mogong, see Zhou, *Mojiao yu Mo wenhua*.

42. Holm, "The Tao among the Zhuang," 387.

43. For an overview of Zhuang language and religious culture, see Holm, *Recalling Lost Souls*.

44. The Mogong traditions studied by Wang Xiyuan also draw from several Daoist traditions, including Qingwei 請微, Tianxin Zhengfa 天心正法, Hunyuan 混元, and Lingbao 靈寶.

45. Wang, *Guixi minjian mimi zongjiao*, 493.

46. The entire text is transcribed in Wang, *Guixi minjian mimi zongjiao*, 493–505.

47. Wang, *Guixi minjian mimi zongjiao*, 136. Che Xilun has suggested that this ritual belongs to a genre of mortuary rites known as "parting rituals" (*jianxing daochang* 餞行道場) that were performed by Buddhist monks for the laity after the Song dynasty. Che, *Zhongguo baojuan yanjiu*, 80.

48. Wang, *Guixi minjian mimi zongjiao*, 517–521.

49. See Che, *Zhongguo baojuan yanjiu*, 79–80; and "Fojiao yu Zhongguo baojuan," 319–322.

50. Chen, "Xin faxian de liang zhong *Xiyou baojuan* kaobian," 48.

51. These traditions have been documented in detail by David Holm. See his *Killing a Buffalo for the Ancestors;* "The Ancient Song of Doengving"; and "The Exemplar of Filial Piety."

52. In central Guangxi province, ritual masters, ethnically Han "military" priests of the Plum Mountain (Meishan 梅山) Daoist tradition, are traditionally called to officiate at funerals. See Alberts, "From Yao to Now"; and Sing, "The Interrelation between Dao-Fa and the Meishan Daoism."

53. Qin, "Yishi chuancheng zhi wenben meijie," 233.

54. "Tang seng qing jing chang" 唐僧请经唱, handwritten manuscript, summarized in Qin, *Yishi chuantong yu difang wenhua jian'gou*, 116–117.

55. Another oral account, also recorded by Qin Yanjia, tells how ritual masters and Daoist priests once held a contest of magical powers. The ritual masters lost, but Taishang Laojun (Laozi) took pity on them and sent the Tang Monk to Western Heaven to obtain the scriptures. The texts the Tang Monk brought back now are used by both Daoists and ritual masters, who frequently work together to save the souls of the dead (Qin, "Yishi chuancheng zhi wenben meijie," 233). A separate hymn describes how, when the Tang Monk and his companions were returning to China, they fell in a river,

soaking the scriptures. As the texts were drying, an old ox came along and ate them. Sun Wukong shrank himself down and entered the ox's stomach and read the texts aloud so the Tang Monk could transcribe them outside. Some of the texts were chewed beyond recognition, however, and could not be reconstituted. It is for this reason that the ritual texts can only liberate the spirits of the dead. In their complete form, they had the power to bring the dead back to life. See "Qu Xitian qing jingjiao change" 去西天请经教唱歌, summarized in Tan, "Zhuangzu qu jing gushi de tese," 78–81.

56. According to Meng Yuanyao 蒙元耀, a specialist in Zhuang manuscripts, ritual texts based on Obtaining the Scriptures narratives written in Zhuang script are widespread throughout Zhuang regions. Personal communication: July 16, 2019. For a brief discussion of ritual dramas involving Xuanzang performed in Hainan, Bangkok, and Singapore, see van der Loon, "Fashi xi chutan."

57. "Fomen qing jing ke" 佛門請經科. Hou, "*Fomen qing jing ke*," 371–496. I am grateful to professor Hou for sharing these materials with me prior to their publication.

58. For example, two liturgical texts collected from the Tujia 土家 village of Qinggang ping 青岡坪 contain entire passages that are identical to the *Ritual of the Buddhist's Obtaining the Scriptures*. The two texts are transcribed in Zuo, "*Yujia qu jing daochang*," 132–133. In two other Tujia villages (Huangmao ping 黃茅坪 and Lan'gan ping 栏杆坪), located roughly one hundred and twenty miles from Qinggang ping, yet another version of the Obtaining the Scriptures narrative is performed during funerals. This text, which takes about forty minutes to recite, contains some of the same passages found in the *Buddhist's Journey*. See Qi, *Exi Tujiazu sangzang yishi yinyue de wenhua yanjiu*, 106–107, 123–124, 149, 310–312, 350–351.

59. Yang, "Dongting hu yuanqu Fojiao daochang," 285–286. On the Pu'an tradition, see Lagerwey, "Popular Ritual Specialists in West Central Fujian."

60. The manuscripts are transcribed by Liu in "Dushan Buyizu minjian xinyang," 139–143.

61. Buyi communities in Guangxi also maintain traditions of *nuo*-style masked dances featuring the Tang Monk and other figures from the Obtaining the Scriptures narrative. See Wu, "Wenhua dili shiyu zhong."

62. *Fomen qing jing kai chan ke* 佛門請經開懺科. Hou, "*Fomen qing jing ke*," 389–401.

63. Other liturgies give slightly different lists of the sutras and repentance texts obtained by the Tang Monk. For a list of all texts mentioned in Obtaining the Scriptures liturgies, see Hou, "*Fomen qing jing ke*," 105. Xuanzang's catalogue is reproduced in the "Xitian daxiaosheng jinglü lun bing zai Tangdu shu mulu," 127. The "Tangseng wang Xitian qu jing mulu" 唐僧往西天取經目錄, published in 1427, appears to be the basis for the texts listed in the hundred-chapter novel.

64. "Fomen yin jing kefan" 佛門迎經科範. Hou, "*Fomen qing jing ke*," 429–440. Similar scenes continue to be played out during funerals in Taiwan. In rituals performed

by Shijiao masters, for example, there is a standard rite held toward the beginning of the ceremony known as "requesting the scriptures" (*qing jing* 請經). The performance begins with a ritual master playing Śākyamuni Buddha speaking to another master playing the Tang Monk. The Buddha asks the Tang Monk why he has come from such a great distance, and the Tang Monk explains that he has come in search of repentance texts. After successfully answering a series of questions posed by the Buddha, the Tang Monk receives the requested volumes along with instructions on their proper use for the salvation of the dead. Yang, "Taiwan Shijiao sangzang badu fashi," 146–147.

65. *Qing jing ke* 請經科. Hou, "*Fomen qing jing ke*," 378–383.

66. There also is a vague reference to an earlier ritual drama performed in Xiamen in the 1830s that featured Mulian as well as a pig, a monkey, and various spirits and ghosts. According to Zhou Kai 周凱 (1779–1837), "The custom in Xia[men] is to put on plays, commonly called '*zachu*' 雜出. Taking 'Mulian Rescues his Mother' as the [main] theme, they mix in scenes involving Pig, Monkey, spirits, and ghosts. In addition to shaven-headed monks, there are also [exorcistic] performance troupes dressed in hideous fashion, with foul language of all manner on display. Men and women assemble to watch without the slightest chaperoning or restriction, mingling with the mourning family as a group . . . In disordering social norms, injuring manners, and destroying customs, nothing is more serious than these [funeral practices]." Zhou, (*Daoguang*) *Xiamen zhi,* 15:6b–7a. Translation after Flanigan, "Sacred Songs of the Central Altar," 502.

67. Chen, *Hexiao zuben Xinzhu xian caifang ce,* 386.

68. On these figures, see Chen, "Taiwan chuantong Fojiao yishi."

69. For a contemporary account of Shijiao funeral rites in Xinzhu county, which still include masked performers representing the Tang Monk, Sun Wukong, and Zhu Bajie, see Liu, "Shijiao da xuepen yishi de yihan," 108–109, 149.

70. See Xie, "Local Community Ritual Theatre in Guangxi, South China," 207.

71. Holm, "The Ancient Song of Doengving," 72.

72. Zhou, *Mojiao yu Mo wenhua,* 37.

73. Berëzkin, *Many Faces of Mulian,* 57–58.

74. Che, *Zhongguo baojuan yanjiu,* 65–80.

75. The author and sectarian affiliation of the *Xiaoshi zhenkong baojuan* has long been debated, but Yu Songqing has made a convincing argument that it was written by Yinzong 印宗, a member of the Non-Action sect in the Shaanxi region, sometime between 1596 and 1620. (Yu, "*Xiaoshi zhenkong baojuan* kao.") The "Verse for Opening the Scriptures" (Kai jing jie 開經偈) in the *Xiaoshi zhenkong baojuan* begins with lines that are conventionally recited prior to receiving Buddhist teachings. It then goes on to extol the teachings of Śākyamuni, Laozi, and Confucius, asserting that, "The Daoists are the cap, the Confucians the shoes, and the Buddhists the robe. The three teachings are fundamentally part of one single family." These same lines appear in the *Buddhist's Journey* liturgy, suggesting a common source if not a shared origin for the two texts.

76. Chen, "Xin faxian," 57. The dating of this text is a matter of some debate. Hou Chong (*"Fomen qing jing ke,"* 106) agrees with Chen's assessment, while Che Xilun (*Zhongguo baojuan yanjiu,* 107) argues for an early Ming date.

77. Wheelock, "The Problem of Ritual Language," 66.

78. Che Xilun observed the practice of placing small clay figures of the Tang Monk and his companions in grave sites in Anhui's Tianchang county 天长县 in the 1990s. See his *Zhongguo baojuan yanjiu,* 80n3. I have seen clay figures of the five pilgrims situated on the altar at a funeral held in Taiwan in 2016.

Chapter 5: Savior

Epitaph: McCarthy, *The Crossing,* 142.

1. Chen and Cheng, *Yihetuan wenxian bianzhu yu yanjiu,* 147–148.

2. Translation slightly modified from Cohen, *History in Three Keys,* 97–98.

3. One infamous anti-Christian polemic was republished in 1891 by the Christian missionary Griffith John as *The Cause of the Riots in the Yangtse Valley.*

4. Cheng et al., *The Search for Modern China: A Documentary Collection,* 185–186.

5. Prazniak, *Of Camel Kings and Other Things,* 16. The Red Lantern Teachings (Hongdeng jiao 紅燈教) also were known as the Red Lantern Shining (Hongdeng zhao 紅燈照). On this movement, see Ono, "The Red Lanterns and the Boxer Rebellion."

6. Zhongguo shehui kexue yuan jindaishi yanjiusuo "jindaishi ziliao" bianji zubian, *Yihetuan shiliao,* 1065.

7. Peill, *The Beloved Physician of Tsang Chou,* 46.

8. Bai, *(Minguo) Hailong xian zhi,* 17:21.

9. Wu, *Gengzi xishou congtan,* 9.

10. Guan, *Quan luan wenjian lu,* 2a.

11. Kui, *Sichuan xinhai geming shiliao,* 62. Translation slightly modified from Chen, *Chinese Shadow Theater,* 124–125.

12. Chen, *(Minguo) Dazu xianzhi,* 7:7.

13. Yang, *Dongtian xuan ji,* (preface) 1a. Cf. translation in Dudbridge, *The Hsi-yu Chi,* 172–73.

14. Ibid.

15. Chen Yuanzhi 陳元之, "Xiyou ji xu" 西遊記序. In Cai, *Xiyou ji ziliao huibian,* 577–578.

16. Wang and Huang, *Xiyou zhengdao shu* (prechapter commentary on chap. 1) 5. On Wang Xiangxu and his involvement with the *Xiyou zhengdao shu,* see Widmer, "Hsi-yu Cheng-tao Shu."

17. Studies of the commentaries on the *Journey to the West* novel are too numerous to list in full, but key works include Dudbridge, "The Hundred-Chapter *Hsi-yu chi*";

Yu, "Liu I-ming on How to Read the *Hsi-yu chi*"; Robertson, "Untangling the Allegory;" Wang, "Reading the *Journey to the West*"; and Lin, "Qing sanjia *Xiyou.*"

18. For a mid-nineteenth century Buddhist commentary on the novel, see Huaiming, *Xiyou ji ji.*

19. See, for example, Yu Ji, "*Xiyou ji xu*" 西遊記序 in Cai, *Xiyou ji ziliao huibian,* 596–597. This preface claims that "the essential point [of the novel] can be summed up in one phrase: 'regain the lost mind.'" This appears to be a reference to *Mengzi* 11:11: "Mencius said, 'Benevolence is the human mind, and righteousness is the human path. To abandon this path and not follow it, to lose this mind and not know how to find it—what a pity! People lose chickens and dogs but know how to find them, yet when they lose their mind, they do not know how to find it. The way of learning is nothing other than finding this lost mind.'" According to the seventeenth-century commentator Zhang Shushen, *Journey to the West* mirrored the Confucian classic *Great Learning* (*Daxue* 大學). The path traversed by the Tang Monk and his fellow pilgrims on their way to Western Heaven was, therefore, none other than the way of filiality (*xiao dao* 孝道). Zhang, *Xin shuo* Xiyou ji, 50:1. On Zhang and his commentary, see Wang, "Rereading the *Journey to the West*," 50.

20. In Chosŏn Korea, the scholar Hŏ Kyun (1569–1618), writing just decades after the novel's publication, noted: "Although its language is not dignified, its words contain instructions for [concocting] the elixir and certainly cannot be ignored." Hŏ, "Sŏyurok pal," 249. Quanzhen inflected commentaries include Wang and Huang, *Xiyou zhengdao shu*; Chen, *Xiyou zhenquan*; and Liu, *Xiyou yuanzhi.*

21. This quote was made famous by Anaïs Nin in *Seduction of the Minotaur*, but various English versions appear in print as far back as the beginning of the nineteenth century.

22. Wang and Huang, *Xiyou zhengdao shu* (prechapter commentary on chap. ninety-seven), 1900. On the tension between reality and fantasy in commentaries on *Journey to the West*, see Robertson, "Untangling the Allegory."

23. See, for example, Luhrmann, *How God Becomes Real.*

24. Pu, "Qitian dasheng." Cf. Zeitlin, *Historian of the Strange,* 167–168.

25. *Hongyang kugong wudao jing,* 2:108.

26. On Han Taihu and the Vast Yang sect, see Seiwert and Ma, *Popular Religious Movements*, 318–342; and Shek, *Religion and Society in Late Ming,* 167–177, 276–287.

27. The history of salvational associations in China is documented in Ma and Han, *Zhongguo minjian zongjiao shi,* and Seiwert and Ma, *Popular Religious Movements.* On precious scrolls in general, see Sawada, *Zōho hōkan no kenkyū*; Overmyer, *Precious Volumes*; and Che, *Zhongguo baojuan yanjiu.* Studies of *Journey to the West* in the context of precious scrolls include Wan and Zhao, "Xiyou gushi zai Ming-Qing mimi zongjiao"; Tan, "Tong yuan er yi pai"; and Cai, "Lun Song-Yuan yilai minjian zongjiao."

28. Che Xilun argues that precious scrolls developed out of Tang and Five dynasties sutra lectures (*jiang jing wen* 講經文), liturgies (*keyi* 科儀), and repentance texts (*chanshu* 懺書). Che, *Xinyang, jiaohua, yule,* 43–63. Overmyer traces their antecedents to indigenous Buddhist sutras, transformation texts (*bianwen*), sutra lectures, Chan texts, Pure Land writings, and the teachings of Quanzhen Daoism. Overmyer, *Precious Volumes,* 9–50.

29. Luo's traditional dates are derived from a biography inserted into his writings sometime in the late sixteenth century and thus may not be reliable. Even the full name of Patriarch Luo is unknown, with different personal names given in different sources. On Patriarch Luo and the Wuwei Teachings, see ter Haar, *Practicing Scripture.*

30. *Zhengxin chuyi wu xiuzheng zizai baojuan,* 304–305.

31. *Kugong wudao juan,* 412–413. This brief biography, which appears to be a late sixteenth-century addition to Luo's earlier writings, is translated in Overmyer, *Precious Volumes,* 95.

32. ter Haar, *Practicing Scripture,* 4–5.

33. *Tanshi wuwei juan,* 185. Patriarch Luo's followers made no distinction between the historical Xuanzang and the Tang Monk of later legend. In a commentary on Patriarch Luo's *Five Books in Six Volumes* published in 1596, for example, the monk Lanfeng 蘭風 identifies the Tang Monk as Xuanzang before quoting from Emperor Taizong's celebration of Xuanzang in the imperial preface to Xuanzang's translations. *Poxie xianzheng yaoshi jing,* 119.

34. *Tanshi wuwei juan,* 159.

35. *Weiwei budong Taishan shengen jieguo baojuan,* 348–349.

36. *Hunyuan hongyang linfan Piaogao jing,* 718–719.

37. Seidel, "Taoist Messianism," 173.

38. See, for example, the sources and discussion in Kleeman, *Celestial Masters,* 128–146.

39. *Cakkavatti-sīhanāda-sutta* sections 19–20 in the *Dīgha Nikāya.* Translated by Walsh in *The Long Discourses of the Buddha,* 401–402.

40. The historical Xuanzang himself was a devotee of Maitreya. While traveling in India, he stood in wonder before the mountain where the Buddha's disciple Mahākāśyapa sat in a state of samādhi waiting to pass the Buddha's robe to Maitreya after the dissolution of the present *kalpa. Xiyu ji,* 919, c16–24; *Record,* 265. Before his death, Xuanzang vowed to be reborn among Maitreya's inner circle in *Tuṣita* Heaven so that he, too, could descend to earth together with the future Buddha. *Zhuan,* 277b4–6; *Biography,* 334.

41. On millenarian prophecies in Chinese Buddhist traditions, see Overmyer, "Folk-Buddhist Religion; Zürcher, "Prince Moonlight"; and Nattier, "Buddhist Eschatology."

42. The term "Wanli Slough" was coined by Timothy Brook. This paragraph is indebted to his discussion in *The Troubled Empire,* 64–73.

43. Plaks, *Four Masterworks,* 258.

44. Anthony Yu identified at least twenty-one passages from the novel that are lifted nearly verbatim from Daoist sources. *Journey,* 1: 43–51. Toward the end of his life, in 1222, Qiu Changchun was summoned to the court of the Mongol emperor Ghengis Khan (r. 1206–27) in Samarkand. The account of Qiu's journey is titled *Changchun zhenren xiyou ji* 長春真人西遊記 (Records of a Journey to the West by the Real Man Changchun), leading many scholars to suspect that the attribution of the *Journey to the West* novel to Qiu Changchun stems from a conflation of the titles of these two works.

45. Yang Ti's contemporary Sun Xu (1474–1547), holder of the prestigious *jinshi* degree, claimed that the demons in the narrative represent negative emotions. One should therefore, "Rely on the Novice to drive out all these enemies and know that they are controlled with the mind. The white horse carries the scriptures. The Novice [subdues] enemies and demons. Refining the elixir and gathering medicine stems completely from the mind and will." Sun, *Shaxi ji,* 15:4–5.

46. On the Yellow Teachings sect, see Seiwert and Ma, *Popular Religious Movements,* 293–318, and Shek, "Millenarianism Without Rebellion."

47. *Puming rulai wuwei liaoyi baojuan,* 158–159.

48. *Pujing rulai yaoshi tongtian baojuan,* 748.

49. Later leaders of the Yellow Heaven association listed ten generations of divine ancestors. Prior to Puming, there had been the Buddha, Zhuangzi, the Tang Monk, Kumārajīva, Mahasattva Fu, and Dīpankara. *Zhongxi cuyan baojuan,* 5:744–745.

50. The same point, that "the Tang Monk is an allegory for [what takes place] within the body," is made in the *Qingyuan miaodao xiansheng zhenjun yiliao zhenren huguo youmin zhongxiao Erlang kaishan baojuan,* 2:119. Both fascicles of this precious scroll record a publication date in the thirty-fourth year of the Jiajing era of the Great Ming [1555]. Chen Hong has argued, however, that based on references within the text, the current version must have been produced either in 1587 or 1628. Chen, "Erlang baojuan yu xiaoshuo."

51. See, for example, Xiao Tingzhi 蕭廷芝 (fl. 1260), *Jindan wenda* 金丹問答 (Questions and Answers on the Golden Elixir), translated in Pregadio, *Taoist Internal Alchemy,* 137–151.

52. Other precious scrolls replicate this system of identifications. For example, the *Precious Scroll of the Muddy Millet Water, the Marvelous Method of the Golden Elixir* (黍米泥水妙訣金丹寶卷), published anonymously in 1598, states: "the Tang Monk is the ancestor who obtained the scrolls. He transformed and became five people. At Thunderclap Monastery in Western Heaven, they obtained the *Precious Scroll of the Golden Elixir.* Of these five people, the Tang Monk is my mind; the White Horse is my will;

Bajie is my essence; Sha Monk is my life force; and Wukong is my nature. These are the five breaths having an audience at the origin, the three flowers gathering at the summit. [My] nature entered Thunderclap Monastery and obtained all sorts of scriptures and precious scrolls to deliver nine generations of deceased ancestors." *Shumi nishui miaojue jindan baojuan,* 2:69.

53. *Fo shuo lisheng liaoyi baojuan,* 5:429.

54. A disciple of Patriarch Luo, the monk Daning 大寧, correlated the pilgrims with the continents of Indian cosmology: Sun Wukong was Pūrvavideha in the east; the Dragon Horse was Jambudvīpa in the south; Sha Monk was Avaragodānīya in the west; and Zhu Bajie was Uttarakuru in the north. Xuanzang alone has no location: "Trepiṭaka Tang is the original face. Trepiṭaka is fundamentally the original person." *Mingzong xiaoyi daben baojuan,* 6:235. See also, *Yuanliu famai,* 290, and *Fozu miaoyi zhizhi xunyuan jiapu,* 300.

55. On the role of Quanzhen thought among Ming literati, see Liu, "The Penetration of Taoism into the Ming Neo-Confucianist Elite."

56. The Incense Smelling sect was alternatively known as the Teachings of the Great Seal (Hongfeng jiao 弘封教) or the Teachings of the Great Vehicle (Dacheng jiao 大乘教).

57. Naquin, "Connections between Rebellions," 340. See, also, Goodrich et al., *Dictionary of Ming Biography,* 587–589; Asai, "Minmatsu Jo Kōju no ran no shiryō nitsuite," 54–92; and de Groot, *Sectarianism and Religious Persecution in China,* 167–168.

58. Shek, "Religion and Society in Late Ming," 352.

59. *Gufo tianzhen kaozheng Longhua baojing,* 2:75–76.

60. The text of the edict is reproduced in Ma and Han, *Zhongguo minjian zongjiao shi,* 590–591.

61. Sawada, *Kōchū Haja shōben.*

62. Ibid., 57.

63. Ibid., 130. Cf. Shek, "Challenge to Orthodoxy," 379.

64. Seiwert and Ma, *Popular Religious Movements,* 333–334.

65. Naquin, *Millenarian Rebellion in China.*

66. Among the sects that resurfaced in the mid-nineteenth century was the Way of the Nine Palaces (*Jiugong dao* 九宮道), a branch of the Eight Trigrams led by the monk Li Xiangshan 李向善 (a.k.a. Puji 普濟, 1843/1850–1912). Like other communities associated with the Eight Trigrams, members of this organization actively prepared for the apocalypse but did not advocate the use of violence. Li Xiangshan, a self-proclaimed incarnation of Maitreya, claimed an ancestry that included Confucius, various buddhas, Xuanzang, Puming (the leader of the Yellow Heaven Teachings), and the reputed founder of the Eight Trigrams Teachings, Li Tingyu 李廷玉 (ca. 1643–1722). *Genben jing,* 809–814. On the history and teachings of this group, see ter Haar, "The Way of the Nine Palaces."

67. Qiao, *Cao Shun qiyi shiliao huibian*, 16, 24, and 64. On this movement, see Ma, "Xiantian jiao yu Cao Shun shijian shimo."

68. On the relationship between the Boxers, the Eight Trigrams and the Teachings of Former Heaven, see Satō, "Giwadan (ken) genryū."

69. For a brief overview of the ritualistic elements of Triad groups, see Ownby, "The Heaven and Earth Society as Popular Religion." A more comprehensive treatment is provided in ter Haar, *Ritual & Mythology of the Chinese Triads*.

70. See Pickering, "Chinese Secret Societies," 5, and Schlegel, *Thian Ti Hwui*, 109–111. The manual reproduced and translated by Schlegel was obtained in Sumatra in 1845, but similar accounts have been reported elsewhere. The scene of the Hong Child on Fire Mountain is illustrated in a manual printed in 1892 now in the collection of the Clinton Museum in British Columbia. Images of the text are available on the website of the Chinese in Northwest America Research Committee: http://www.cinarc.org/Freemasons .html.

71. The crossing of Fire Mountain is a common motif in ritual traditions deriving from mainland China. As in Triad ceremonies, the passage typically symbolizes rebirth and has been incorporated into mortuary rites—the crossing of the deceased into the ancestral realm—and shamanic initiation rites. For an example of the former, see the description of "Teasing Guanyin" (Nong Guanyin 弄觀音) in Yang, "Taiwan Shijiao sangzang badu fashi," 247–249. On the latter, see Guo, "Mongolian Shaman Initiation Rites," 360.

72. *Guiyuan baofa*, 19–20.

73. Ibid., 42.

74. Stenz and Conrady, *Beiträge Zur Volkskunde Süd-Schantungs*, 48. See also Esherick, *The Origins of the Boxer Uprising*, 62.

75. *Pekin Mantetsu geppō*, 43. See also Baba, *Kindai chūgoku kahoku minshū to kōsōkai*, 32–38.

76. Red Guards, "Long Live the Revolutionary Rebel Spirit of the Proletariat," 21.

77. The various political interpretations of the *Journey to the West* narrative by members of the Chinese communist party are discussed in detail in Wagner, "Monkey King Subdues the White-Bone Demon."

Epilogue

Epigraph: Landy, *How to Do Things with Fictions*, 43.

1. *Xiyou ji*, vol. 2, 1164–1166; *Journey*, vol. 4, 344–346.

2. Damrosch, *What Is World Literature?*, 22.

3. In the ninety-eighth chapter of *Journey to the West*, the wordless scriptures are eventually exchanged for those with words because, according the buddha Dīpankara, Buddhist monks in China are "so stupid and blind that they will not recognize the value of these wordless scriptures." *Xiyou ji,* vol. 2, 1170; *Journey,* vol. 4, 351–352.

4. *Zhuan,* 277a17–21; *Biography,* 333.

5. Bernstein, *The Delusions of Crowds,* 7.

6. Stuart Earle Strange, personal communication (March 8, 2021).

7. *Zhuan,* 261b21–262a27; *Biography,* 230–235.

8. *Zhuan,* 249b23–c4; *Biography,* 156–157.

9. *Xiyou ji,* vol. 2, 1178–1179; *Journey,* vol. 4, 363–366.

10. Other locations include the counties of Gaotai 高台, Linze 临泽, Xiahe 夏河, and the city of Tianshui 天水, all in Gansu province; and Hejing 和静 county in Xinjiang province.

11. For an overview of the place of Obtaining the Scriptures narratives in the regional cultures of Gansu province, see Tang, *Tushuo Xiyou ji yu Zhangye.*

12. *Xiyou ji,* vol. 2, 1181; *Journey,* vol. 4, 366–368.

Appendix

1. The badly damaged Zhaoan caves are in Ansai 安塞 county. On this and other caves in this vicinity, see Yang, "Ansai xian shiku si diaocha baogao." Images of the Water Moon Avalokiteśvara from this cave are reproduced in Wei and Zhang, *Xiyou ji bihua,* 11–13.

2. Shi, Yang, and Bai, "Shaanxi Yichuan Beisong Hejiagou Foye dong shiku."

3. For surveys of this site, see Qi, "Zichang xian Zhongshan shiku," and Lü, "Shaanbei Zichang xian Zhongshan shiku."

4. This image was carved on a rock outcropping on the grounds of Yanfu Temple in Lu County 瀘縣. The scene centers on Śakyamuni, who is situated between his two disciples Mahākāśyapa and Ananda. These disciples are, in turn, flanked by the bodhisattvas Avalokiteśvara and Mahāsthāmaprāpta. Below Avalokiteśvara, who sits in the posture of royal ease, stands a monk with palms together beside a horse carrying a bundle radiating five beams of light. Another, smaller figure that resembles a monkey is positioned below Mahāsthāmaprāpta. The original stone carvings have been twice "restored" with clay and paint, but it is not clear whether the underlying forms were altered. See Mei, "Gongjiang Wen Juli, Huseng qu jing xiang ji qita."

5. Yang, "Ansai xian shiku," 66–68; Wei and Zhang, *Xiyou ji bihua,* 9–10.

6. Yang and Bai, "Yan'an shi Baota qu Shiyao shiku."

7. Liu and Wang, "Fu xian Shihong si shiku."

8. For a comprehensive study of this site, see Zhang, *Guazhou dong qian fo dong.*

9. These carvings, located on Mt. Wenshu 文殊山 near Qifengzangzu 祁丰藏族 village, are discussed in Zhang and Guo, "Wenshu shan shiku."

10. The best catalog of the Yulin cave murals is Dunhuang Yanjiu Yuan, *Zhongguo shiku: Anxi Yulin ku.*

11. The sculpture is in the Old Master Cave (Laoshi dong 老師洞) on Mount Zijin 紫金山. See An, "Shanxi Jincheng Zijin shan."

Bibliography

Abe Yasurō 阿部泰郎. "Koramu 1: shōgyō no sekai" コラム 1「聖教」の世界. In *Shin Ajia bukkyōshi 12: Nihon 2: Yakudōsuru chūsei Bukkyō* 新アジア仏教史 12 日本 II 躍動 する中世仏教, edited by Sueki Fumihiko 末木文美士, Matsuo Kenji 松尾剛次, Satō Hiroo 佐藤弘夫, Hayashi *Makoto* 林淳, and Ōkubo Ryōshun 大久牟保良峻. Tokyo: Kōsei shuppansha 佼成出版社, 2010, 58–63.

Abel, Johanna. "Ritual Drama and Dramatic Ritual in Spanish Sacramental Plays: La Margarita Preciosa (1616) between Procession and Stage." *Convivium* 6, no. 1 (2019): 148–165.

Alberts, Eli Noah. "From Yao to Now: Daoism and the Imperialization of the China/ Southeast Asia Borderlands." *Asian Ethnicity* 18, no. 2 (2017): 156–172.

An Jianfeng 安建峰. "Shanxi Jincheng Zijin shan Dayun yuan kaogu diaocha" 山西晋城 紫金山大云院考古调查. *Kaogu faxian yu diaocha* 考古发现与调查 (2016.3): 24–35.

Asai Motoi 浅井紀. "Minmatsu Jo Kōju no ran no shiryō ni tsuite 明末徐鴻儒の乱の史 料について. *Tōyō gakuhō* 東洋学報 60, no. 1–2 (1978): 54–91.

Asano Haruji 浅野春二. *Hishō tenkai: dōshi no gihō* 飛翔天界: 道士の技法. Tōkyō: Shunjūsha, 2003.

Baba Takeshi 馬場毅. *Kindai chūgoku kahoku minshū to kōsōkai* 近代中国華北民衆と紅 槍會. Tōkyō: Kyūko Shoin, 2001.

Bai Yongzhen 白永貞, ed. *(Minguo) Hailong xian zhi* (民國) 海龍縣志. Beijing: Beijing airusheng shuzihua jishu yanjiu zhongxin, 1990.

Balazs, Etienne. *Chinese Civilization and Bureaucracy: Variations on a Theme*. New Haven: Yale University Press, 1964.

Ball, Dyer. "Scraps from Chinese Mythology." *China Review* 13, no. 2 (1884): 75–85.

Beck, L. Adams. "The Chinese Pilgrim's Progress: A History of the Mind of Man." *Hibbert Journal* XX (Oct. 1921–July 1922): 5–19.

Beckwith, Sarah. *Signifying God: Social Relation and Symbolic Act in the York Corpus Christi Plays*. University of Chicago Press, 2001.

Bender, Mark. "A Description of 'Jiangjing' (Telling Scriptures) Services in Jingjiang, China." *Asian Folklore Studies* 60.1 (2001): 101–133.

Berëzkin, Rostislav. *Many Faces of Mulian: The Precious Scrolls of Late Imperial China.* Seattle: University of Washington Press, 2017.

———. "On the Survival of the Traditional Ritualized Performance Art in Modern China: A Case of Telling Scriptures by Yu Dingjun in Shanghu Town Area of Changshu City." *Journal of Chinese Ritual, Theatre and Folklore/Minsu quyi* 181 (2013): 167–222.

———. "Scripture-telling (*jiangjing*) in the Zhangjiagang Area and the History of Chinese Storytelling." *Asia Major,* 3rd Series 24, no. 1 (2011): 1–42.

Bernstein, William J. *The Delusions of Crowds: Why People Go Mad in Groups.* London: Grove Press UK, 2021.

Bin Jiang 姜彬. *Wuyue minjian xinyang minsu: Wuyue diqu minjian xinyang yu minjian wenyi guanxi de kaocha he yanjiu* 吴越民间信仰民俗: 吴越地区民间信仰与民间文艺关系的考察和研究. Shanghai: Shanghai wenyi chubanshe, 1992.

Bodde, Derk. *Festivals in Classical China: New Year and Other Annual Observances during the Han Dynasty, 206 B.C.–A.D. 220.* Princeton, NJ: Princeton University Press, 1975.

Brother Anthony of Taize. "Bethell, Hulbert, Gale and the Epic Stories of Two Pagodas." http://hompi.sogang.ac.kr/anthony/SeoulPagodaStory.html.

Brook, Timothy. *The Troubled Empire: China in the Yuan and Ming Dynasties.* Belknap Press of Harvard University Press, 2010.

Brose, Benjamin. "The Pig and the Prostitute: The Cult of Zhu Bajie in Modern Taiwan." *Journal of Chinese Religions* 46 (2018): 167–196.

———. "Resurrecting Xuanzang: The Modern Travels of a Medieval Monk." In *Recovering Buddhism in Modern China,* edited by Jan Kiely and Brooks Jessup. New York: Columbia University Press, 2016, 143–176.

———. "Taming the Monkey: Reinterpreting the *Xiyou ji* in the Early Twentieth Century." *Monumenta Serica* 68 (2020): 169–196.

———. *Xuanzang: China's Legendary Pilgrim and Translator.* Boulder, CO: Shambhala Publications, 2021.

Cai Tieying 蔡铁鹰. "Lun Song Yuan yi lai minjian zongjiao dui *Xiyou ji* de yinxiang" 论宋元以来民间宗教对 "西游记" 的影响. *Minzu wenxue yanjiu* 民族文學研究 2 (2008): 134–140.

Cai Tieying 蔡鐵鷹, ed. *Xiyou ji ziliao huibian* 西遊記資料彙編. Beijing: Zhonghua Shuju, 2010.

Candlin, George T. *Chinese Fiction.* Chicago: The Open Court Publishing Company, 1898.

———. "What Should Be Our Attitude towards the False Religions?" *Chinese Recorder and Missionary Journal* 23, no. 3 (1892): 99–110.

Cao Bingjian 曹炳建 and Yang Jun 杨俊. "*Lijie chuanbu* suo zai *Xiyou* xiqu kao—jian yu Cai Tieying deng xiansheng shangque"《礼节传簿》所载 "西游" 戏曲考—兼与蔡铁鹰等先生商榷. *Ming-Qing xiaoshuo yanjiu* 明清小说研究 76 (2005:2): 65–76.

Cao Lin 曹琳. "Jianghai pingyuan shang de gu nuo yufeng—Nantong tongzi jisi huodong gailan" 江海平原上的古儺餘風—南通童子祭祀活動概覽. *Minsu quyi* 民俗曲藝 70 (1991): 183–216.

———. *Jiangsu Nantong tongzi jisi yishi juben* 江蘇南通童子祭祀儀式劇本. Taipei: Shi Hezheng jijinhui, 2000.

———. *Jiangsu sheng Nantong shi Zhadong xiang Gongyuan cun Hanren de mianzai shenghui* 江蘇省南通市閘東鄉公園村漢人的免災勝會. *Minsu quyi* 民俗曲藝 42, 1996.

———. *Jiangsu sheng Tongzhou shi Henggang xiang Beidian cun Hushi shang tongzi yishi* 江蘇省通州市橫港鄉北店村胡氏上童子儀式. *Minsu quyi* 民俗曲藝 31, 1995.

Cedzich, Ursula-Angelika. "The Cult of Wu-t'ung/Wu-hsien in History and Fiction: The Religious Roots of the *Journey to the South*." In *Ritual and Scripture in Chinese Popular Religion: Five Studies,* edited by David Johnson. Berkeley, CA: University of California. Institute of East Asian Studies, 1995, 137–218.

Chang Yŏng-gi 張永起. "Chosŏn sidae kunggwŏl changsikki wa chapsang ŭi kiwŏn kwa ŭimi" 조선시대 궁궐 장식기와 雜像의 기원과 의미. MA thesis, Kungmin Taehakkyo Taehagwŏn, 2004.

Chanmen risong 禪門日誦. Fujian: Gushan yongquan chan si, 1886.

Chen, Jinhua. "The Tang Buddhist Palace Chapels." *Journal of Chinese Religions* 32 (2004): 101–173.

Che Xilun 车锡伦. "Fojiao yu Zhongguo baojuan" 佛教與中國寶卷. *Yuanguang Foxue xuebao* 圓光佛學學報 4 (1999.12): 293–323.

———. *Xinyang, jiaohua, yule: Zhongguo baojuan yanjiu ji qita* 信仰, 教化, 娛樂: 中國寶卷研究及其它. Taibei: Xuesheng shuju, 2002.

———. *Zhongguo baojuan yanjiu* 中国宝卷研究. Guilin: Guangxi shifan daxue chubanshe, 2009.

Che Xilun, Jin Xin 金鑫, and Yin Yi 殷仪. "Jiangsu Nantong de Tongzi xi he Taiping hui" 江苏南通的童子戏和太平会. *Dongnan wenhua* 东南文化 1 (1989): 173–181.

Chen, Fan-Pen Li. *Chinese Shadow Theatre: History, Popular Religion, and Women Warriors*. Montreal: McGill-Queen's University Press, 2007.

———. "Ritual Roots of the Theatrical Prohibitions of Late-Imperial China." *Asia Major* (Third Series), 20.1 (2007): 25–44.

Chen Guofu 陳郭甫. *Xiyou ji shiyi (Longmen xinchuan)* 西遊記釋義 (龍門心傳). Taipei: Quanzhen jiao chubanshe, 1976.

Chen Hong 陈宏. "*Erlang baojuan* yu xiaoshuo *Xiyou ji* guanxi kao"《二郎宝卷》与小说《西游记》关系考. *Gansu shehui kexue* 甘肃社会科学 (2004:2): 21–24.

Chen Shengshen 陳省身. "Taiwan chuantong Fojiao yishi senglü de wenhua jiazhi 台灣傳統佛教儀式僧侶的文化價值." *Xuanzang Foxue yanjiu* 玄奘佛學研究 27 (2017.3): 165–198.

Chen Shibin 陳士斌. *Xiyou zhenquan* 西遊真詮. Shanghai: Shanghai guji chubanshe, 1990.

Chen Wannai 陳萬鼐. "Shu 'Wenshu pusa xiang shizi' zaju" 述「文殊菩薩降獅子」雜劇. *Guoli zhongyang tushuguan kan* 國立中央圖書館館刊 2.2 (1968): 34–45.

Chen Xishan 陳習珊. (*Minguo*) *Dazu xianzhi* (民國)大足縣志. Beijing: Beijing airusheng shuzihua jishu yanjiu zhongxin, 2009.

Chen Yinchi 陈引驰. "*Da Tang Sanzang qu jing shihua* shidai xing zaiyi: yi yunwen tizhi de kaocha wei zhongxin"《大唐三藏取经诗话》时代性再议：以韵文体制的考察为中心. *Fudan xuebao (shehui kexue ban)* 复旦学报 (社会科学版) 5 (2014): 69–80.

Chen Yupi 陳毓羆. "Xin faxian de liang zhong *Xiyou baojuan* kaobian" 新發現的兩種 '西遊寶卷' 考辨. *Zhongguo wenhua* 中國文化 13 (1996.6): 48–58.

Chen Zhaolong 陳朝龍. *Hexiao zuben Xinzhu xian caifang ce* 合校足本新竹縣采訪冊. Nantou: Sheng wen xian hui, 1999.

Chen Zhenjiang 陈振江 and Cheng Xiao 程歗. *Yihetuan wenxian bianzhu yu yanjiu* 义和团文献辑注与研究. Tianjin: Tianjin renmin chubanshe, 1985.

Cheng, Pei-kai, Michael Lestz, and Jonathan Spence, eds. *The Search for Modern China: A Documentary Collection*. New York: W. W. Norton, 1999.

Chengzu 成祖. *Shen seng zhuan* 神僧傳. T50, no. 2064.

Cho Wŏn-chʼang 조원창. "Koryŏ sigi chapsang yŏnʼgu" 고려시기 잡상 연구. *Chibangsa wa chibang munhwa* 지방사와 지방문화16.1 (2013): 7–40.

Chŏng Ŭn-u 鄭恩雨, "Kyŏngchʼŏn-saji 10 chʼŭng sŏktʼap kwa samse pul hoego" 敬天寺址 10 層石塔과 三世佛會考. *Misulsa Yŏnʼgu* 美術史研究 19 (2005.12): 31–58.

Chūbachi Masakazu 中鉢雅量. "*Saiyūki* no seiritsu" 西遊記の成立. *Chūgoku bungakuhō* 中國文學報 35 (October, 1983): 54–90.

Clart, Philip. "The Relationship of Myth and Cult in Chinese Popular Religion: Some Remarks on Han Xiangzi." *Xingda zhongwen xuebao* 興大中文學報 23 (2008) (Supplementary issue, zengkan 增刊): 479–513.

Cohen, Paul A. *History in Three Keys: The Boxers as Event, Experience, and Myth*. New York: Columbia University Press, 1997.

Cordier, Henri. "Théodore Pavie: Nécrologie." *T'oung Pao* 7, no. 4 (1896): 417–423.

Crosnier, Alexis. *Théodore Pavie: Le Voyageur, Le Professeur, L'écrivain, L'homme et Le Chrétien*. Angers: Lachèse, 1897.

Da fanguang Fo huayan jing 大方廣佛華嚴經. T09, no. 278.

Damrosch, David. *What Is World Literature?* Princeton, NJ: Princeton University Press, 2003.

Daoxuan 道宣. *Xu gaoseng zhuan* 續高僧傳. T50, no. 2060.

Dean, Kenneth. "Lei Yu-sheng ("Thunder Is Noisy") and Mu-Lien in the Theatrical and Funerary Traditions of Fukien. In *Ritual Opera, Operatic Ritual,* David Johnson and Beata Grant, editors, 47–85.

Deeg, Max. "Has Xuanzang Really Been in Mathurā? Interpretatio Sinica or Interpretatio Occidentalia—How to Critically Read the Records of the Chinese Pilgrim." In *Essays on East Asian Religion and Culture: Festschrift in Honour of Nishiwaki Tsuneki on the Occasion of his 65th Birthday,* edited by Christian Wittern and Shi Lishan. Kyoto, 2007, 35–73.

———. "'Show Me the Land Where the Buddha Dwelled . . .' Xuanzang's 'Record of the Western Regions' (*Xiyu ji*): A Misunderstood Text?" *China Report* 48.1–2 (2012): 89–113.

de Groot, Johann Jacob Maria. *Sectarianism and Religious Persecution in China: A Page in the History of Religions.* Amsterdam: J. Miller, 1903–1904.

de la Vaissière, Etienne. "Note sur la chronologie du voyage de Xuanzang." *Journal Asiatique* 298.1 (2010): 157–168.

Despeaux, Catherine. "*Les lectures alchimiques du Hsi-yu-chi.*" In *Religion Und Philosophie in Ostasien: Festschrift Für Hans Steininger Zum 65. Geburststag.* Hans Steininger, Hans-Hermann Schmidt, Karl-Heinz Pohl, and Gert Naundorf. Würzburg: Königshausen und Neumann, 1985, 61–75.

Didion, Joan. *We Tell Ourselves Stories in Order to Live: Collected Nonfiction.* New York: Alfred A. Knopf, 2006.

Dong You 董逌. *Guang chuan hua ba* 廣川畫跋. SKQS.

Doniger, Wendy. *The Implied Spider: Politics & Theology in Myth.* New York: Columbia University Press, 1998.

Doré, Henry. *Researches into Chinese Superstitions,* part 2, vol. VIII. Translated from the French with notes, historical and explanatory, by M. Kennelly. Shanghai: T'usewei Printing Press, 1926.

Du, Daisy Yan. *Animated Encounters: Transnational Movements of Chinese Animation, 1940s-1970s.* Honolulu: University of Hawai'i Press, 2019.

Du Guichen 杜贵晨. "Gujin zailun zhong de Sun Wukong congsi zhi su" 古今载论中的孙悟空崇祀之俗. *Jining xueyuan xuebao* 济宁学院学报 31, no. 1 (2010): 20–23.

Duan Chengshi 段成式. *Youyang zazu* 酉陽雜俎. SKQS.

Duara, Prasenjit. "Superscribing Symbols: The Myth of Guandi, Chinese God of War." *Journal of Asian Studies* 47, no. 4, 1988, 778–795.

Dudbridge, Glen. *The Hsi-yu Chi: A Study of Antecedents to the Sixteenth-Century Novel.* Cambridge: Cambridge University Press, 1970.

———. "The Hsi-yu Chi Monkey and the Fruits of the Last Ten Years." In *Books, Tales and Vernacular Culture: Selected Papers on China.* Glen Dudbridge. Leiden: Brill, 2005, 254–274.

———. "The Hundred-Chapter Hsi-yu chi and its Early Versions." *Asia Major,* 2nd series, 14 (1969): 141–191.

———. *The Legend of Miaoshan.* London: Ithaca Press, 1978.

Dunhuang Yanjiu Yuan 敦煌研究院, ed. *Zhongguo shiku: Anxi Yulin ku* 中国石窟: 安西榆林窟. Beijing: Wenwu chubanshe, 1997.

Durand-Dastes, Vincent. "A Late Qing Blossoming of the Seven Lotus: Hagiographic Novels about the Qizhen." In *Quanzhen Daoists in Chinese Society and Culture*

1500–2010, edited by Xun Liu and Vincent Goossaert. Berkeley: University of California Press, 2013, 78–112,

Ecke, Gustav, and Paul Demieville. *The Twin Pagodas of Zayton: A Study of Later Buddhist Sculpture in China.* Cambridge: Harvard University Press, 1935.

Edgren, Soren. *Southern Song Printing at Hangzhou.* Stockholm: Östasiatiska museet, 1989.

Elliott, Alan J. A. *Chinese Spirit-Medium Cults in Singapore.* London: Dept. of Anthropology, London School of Economics and Political Science, 1955.

Elman, Benjamin. *Civil Examinations and Meritocracy in Late Imperial China.* Cambridge: Harvard University Press, 2013.

Enchin 圓珍. *Nihon biku Enchin nittō guhō mokuroku* 日本比丘圓珍入唐求法目錄. T55, no. 2172.

Esherick, Joseph. *The Origins of the Boxer Uprising.* Berkeley: University of California Press, 1987.

Fan Ye 范曄. *Hou Han shu* 後漢書. Beijing: Zhonghua Shuju, 1965.

Fang Chengyu (Alex) 方称宇. *Zhongguo huaqian yu chuantong wenwua* 中国花钱与传统文化. Beijing: Shangwu yinshuguan, 2008.

Fashi xuanze ji 法師選擇記. *Zhentong Daozang* 正統道藏, no. 1481. Shanghai: Shanghai Commercial Press, 1923–1926.

Faure, Bernard. *Protectors and Predators.* Honolulu: University of Hawaiʻi Press, 2016.

Flanigan, Stephen M. "Sacred Songs of the Central Altar: Texts and Histories of the Ritual Master in the Religious World of Southern Taiwan." PhD dissertation, University of Hawaiʻi at Mānoa, 2019.

Fo shuo dasheng zhuangyan baowang jing 佛說大乘莊嚴寶王經. T20, no. 1050.

Fo shuo lisheng liaoyi baojuan 佛說利生了義寶卷. MQMZ, vol. 5.

Fo shuo yuxiu shiwang sheng qi jing 佛說預修十王生七經. *Xuzang jing* 續藏經1, no. 21. Taipei: Xinwenfeng, 1968–1970.

Fozu miaoyi zhizhi xunyuan jiapu 佛祖妙意直指尋源傢譜. MQMZ, vol. 8.

Frankfurter, David. "Narrating Power: The Theory and Practice of the Magical Historiola in Ritual Spells." In *Ancient Magic and Ritual Power,* edited by Marvin Meyer and Paul Mirecki. Leiden: Brill, 1995: 457–476.

Ganany, Noga. "Origin Narratives: Reading and Reverence in Late-Ming China." PhD dissertation, Columbia University, 2018.

Gao Dengzhi 高登智. "Shua shizi yu nuo wenhua guanxi lice" 耍狮子与傩文化关系蠡测. *Minzu yishu yanjiu* 民族艺术研究 1 (1994): 10–19.

Genben jing 根本經. MQMZ, vol. 3.

Goethe, Johann Wolfgang von, and Johann Peter Eckermann. *Conversations of Goethe with Eckermann and Soret.* Revised edition. London: G. Bell & Sons, 1883.

Goldblatt, Howard. "The *Hsi-yu chi* Play: A Critical Look at its Discovery, Authorship, and Content." *Asian Pacific Quarterly* 5–1 (1973): 31–46.

Goodrich, Luther C., and Zhaoying Fang. *Dictionary of Ming Biography, 1368–1644.* New York: Columbia University Press, 1976.

Gopnik, Adam. *Angels and Ages: A Short Book about Darwin, Lincoln, and Modern Life.* New York: Alfred A. Knopf, 2009.

Gordon, Elizabeth Anna. *Symbols of "The Way"—Far East and West.* Tokyo: Maruzen and Company, Ltd., 1916.

Guo, Qitao. *Ritual Opera and Mercantile Lineage: The Confucian Transformation of Popular Culture in Late Imperial Huizhou.* Stanford, CA: Stanford University Press, 2005.

Gufo tianzhen kaozheng Longhua baojing 古佛天真考證龍華寶經. Beijing: Beijing Airusheng shuzihua jishu yanjiu zhongxin, 2011.

Gu Puguang 顾朴光, Chen Rong 陈荣, and Zhang Shishen 张世申. *Zhongguo Guizhou minzu minjian meishu quanji: nuo mian* 中国贵州民族民间美术全集: 傩面. Guizhou: Guizhou renmin chubanshe, 2009.

Guan Hanqing 關漢卿 (13th century), attributed. *Zhuangyuan tang Chen mu jiu zi* 狀元堂陳母教子. In *Quan Yuan zaju* 全元雜劇, vol. 2, edited by Yang Jialuo 楊家駱. Taibei: Shijie shuju, 1963.

Guan He 管鶴. *Quan luan wenjian lu* 拳亂聞見錄. Shanghai: Shanghai guji chubanshe, 1995.

Guattari, Félix, and Gilles Deleuze. *A Thousand Plateaus.* London: Athlone, 1988.

Guiyuan baofa 歸原寶筏. MQMZ, vol. 9.

Guo Shuyun, "Mongolian Shaman Initiation Rites." In *Popular Religion and Shamanism.* Ma Xisha, et al. Brill, 2011, 353–374.

Han Sheng 寒声, Li Shoutian 栗守田, Yuan Shuangxi 原双喜, and Chang Zhitan 常之坦. "*Ying shen saishe lijie chuanbu sishi qu gongdiao:* zhushi"《迎神赛社礼节传簿四十曲官调》注释. *Zhonghua xiqu* 中華戲曲3 (1987): 55–117.

Hansen, Valerie. *Changing Gods in Medieval China, 1127–1276.* Princeton, NJ: Princeton University Press, 1990.

Hao Yuxiang 郝譽翔. "Cong yishi dao xiju: yige yi Zhongguo minjian ying shen saishe weili de chubu yanjiu" 從儀式到戲劇: 一個以中國民間迎神賽社為例的初步研究. *Donghua renwen xuebao* 東華人文學報 1 (August, 1999): 211–234.

Hayes, Helen M. *The Buddhist Pilgrim's Progress.* New York: E. P. Dutton, 1930.

Hŏ Kyun 許筠. "Sŏyurok pal" 西游錄跋. In *Han'guk munjip ch'onggan* 74 韓國文集叢刊. Seoul: Minjok Munhwa Ch'ujinhoe, 1991.

Holm, David L. "The Ancient Song of Doengving: A Zhuang Funeral Text from Donglan, Guangxi." *Monumenta Serica* 49 (2001): 71–140.

———. "The Exemplar of Filial Piety and the End of the Ape-Men Dong Yong in Guangxi and Guizhou Ritual Performance." *T'oung Pao,* Second Series, 90, Fasc. 1/3 (2004): 32–64.

———. *Killing a Buffalo for the Ancestors: A Zhuang Cosmological Text from Southwest China.* DeKalb, IL: Southeast Asia Publications, Center for Southeast Asian Studies, Northern Illinois University, 2003.

———. *Recalling Lost Souls: The Baeu Rodo Scriptures, Tai Cosmogonic Texts from Guangxi in Southern China.* Bangkok: White Lotus, 2004.

———. "The Tao among the Zhuang: Imported and Indigenous Aspects of Zhuang Ritual." *Minsu quyi* 民俗曲藝 117 (1999): 371–388.

Hongyang kugong wudao jing 弘陽苦功悟道經. Beijing: Beijing Airusheng shuzihua jishu yanjiu zhongxin, 2011.

Hou Baolin 侯宝林. *Hou Baolin zizhuan* 侯宝林自传. Harbin: Heilongjiang renmin chubanshe, 1982.

Hou Chong 侯冲. "*Fomen qing jing ke: Xiyou ji* yanjiu de xin ziliao"《佛门请经科》:《西游记》研究的新资料. *Zhongjiao xue yanjiu* 宗教學研究 (2013): 104–109.

———. "*Fomen qing jing ke: Xiyou ji* yanjiu de xin ziliao"《佛門請經科》:《西遊記》研究的新資料. In Xiyou ji *xinlun ji qita,* edited by Hou Chong and Wang Jianchuan: 357–496.

———. "Xuanzang: cong sengren dao xingxiang dashi" 玄奘: 從僧人到形象大使. In Xiyou ji *xinlun ji qita,* edited by Hou Chong and Wang Jianchuan, 33–62.

Hou Chong and Wang Jianchuan, eds. Xiyou ji *xinlun ji qita: laizi Fojiao yishi, xisu yu wenben de shijiao*《西遊記》新論及其他: 來自佛教儀式, 習俗與文本的視角. Xinbei: Boyang wenhua shiye youxian gongsi, 2020.

Hsia, C. T. *Classic Chinese Novel: A Critical Introduction.* Hong Kong: Chinese University Press, 2018.

Hu Shih 胡適. "The Chinese Novel." In *The English Writings of Hu Shih: Literature and Society,* vol. 1. Berlin: Springer; Beijing: Foreign Language Teaching and Research Press, 2013, 55–64.

———. "The Literary Renaissance." In *The English Writings of Hu Shih: Literature and Society,* vol. 1. Berlin: Springer; Beijing: Foreign Language Teaching and Research Press, 2013, 41–50.

———. "Lun huichu shenfo" 論毀除神佛. In *Hu Shi zaonian wencun* 胡適早年文存, Taipei: Yuanliu chuban shiye gufen youxian gongsi, 1995, 164–167.

———. "*Xiyou ji* di jiushijiu hui"《西游记》第九十九回. In *Hu Shi wencun* 胡適文存 vol. 4. Taibei: Yuandong tushu gongsi, 1953, 417–428.

———. "*Xiyou ji* kaozheng" 西游记考證. In *Hu Shi wencun* 胡適文存 vol. 2. Taibei: Yuandong tushu gongsi, 1953, 354–399.

Huaiming 懷明. *Xiyou ji ji* 西遊記記. Beijing: Shumu wenxian chubanshe, 1996.

Huang, Susan. "Reassessing Printed Buddhist Frontispieces from Xi Xia." *Zhejiang University Journal of Art and Archaeology* 1 (2014): 129–182.

Huang Wenbo 黃文博. *Genzhe xiangzhen zou* 跟著香陣走. Taipei: Taiyuan chuban, 1991.

Huang Wenhu 黃文虎. *Jiangsu Liuhe xian Ma'an xiang Wuxing cun Songzhuang ji Maji zhen Jianshan cun Longying Hanren de jiapu xianghuo shenhui* 江蘇六合縣馬鞍鄉五星村宋莊及馬集鎮尖山村壟營漢人的家譜香火神會. *Minsu quyi* 民俗曲藝 41, 1996.

"Huayi bai shan xiao wei xian *Xiyou ji* renwu songbin" 華裔百善孝為先 "西游記" 人物送殯. *Sinchew Daily* 星洲日報 (12/5/2008). http://www.sinchew.com.my/node/734416.

Huili et al. *A Biography of the Tripiṭaka Master of the Great Ci'en Monastery of the Great Tang Dynasty*. Translated by Li Rongxi. Berkeley, CA: Numata Center for Buddhist Translation and Research, 1995.

———. *Da Tang da Ci'en si Sanzang fashi zhuan* 大唐大慈恩寺三藏法師傳. T50 no. 2053.

Huitu Sanjiao yuanliu soushen daquan: fu Soushen ji 繪圖三教源流搜神大全: 附搜神記. Taibei: Lianjing chuban shiye gongsi, 1980.

Hunyuan hongyang linfan Piaogao jing 混元弘陽臨凡飄高經. MQMZ, vol. 6.

Idema, Wilt L. "The Capture of the Tsou-yü." In *Leyden Studies in Sinology: Papers Presented at the Conference Held in Celebration of the Fiftieth Anniversary of the Sinological Institute of Leyden University, December 8–12, 1980*. W. L. Idema. Leiden: Brill, 1981, 57–74.

———. "Narrative daoqing, the Legend of Han Xiangzi and the Good Life in the *Han Xiangzi jiudu Wengong daoqing quanben*." *Daoism: Religion, History and Society* no. 8 (2016): 93–150.

———. *Personal Salvation and Filial Piety: Two Precious Scroll Narratives of Guanyin and Her Acolytes*. Honolulu: University of Hawai'i Press, 2008.

Ikeda On 池田温. *Chūgoku kodai shahon shikigo shūroku* 中国古代写本識語集録. Tokyo: Tōkyō Daigaku Tōyō Bunka Kenkyūjo Kenkyū Hōkoku, 1990.

Ishii Kōsei. "Issues Surrounding the *Heart Sūtra*: Doubts Concerning Jan Nattier's Theory of a Composition by Xuánzàng." *Journal of Indian and Buddhist Studies* (Indogaku Bukkyo-gaku Kenkyu) 64.1 (2015): 499–492.

Isobe Akira 礒部彰. Saiyūki *shiryō no kenkyū* 「西遊記」資料の研究. Sendai: Tōhoku daigaku shuppansha, 2007.

———. *Tabiyuku Son Gokū: Higashi Ajia no Saiyūki* 旅行く孫悟空: 東アジアの西遊記. Tōkyō: Hanawashobō, 2011.

Ji Dejun 纪德君. "Ming-Qing xiaoshuo jieshou zhong 'bushan du' xianxiang tanlun" 明清小说接受中 "不善读" 现象探论. *Wenyi yanjiu* 文艺研究 6 (2012): 62–70.

Jiang Yan 姜燕. *Xianghuo xi kao* 香火戏考. Yangzhou: Guangling shushe, 2007.

John, Griffith. *The Cause of the Riots in the Yangtse Valley: A "Complete Picture Gallery."* Hankow, 1891. https://visualizingcultures.mit.edu/cause_of_the_riots/cr_book_02.html).

Johnson, David. "Actions Speak Louder than Words: The Cultural Significance of Chinese Opera." In David Johnson and Beata Grant, eds, *Ritual Opera, Operatic Ritual*, 1–45.

———. *Spectacle and Sacrifice: The Ritual Foundations of Village Life in North China.* Cambridge: Harvard University Asia Center, 2009.

Johnson, David G., and Beata Grant, eds. *Ritual Opera, Operatic Ritual: "Mu-lien Rescues His Mother" in Chinese Popular Culture.* Berkeley, CA: University of California, 1989.

Johnston, Sarah. *The Story of Myth.* Cambridge: Harvard University Press, 2019.

Julien, Stanislas. *Histoire de la vie de Hiouen-Thsang et de ses voyages dans l'inde, depuis l'an 629 jusqu'en 645.* Paris: Imprimerie impériale, 1853.

———. *Mémoires sur les contrées occidentales, traduit du sanscrit en chinois, en l'an 648, par Hiouen-Tshang.* Paris: Imprimerie Impériale, 1857–1858.

Jullien, François. "Naissance de l'imagination: Essai de problématique au travers de la réflexion littéraire de la Chine et de l'Occident." *Extrême-Orient, Extrême-Occident* 7 (1985): 23–81.

Kaiser, Andrew T. *Encountering China: The Evolution of Timothy Richard's Missionary Thought (1870–1891).* Eugene: Pickwick Publications, 2019.

Katz, Paul R. *Images of the Immortal: The Cult of Lü Dongbin at the Palace of Eternal Joy.* Honolulu: University of Hawai'i Press, 1999.

———. *Religion in China & Its Modern Fate.* Waltham, MA: Brandeis University Press, 2014.

Khoury, Elias. *Broken Mirrors: Sinalcol.* Humphrey Davies, trans. Brooklyn: Archipelago Books, 2015.

Kim, Jeong-Eun. "Sabangbul during the Chosŏn Dynasty: Regional Development of Buddhist Images and Rituals." PhD thesis, School of Oriental and African Studies, 2011.

Kleeman, Terry. *Celestial Masters: History of Ritual in Early Daoist Communities.* Harvard: Harvard University Asia Center, 2016.

Ko Yu-sŏp. *Songdo ŭi kojŏk* 松都 의 古蹟. Kyŏnggi-do P'aju-si: Yŏrhwadang, 2007.

Kotyk, Jeffrey. "Chinese State and Buddhist Historical Sources on Xuanzang: Historicity and the *Daci'en si sanzang fashi zhuan* 大慈恩寺三藏法師傳." *T'oung Pao* 105 (2019): 513–554.

Kōzanji Tenseki Monjo Sōgō Chōsadan 高山寺典籍文書綜合調査團, ed. *Kōzanji kyōzō komokuroku* 高山寺經藏古目錄. Tōkyō: Tōkyō Daigaku Shuppankai, 1985.

Kugong wudao juan 苦功悟道卷. MQMZ, vol. 1.

Kui Yingtao 隗瀛涛, et al. *Sichuan xinhai geming shiliao* 四川辛亥革命史料, vol 1. Chengdu: Sichuan renmin chubanshe, 1981.

Kungnip Munhwajae Yŏn'guso 국립 문화재 연구소, eds. *Kyŏngch'ŏnsa sipch'ŭng sŏkt'ap* 경천사 십층 석탑, 3 vols. Taejŏn Kwangyŏksi: Kungnip Munhwajae Yŏn'guso, 2005.

Kuusi, Matti, et al. *Finnish Folk Poetry: Epic: An Anthology in Finnish and English.* Finnish Literature Society, in assoc. with C. Hurst, London, 1977.

Kuwayama Shōshin. "How Xuanzang Learned about Nālandā." *China Report* 48: 1–2 (2012): 61–88.

Lagerwey, John. "Popular Ritual Specialists in West Central Fujian." In *Shehui, minzu yu wenhua zhanyan guoji yantao huilun wenji* 社會, 民族與文化展演國際研討會論文集. Wang Qiugui 王秋桂 et al. Taibei: Hanxue yanjiu zhongxin, 2001, 435–507.

Landy, Joshua. *How to Do Things with Fictions.* Oxford: Oxford University Press, 2014.

Lazarus, H. P. *The Nation* 156, issue 14 (April 3, 1943).

Lévi-Strauss, Claude. *The Naked Man: Introduction to a Science of Mythology,* vol. 4. New York: Harper & Row, 1981.

Li Baochuan 李保传. *Wan Laiming yanjiu* 万籁鸣研究. Chengdu: Sichuan meishu chubanshe, 2016.

Li Gang 李綱. *Liang xi ji* 梁谿集. SKQS.

Li Guotao 黎国韬. "Zai lun Sun Wukong yu nuoyi Fangxiang shi" 再论孙悟空与傩仪方相氏. *Zongjiao xue yanjiu* 宗教学研究 4 (2014): 273–278.

Li Ling 李翎, "Xuanzang huaxiang jiedu: tebie guanzhu qi mijiao tuxiang yuansu" 玄奘画像解读—特别关注其密教图像元素. *Gugong bowuyuan yuankan* 故宮博物院院刊, no. 4 (2012): 40–52.

"Ling lei songxing! Tang Sanzang songwang shengzhe dao xifang jile 另類送行! 唐三藏送往生者到西方極樂." *ETtoday* 新聞雲 (April 21, 2012). https://www.ettoday.net /news/20120421/40824.htm.

Liu Jiaji 陸家驥. *Wubai luohan faxiang* 五百羅漢法相. Taipei: Daqian Chubanshe, 2004.

Li, Qiancheng. "Rewriting of Chapter 99 of *The Journey to the West.*" *Renditions: A Chinese-English Translation Magazine* 67 (Spring 2007): 28–45.

———. "Transformations of Monkey: *Xiyou ji* Sequels and the Inward Turn." In *Snakes' Legs: Sequels, Continuations, Rewritings, and Chinese Fiction,* edited by Martin W. Huang. Honolulu: University of Hawaiʻi Press, 2004.

Li Maoshun 李茂順. "Miaoli Kejia Zhuang zuo gongde yishi" 苗栗客家莊做功德儀式. Taipei: Guoli Taibei jishu daxue tushuguan, 2001.

Li Shiren 李時人, ed. *Zhongguo jinhui xiaoshuo daquan* 中国禁毁小说大全. Hefei: Huangshan shushe, 1992.

Li Shiren 李時人 and Cai Jinghao 蔡鏡浩. "*Da Tang Sanzang qu jing shihua* chengshu shidai kaobian《大唐三藏取經詩話》成書時代考辨." *Xuzhou shifan xueyuan xuebao* 徐州師範學院學報 3 (1982): 22–30.

———. Da Tang Sanzang qu jing shihua *jiaozhu* 大唐三藏取經詩話校注. Beijing: Zhonghua shu ju, 1997.

Li Xiaoqiang 李小强 and Yao Qilin 姚淇琳. "Dazu shike Songdai liang zu qu jing tu jian shuo" 大足石刻宋代两组取经图简说. *Dunhuang yanjiu* 敦煌研究 154, no. 6 (2015): 68–74.

Li Xu 李詡. *Jie'an laoren manbi* 戒安老人漫筆. Beijing: Zhonghua shuju, 1982.

Li Yuan 李元. *Shu shui jing* 蜀水经. Shanghai: Shanghai guji chuban she, 1995.

Liang Qichao 梁啟超. "Lun xiaoshuo yu qunzhi zhi guanxi" 論小說與群治之關係. Gek Nai Cheng, trans., "On the Relationship between Fiction and the Government of the People." In *Modern Chinese Literary Thought: Writings on Literature, 1893–1945*, edited by Kirk A. Denton. Stanford: Stanford University Press, 1996, 74–81.

Lin, Ching-chih. "The Life and Religious Culture of the Freshwater Boat People of North China, 1700–Present." PhD dissertation, University of California, Berkeley, 2012.

Lin Yaling 林雅玲. "Qing sanjia *Xiyou* pingdian yuyi quanshi yanjiu" 清三家《西遊》評點寓意詮釋研究. PhD dissertation, Tunghai University, 2002.

Lin Zhili 林智莉. *Mingdai zongjiao xiqu yanjiu* 明代宗教戲曲研究. Taipei: Guojia chubanshe, 2013.

Liu Dajie 劉大杰. *Zhongguo wenxue fada shi* 中國文學發達史. Taibei: Zhonghua shuju, 1967.

Liu Lin 刘琳. "Dushan Buyizu minjian xinyang yu Hanwen zongjiao dianji yanjiu" 独山布依族民间信仰与汉文宗教典籍研究. MA thesis, Guizhou shifan daxue, 2008.

Liu Meiling 劉美玲. "Shijiao da xuepen yishi de yihan, liubian yu chuancheng: yi Xinzhu xian Hengshan xiang Chunsheng tan weili" 釋教打血盆儀式的意涵, 流變與傳承: 以新竹縣橫山鄉春盛壇為例. MA thesis, Guoli jiaotong daxue, 2011.

Liu Shufen 劉淑芬, "Gaoseng xingxiang de chuanbo yu huiliu—cong 'Xuanzang fuji tu' tanqi" 高僧形像的傳播與回流——從「玄奘負笈圖」談起. *Xu Pingfang xiansheng jinian wenji* 徐苹芳先生紀念文集. Shanghai: Shanghai guji chubanshe (2012): 333–359.

———. "Songdai Xuanzang de shenghua: tuxiang, wenwu he yiji" 宋代玄奘的聖化: 圖像, 文物和遺迹. *Zhonghua wenshi luncong* 中華文史論叢 133 (2019): 161–219.

———. "Tangdai Xuanzang de shenghua" 唐代玄奘的聖化. *Zhonghua wenshi luncong* 中華文史論叢 125 (2017): 1–57.

Liu Tingji 劉廷璣. *Zai yuan za zhi* 在園雜志. Beijing: Zhonghua shuju, 2005.

Liu Ts'un-yan [Liu Cunren] 劉存仁. "Quanzhen jiao he xiaoshuo *Xiyou ji*" 全真教和小說西遊記. *Mingbao yuekan* 明報月刊 part 1 (May 1985): 55–62; part 2 (June 1985): 59–64; part 3 (July 1985): 85–90; part 4 (August 1985): 85–90; and part 5 (September 1985): 70–74.

———. "The Penetration of Taoism into the Ming Neo-Confucianist Elite." *T'oung Pao* 57 (1971): 31–102.

Liu Yiming 劉一明. *Xiyou yuanzhi* 西遊原旨. Beijing: Zongjiao wenhua chubanshe, 2015.

Liu Yinbai 刘荫柏. Xiyou ji *yanjiu ziliao* 西游记研究资料. Shanghai: Shanghai guji chubanshe, 1990.

Liu Zhengang 刘振刚 and Wang Yufang 王玉芳. "Fu xian Shihong si shiku lidai tiji shidu yu fenxi" 富县石泓寺石窟历代题记识读与分析. *Dunhuang xue jikan* 敦煌学辑刊 no. 3 (2016): 141–152.

Liu Zhiwan 劉枝萬. *Taibei shi Songshan qi an jian jiao jidian* 臺北市松山祈安建醮祭典. Nangang: Zhongyang yanjiuyuan minzu xue yanjiusuo, 1967.

Lü Chunxiang 呂春祥. "Shaanbei Zichang xian Zhongshan shiku kaocha shilu" 陕北子长县钟山石窟考察实录. *Xibei meishu* 西北美术 no. 2 (2014): 84–87.

Lu Xun 魯迅. *Zhongguo xiaoshuo shilüe* 中國小說史略. Beijing: Renmin wenxue chubanshe, 1973. Translated into English as *A Brief History of Chinese Fiction*. Peking: Foreign Language Press, 1964.

Luhrmann, T. M. *How God Becomes Real: Kindling the Presence of Invisible Others*. Princeton, NJ: Princeton University Press, 2020.

Luo Zhenyu 羅振玉. *Jishi an congshu (chuji)* 吉石庵叢書 (初集). Shangyu: Luo shi, 1914.

Ma Xisha 马西沙. "Xiantian jiao yu Cao Shun shijian shimo" 先天教与曹顺事件始末. *Qingshi yanjiu* 清史研究 1 (1988): 16–21.

Ma Xisha and Han Bingfang 韩秉方. *Zhongguo minjian zongjiao shi* 中国民间宗教史. Beijing: Zhongguo shehui kexue chubanshe, 2017.

Mackenzie-Grieve, Averil. *A Race of Green Ginger*. London: Putnam, 1959.

Mair, Victor. "Parallels between Some Tun-huang Manuscripts and the 17th Chapter of the Kōzanji *Journey to the West*." *Cahiers d'Extrême-Asie* 3.1 (1987): 41–53.

———. "Suen Wu-kung = Hanumat? The Progress of a Scholarly Debate." *Proceedings of the Second International Conference on Sinology*. Taibei: Academia Sinica, 1989, 659–753.

———. *T'ang Transformation Texts: A Study of the Buddhist Contribution to the Rise of Vernacular Fiction and Drama in China*. Cambridge: Council on East Asian Studies, 1989.

Mao Gengru 茆更茹. *Anhui Mulian xi ziliao ji* 安徽目連戲資料集. Taibei: Shihezheng jijin hui, 1997.

Matsumoto Nobuhiro 松本信廣. *Chōsen koseki zufu* 朝鮮古蹟図譜. Keijō: Chōsen Sōtokufu, 1915.

McCarthy, Cormac. *The Crossing*. New York: Alfred A. Knopf, 1994.

McLean, Archibald. *The History of the Foreign Christian Missionary Society*. New York: Fleming H. Revell, 1919.

Mei Lin 梅林. "Gongjiang Wen Juli, Huseng qu jing xiang ji qita: Sichuan Lu xian Yanfu si Beisong shike zaoxiang kaocha jianji" 工匠文居禮、胡僧取經像及其他: 四川瀘縣延福寺北宋石刻造像考察簡記. *Yishu shi yanjiu* 藝術史研究 12 (2010): 167–187.

Meulenbeld, Mark. *Demonic Warfare: Daoism, Territorial Networks, and the History of a Ming Novel*. Honolulu: University of Hawai'i Press, 2016.

Miao Huaiming 苗怀明. "Liang tao xiyou gushi de niujie—dui *Xiyou ji* chengshu guocheng de yige cemian kaocha" 两套西游故事的扭结—对《西游记》成书过程的一个侧面考察. *Ming-Qing xiaoshuo yanjiu* 明清小说研究 83 (2007): 108–121.

———. "Lun Ming-Qing shiqi de Qitian Dasheng chongbai" 论明清时期的齐天大圣崇拜. *Kukche ŏnŏ munhak* 국제언어문학 (International Language and Literature) 24 (2011.10): 105–119.

Ming-Qing minjian zongjiao jingjuan wenxian 明清民间宗教经卷文献. Taipei: Xinwen-feng chuban gongsi, 1999.

Mingxiang 冥詳. *Datang gu sanzang Xuanzang fashi xingzhuang* 大唐故三藏玄奘法師行狀. T50, no. 2052.

Mingzong xiaoyi daben baojuan 明宗孝義達本寶卷. MQMZ, vol. 6.

Mino, Yutaka, and Katherine R. Tsiang. *Freedom of Clay and Brush through Seven Centuries in Northern China: Tz'u-chou Type Wares, 960–1600 A.D.* Bloomington: Indiana University Press, 1980.

Nakano Miyoko 中野美代子. *Son Goku no tanjō: saru no minwagaku to Saiyūki* 孫悟空の誕生: サルの民話学と「西遊記」. Tokyo: Fukutake Shoten, 1987.

———. *Xiyou ji de mimi (wai er zhong)* 西遊记的秘密 (外二种). Beijing: Zhonghua shuju, 2002.

Naquin, Susan. "Connections between Rebellions: Sect Family Networks in Qing China." *Modern China* 8, no. 3 (Jul., 1982): 337–360.

———. *Millenarian Rebellion in China: The Eight Trigrams Uprising of 1813.* New Haven: Yale University Press, 1976.

Nara Kokuritsu Hakubutsukan 奈良国立博物館. *Daitokuji denrai Gohyaku rakanzu* 大德寺伝来五百羅漢図. Nara Kokuritsu Hakubutsukan, 2014.

———. *Tenjiku e: Sanzō hōshi 3-man kiro no tabi* 天竺へ: 三蔵法師３万キロの旅 (On to India! Xuanzang's 30,000-Kilometer Trek). Nara Kokuritsu Hubutsukan, 2011.

Nara Kenritsu Bijutsukan. Saiyūki *no shiruku rōdo: Sanzō hōshi no michi:* 西遊記のシルクロ-ド: 三蔵法師の道 (*The Silk Road and the World of Xuanzang*). Tokyo: Asahi Shinbunsha, 1999.

Nattier, Jan. "Buddhist Eschatology." In *The Oxford Handbook of Eschatology,* edited by Jerry L Wallis. Oxford University Press, 2008, 151–169.

———. "The *Heart Sūtra:* A Chinese Apocryphal Text?" *Journal of the International Association of Buddhist Studies* 15, no. 2 (1992): 153–223.

Nickerson, Peter. "'Opening the Way': Exorcism, Travel, and Soteriology in Early Daoist Mortuary Practice and Its Antecedents." In *Daoist Identity: History, Lineage and Ritual,* edited by Livia Kohn and Harold D. Roth. Honolulu: University of Hawai'i Press, 2002, 58–78.

Nin, Anaïs. *Seduction of the Minotaur.* London: P. Owen, 1961.

Oldstone-Moore, Jennifer. "Alchemy and *Journey to the West:* The Cart-Slow Kingdom Episode." *Journal of Chinese Religions* 26 (1998): 51–66.

Ono, Kazuko. "The Red Lanterns and the Boxer Rebellion." In *Chinese Women in a Century of Revolution, 1850–1950,* edited by Kazuko Ono, Joshua A. Fogel, and Kathryn Bernhardt. Stanford: Stanford University Press, 1989, 47–53.

Oostveen, Daan F. "Religious Belonging in the East Asian Context: An Exploration of Rhizomatic Belonging." *Religions* 10, no. 182 (2019).

Orzech, Charles. "Fang Yankou and Pudu: Translation, Metaphor, and Religious Identity." In *Daoist Identity: History, Lineage and Ritual,* edited by Livia Kohn and Harold D. Roth. Honolulu: University of Hawai'i Press, 2002, 213–234.

Ota Tatsuo. "A New Study on the Formation of the Hsi-yu chi." *Acta Asiatica* 32 (1977): 96–113.

Ou Itaï. *Le Roman Chinois.* Paris: Les Editions Véga, 1933.

Ouyang Xiu. *Wen zhong ji* 文忠集. SKQS.

Overmyer, Daniel L. "Folk-Buddhist Religion: Creation and Eschatology in Medieval China." *History of Religions* 12.1 (1972): 42–70.

———. *Precious Volumes: An Introduction to Chinese Sectarian Scriptures from the Sixteenth and Seventeenth Centuries.* Cambridge: Harvard University Asia Center, 1999.

Ownby, David. "The Heaven and Earth Society as Popular Religion." *Journal of Asian Studies* 54, no. 4 (Nov., 1995): 1023–1046.

Oxfeld, Ellen. "'When You Drink Water, Think of Its Source': Morality, Status, and Reinvention in Rural Chinese Funerals." *Journal of Asian Studies* 63.4 (Nov., 2004): 961–990.

Palmer, David. "Folk, Popular, or Minjian Religion?" *Review of Religion and Chinese Society* 6 (2019): 155–159.

Pavie, M. Théodore. *Choix de contes et nouvelles.* Paris: B. Duprat, 1839.

———. "Etude sur le Sy-yéou-tchiu-tsuen, roman bouddhique chinois." *Journal Asiatique* series 5 vol. IX (April–May 1857): 357–392; vol. X (October–November 1857): 308–374.

———. "La vision de Pao-Ly, Legende Chinoise," *Revue des Deux-Mondes,* 2e période, tome 18, 1858, 854–867.

———. "Les trois religions de la Chine, leur antagonisme, leur developpement et leur influence." *Revue des Deux-Mondes,* Période Initiale, tome 9, 1845, 451–476.

———. *San-koué-tchy Ilan Kouroun-I Pithe: Histoire des trois royaumes, roman historique, traduit sur les textes Chinois Mandchou de la bibliothèque royale.* Tome 1, 2. Paris, 1845.

———. "Yu-Ki le Magicien, Legende Chinoise." *Revue des Deux Mondes,* Nouvelle période, tome 9, 1851, 1129–1144.

Pekin Mantetsu geppō 北京滿鐵月報 4, no. 5 (1928).

Peill, Arthur D. *The Beloved Physician of Tsang Chou: Letters of Arthur D. Peill.* London: Headley Brothers, 1908.

Pickering, W. A. "Chinese Secret Societies." *Journal of the Straits Branch of the Royal Asiatic Society* 3 (1879): 1–18.

Piotrovsky, Mikhail. *Lost Empire of the Silk Road: Buddhist Art from Khara Khoto (x–xiiith century).* Milano: Electa, 1993.

Plaks, Andrew H. *The Four Masterworks of the Ming Novel.* Princeton, NJ: Princeton University Press, 1987.

Potterf, Katheryn. "Ritualizing *The Journey to the West.*" PhD dissertation, Stanford University, 2005.

Poxie xianzheng yaoshi jing (kaixin fayao ban) 破邪顯證鑰匙經 (開心法要版). MQMZ, vol. 2.

Prazniak, Roxann. *Of Camel Kings and Other Things: Rural Rebels against Modernity in Late Imperial China.* Lanham: Rowman & Littlefield, 1999.

Pregadio, Fabrizio. *Taoist Internal Alchemy: An Anthology of Neidan Texts.* Mountain View, CA: Golden Elixir Press, 2019.

Propp, V. I͡A. *Morphology of the Folktale,* 2nd ed. University of Texas Press, 1968.

Pujing rulai yaoshi tongtian baojuan 普靜如來鑰匙通天寶卷. MQMZ, vol. 4.

Puming rulai wuwei liaoyi baojuan 普明如來無為了義寶卷. MQMZ, vol. 6.

Pu Songling 蒲松齡. "Qitian dasheng" 齊天大聖. In *Liaozhai zhiyi* 聊齋志異. Taipei: Shijie shuju, 1975, 199–202.

Qi Baiping 齐柏平. *Exi Tujiazu sangzang yishi yinyue de wenhua yanjiu* 鄂西土家族丧葬仪式音乐的文化研究. Beijing: Zhongyang minzu daxue chubanshe, 2006.

Qi Tiangu 齐天谷. "Zichang xian Zhongshan shiku diaocha ji" 子长县钟山石窟调查记. *Kaogu yu wenwu* 考古与文物 6 (1982): 39–43.

Qian Daxin 錢大昕. *Qian yan tang wen ji* 潛研堂文集. In *Xuxiu siku quanshu* 續修四庫全書 vol. 1438. Shanghai: Shanghai guji chuban she, 1995.

Qian yan qian bi Guanshiyin pusa tuoluoni shenzhou jing 千眼千臂觀世音菩薩陀羅尼神呪經. T20, no. 1057a.

Qiao Zhiqiang 乔志强. *Cao Shun qiyi shiliao huibian* 曹順起义史料汇编. Taiyuan: Shanxi renmin chubanshe, 1957.

Qin Yanjia 覃延佳. *Yishi chuantong yu difang wenhua jian'gou: Guangxi Shanglin shigong de lishi renleixue yanjiu* 仪式传统与地方文化建构: 广西上林师公的历史人类学研究. Beijing: Shehui kexue wenxian chubanshe, 2015.

———. "Yishi chuancheng zhi wenben meijie: Guangxi Shanglin xian Zhuangzu shigong jiedu fashi zhong de changben fenxi" 儀式傳承之文本媒介: 廣西上林縣壯族師公戒度法事中的唱本分析. *Minsu quyi* 民俗曲藝 185 (2014.9): 219–295.

Qingyuan miaodao xiansheng zhenjun yiliao zhenren huguo youmin zhongxiao Erlang kaishan baojuan 清源妙道顯聖眞君一了眞人護國佑民忠孝二郎開山寶卷. Beijing: Beijing Airusheng shuzihua jishu yanjiu zhongxin, 2011.

Qu Liuyi 曲六乙 and Fu Qian 錢茀. *Zhongguo nuo wenhua tonglun* 中國儺文化通論. Taibei: Taiwan xuesheng shuju, 2003.

Ramanujan, A. K. "Three Hundred Ramayanas: Five Examples and Three Thoughts on Translation." In *Many Rāmāyaṇas: The Diversity of a Narrative Tradition in South Asia,* edited by Paula Richman. Berkeley, CA: University of California Press, 1991.

Rawski, Evelyn Sakakida. *Education and Popular Literacy in Ch'ing China*. Ann Arbor: Center for Chinese Studies, 1979.

Red Guards, "Long Live the Revolutionary Rebel Spirit of the Proletariat." *Peking Review* 9.37 (Sept. 9, 1966): 21.

Richard, Timothy. *A Journey to Heaven being a Chinese Epic and Allegory dealing with the Origin of the Universe: the Evolution of Monkey to Man: the Evolution of Man to the Immortal: and Revealing the Religion, Science, and Magic, which moulded the Life of The Middle Ages of Central Asia and which underlie the civilization of the Far East to this day, by Ch'iu Ch'ang Ch'un, A.D. 1208–1288, Born 67 years before Dante*. Shanghai: Christian Literature Society's Depot, 1913.

———. *Forty-five Years in China: Reminiscences*. New York: Frederick A. Stokes, 1916.

Righter, Anne. *Shakespeare and the Idea of the Play*. London: Chatto & Windus, 1962.

Robertson, Carl A. "Untangling the Allegory: The Genuine and the Counterfeit in *Xiyou zhengdao shu* (The book to enlightenment of the journey west)." *Tamkang Review* 38, no. 1 (2007): 213–252.

Rolston, David, ed. *How to Read the Chinese Novel*. Princeton: Princeton University Press, 1990.

Rolston, David. *Traditional Chinese Fiction and Fiction Commentary: Reading and Writing between the Lines*. Stanford: Stanford University Press, 1997.

Ropp, Paul S. *Dissent in Early Modern China: Ju-Lin Wai-Shih and Ch'ing Social Criticism*. Ann Arbor: University of Michigan Press, 1981.

Rösch, Petra. *Chinese Wood Sculptures of the 11th to 13th Centuries: Images of Water Moon Guanyin in Northern Chinese Temples and Western Collections*. Stuttgart: Ibidem-Verlag, 2007.

Saito Tatuya. "Features of the Kongō-ji Version of the Further Biographies of Eminent Monks 続高僧伝: With a Focus on the Biography of Xuanzang 玄奘 in the Fourth Fascicle." *Journal of the International College for Postgraduate Buddhist Studies* 16 (2012): 69–104.

Sakaida Yukiko 坂井田夕起子. *Dare mo shiranai Saiyūki: Genjō Sanzō no ikotsu o meguru Higashi Ajia sengoshi* 誰も知らない<西遊記>: 玄奘三蔵の遺骨をめぐる東アジア戦後史. Tokyo: Ryukei shosha, 2013.

Sango, Asuka. "Buddhist Debate and the Production and Transmission of Shōgyō in Medieval Japan." *Japanese Journal of Religious Studies* 39, no. 2 (2012): 241–273.

Sangren, P. Steven. "Great Tradition and Little Traditions Reconsidered: The Question of Cultural Integration in China." *Journal of Chinese Studies* 1.1 (1984): 1–24.

Satō Kimihiko 佐藤公彦. "Giwadan (ken) genryu: Hakkekyō to Giwaken" 義和団(拳)源流: 八卦教と義和拳. *Shigaku zasshi* 史学雑誌 91.1 (1982): 43–80.

Sawada Mizuho 澤田瑞穂. *Kōchū Haja shōben: Chūgoku minkan shūkyō kessha kenkyū shiryō* 校注破邪詳弁: 中国民間宗教結社研究資料. Tokyo: Dōkyō Kankōkai, 1972.

———. *Zōho hōkan no kenkyū* 増補寶巻の研究. Tokyo: Dōkyō kankōkai, 1975.

Schlegel, Gustaaf. *Thian Ti Hwui: The Hung-League or Heaven-Earth-League. A Secret Society with the Chinese in China and India.* Batavia: Lange, 1866.

Scott, Gregory Adam. "Timothy Richard, World Religion, and Reading Christianity in Buddhist Garb." *Social Sciences and Missions* 25 (2012): 1–23.

Seidel, Anna. "Taoist Messianism." *Numen* 31.2 (1984): 161–174.

———. "Traces of Han Religion in Funeral Texts Found in Tombs." In *Dōkyō to shūkyō bunka* 道教と宗教文化, edited by Akitsuki Kan'ei 秋月觀暎. Tōkyō: Hirakawa Shuppansha, 1987, 21–57.

Seiwert, Hubert, and Xisha Ma. *Popular Religious Movements and Heterodox Sects in Chinese History.* Leiden: Brill, 2003.

Shahar, Meir. *Crazy Ji: Chinese Religion and Popular Literature.* Cambridge, MA: Harvard University Asia Center, 1998.

———. "The Lingyin Si Monkey Disciples and the Origins of Sun Wukong." *Harvard Journal of Asiatic Studies* 52, no. 1 (1992): 193–224.

———. "Vernacular Fiction and the Transmission of Gods' Cults." In *Unruly Gods: Divinity and Society in China,* edited by Meir Shahar and Robert P. Weller. Honolulu: University of Hawai'i Press, 1996, 184–211.

Shandong sheng zhongdian wenhua baohu danwei 山東省重點文物保護單位. "Tengzhou shi Guanyin ge ji ge nei de shike" 滕州市观音阁及阁内的石刻. *Meiri toutiao* 每日头条 (May 15, 2018). https://kknews.cc/zh-my/culture/6l3m2am.html.

Shao Qian 邵潛. *Zhou sheng zi* 州乘資, vol. 1. Yangzhou: Jiangsu Guangling guji keyinshe, 1986.

Shek, Richard. "Challenge to Orthodoxy: Beliefs and Values of the Eternal Mother Sects in Sixteenth- and Seventeenth-Century China." *Journal of Early Modern History* 3, no. 3 (1999): 355–393.

———. "Millenarianism Without Rebellion: The Huangtian Dao in North China." *Modern China* 8, no. 3 (Jul., 1982): 305–336.

———. "Religion and Society in Late Ming: Sectarianism and Popular Thought in 16th- and 17th-Century China." PhD dissertation, University of Michigan, 1987.

Shi Jiangang 石建剛, Yang Jun 杨军, and Bai Xiaolong 白小龙. "Shaanxi Yichuan Beisong Hejiagou Foye dong shiku diaocha yu chubu yanjiu" 陝西宜川北宋贺家沟佛爷洞石窟调查与初步研究. *Dunhuang yanjiu* 186 敦煌研究 no. 2 (2021): 50–62.

Shiga Ichiko 志賀市子. "Kōsoshō Nantsū no minzoku geinō 'Dōjigi' no kenkyū minkan shūkyōsha 'Dōji' to sono kindai 江蘇省南通の民俗芸能 '僮子戲' の研究民間宗教者 '僮子' とその近代. *Hikaku minzoku kenkyū* 比較民俗研究 5 (1992.3): 63–100.

Shumi nishui miaojue jindan baojuan 黍米泥水妙訣金丹寶卷. Beijing: Beijing Airusheng shuzihua jishu yanjiu zhongxin, 2011.

Si shamen Xuanzang shangbiao ji 寺沙門玄奘上表記. T52, no. 2119.

Sin So-yŏn 신소연. "Wŏn'gaksaji sipch'ŭng sŏkt'ap ŭi Sŏyugi puyŏng sogu" 圓覺寺址十層石搭의 西遊記浮影昭究. *Misul sahak yŏn'gu* (*Ku kogo misul*) 미술사학연구 (구 고고미술) (2006.3): 79–112.

Sing, Lui Wing. "The Interrelation between Dao-Fa and the Meishan Daoism in the Central Hunan: A Case Study of Xinhua County." *Minsu quyi* 民俗曲藝 184 (2014): 105–153.

Solonin, Kirill. "The Glimpses of Tangut Buddhism." *Central Asiatic Journal* 52, no. 1 (2008): 64–127.

Son Jihye 孫知慧. "Kindai Bukkyō no tōzai kōshō: Timoshī Richādo no Bussho honyaku to Bukkyō rikai" 近代仏教の東西交渉: ティモシー・リチャードの仏書翻訳と仏教理解. *Kansai daigaku tōzai gakujutsu kenkyūjo kiyō* 関西大学東西学術研究所紀要 48 (2015): 281–305.

Stein, Aurel. *Ruins of Desert Cathay: Personal Narrative of Explorations in Central Asia and Westernmost China*. London: MacMillan, 1912.

Stenz, Georg M., and August Conrady. *Beiträge Zur Volkskunde Süd-Schantungs*. R. Voigtländer, 1907.

Strickmann, Michel, and Bernard Faure. *Chinese Magical Medicine*. Stanford, CA: Stanford University Press, 2002.

Studholme, Alexander. *The Origins of Oṃ Maṇipadme Hūṃ: A Study of Kāraṇḍavyūha Sūtra*. Albany: State University of New York Press, 2002.

Sun Bojun 孫伯君. "Cong liang zhong Xixiawen guashu kan Hexi diqu 'Datang Sanzang' xingxiang de shenhua he zhanbu yu Fojiao de jiaorong" 从两种西夏文卦书看河西地区 "大唐三藏" 形象的神化和占卜与佛教的交融. *Minzu yanjiu* 民族研究 4 (2016): 72–78.

Sun, Hongmei. *Transforming Monkey: Adaptation and Representation of a Chinese Epic*. Seattle: University of Washington Press, 2018.

Sun Xu 孫緒. *Shaxi ji* 沙溪集. SKQS.

Taishō shinshū daizōkyō 大正新脩大藏經. Takakusu Junjirō and Watanabe Kaigyoku, eds. Tokyo: Taishō issaikyō kankōkai, 1924–1932.

Takahashi Masataka 高橋正隆. *Kyūan rokunenbon* Sangoku soshiei *no kenkyū* 久安六年本三国祖師影の研究. Kanda Kiichirō, 1969.

Takimoto Hiroyuki 瀧本弘之. *Chūgoku koten bungaku sōga shūsei* (2): Saiyūki 中国古典文学挿画集成 (2): 西游记. Tōkyō: Yūshikan, 2000.

Tan Lin 谭琳. "Tong yuan er yi pai—'Xiyou' gushi baojuan yu *Xiyou ji* bijiao yanjiu" 同源而异派—"西游" 故事宝卷与《西游记》比较研究. MA thesis, Hubei University, 2012.

Tan Shiguang 谭仕光. "Zhuangzu qu jing gushi de tese" 壮族取经故事的特色. *Guangxi daxue xuebao* (*zhexue shehui kexue ban*) 广西大学学报 (哲学社会科学版) 29 (1990.2): 78–81.

Tanshi wuwei juan 嘆世無為卷. MQMZ, vol. 1.

Tan Shuqin 谭淑琴. "*Qianfo tang bei* yu minsu wenhua"《千佛堂碑》与民俗文化. *Zhongyuan wenwu* 中原文物 6 (2012): 80–85.

Tanaka Issei 田仲一成. *Chūgoku engekishi* 中国演劇史. Tōkyō: Tōkyō Daigaku Shup-pankai, 1998. Translated into Chinese as *Zhongguo xiju shi* 中国戏剧史. Beijing: Beijing guangbo xueyuan chubanshe, 2002.

———. "Chūgoku shoki engeki shiron" 中国初期演劇史論. *Tōyō bunka* 東洋文化 71 (1990): 1–37.

Tanaka Tomoyuki 田中智行. "Ryūkoku daigaku toshokanzō *Genjō Sanzō toten yurai engi* honkoku (ichi) fu kaidai" 龍谷大学図書館蔵『玄奘三蔵渡天由来縁起』翻刻 (1) 附解題. *Tokushima daigaku kokugo kokubungaku* 徳島大学国語国文学 22 (2009.3): 1–20.

Tang Guozeng 唐国增. *Tushuo* Xiyou ji *yu Zhangye* 图说西游记与张掖. Lanzhou: Gansu wenhua chubanshe, 2015.

Taves, Ann. *Revelatory Events: Three Case Studies of the Emergence of New Spiritual Paths.* Princeton, NJ: Princeton University Press, 2016.

Taylor, George. "Chinese Folk Lore." *China Review* 16, no. 3 (1887): 163–177.

Taylor, George, and Glen Dudbridge. *Aborigines of South Taiwan in the 1880s.* Taipei: Shung Ye Museum of Formosan Aborigines, 1999.

Teiser, Stephen F. *The Ghost Festival in Medieval China.* Princeton, NJ: Princeton University Press, 1996.

———. "The Ritual behind the Opera: A Fragmentary Ethnography of the Ghost Festival, A.D. 400–1900." In *Ritual Opera, Operatic Ritual,* 191–223. David G. Johnson and Beata Grant.

ter Haar, Barend J. *Guan Yu: The Religious Afterlife of a Failed Hero.* Oxford: Oxford University Press, 2017.

———. *Practicing Scripture: A Lay Buddhist Movement in Late Imperial China.* Honolulu: University of Hawai'i Press, 2014.

———. *Ritual & Mythology of the Chinese Triads: Creating an Identity.* Leiden: Brill, 2000.

———. "The Way of the Nine Palaces (*jiugong dao* 九宫道): A Lay Buddhist Movement." *Studies in Chinese Religions* 5, no. 3–4 (2019): 415–432.

Thierry, François. *Amulettes De Chine: Catalogue.* Paris: Bibliothèque nationale de France, 2008.

Tie Bao 鐵保. *Qinding baqi tongzhi* 欽定八旗通 7. Changchun: Jilin wenshi chubanshe, 2002.

The Literary Digest, ed. 1900. "Statistics of the Chinese Protestant Missions." *The Literary Digest* 21, no. 6 (Aug. 11, 1900).

"Transformation Text on Mahāmaudgalyāyana Rescuing His Mother from the Underworld, with Pictures, One Scroll, with Preface." Victor Mair, trans. *The Columbia*

Anthology of Traditional Chinese Literature, edited by Victor H. Mair. New York: Columbia University Press, 1994, 1093–1127.

van der Leeuw, G., and John Evan Turner. *Religion in Essence and Manifestation: A Study in Phenomenology.* London: G. Allen & Unwin, Ltd., 1938.

van der Loon, Piet. "Les origines rituelles du theatre chinois." *Journal Asiatique* 215 (1977): 158–162.

van der Loon, Piet [Long Bide 龍彼得]. "Fashi xi chutan" 法事戲初探. *Minsu quyi* 民俗曲藝 84 (1993): 9–30.

Vauchez, André, and Michael F. Cusato. *Francis of Assisi: The Life and Afterlife of a Medieval Saint.* New Haven: Yale University Press, 2012.

Versnel, Henk. *Inconsistencies in Greek and Roman Religion, Volume 2: Transition and Reversal in Myth and Ritual.* Leiden, New York: Brill, 1992.

Wagner, Rudolf G. "Monkey King Subdues the White-Bone Demon: A Study in PRC Mythology." In *The Contemporary Chinese Historical Drama: Four Studies,* Berkeley: University of California Press, 1990, 139–235.

Waley, Arthur. *Monkey.* London: George Allen & Unwin Ltd.

———. "T'ai Tsung in Hell." *Ballads and Stories from Tun-huang.* London: G. Allen & Unwin, Ltd., 1960, 165–174.

———. "The Real Tripitika." In *The Real Tripitika and Other Pieces.* London: G. Allen & Unwin, Ltd., 1952.

Walker, Hera S. "Indigenous or Foreign? A Look at the Origins of the Monkey Hero Sun Wukong." *Sino-Platonic Papers* 81 (September 1998).

Wall, Barbara. "Transformations of *Xiyouji* in Korean Intertexts and Hypertexts." PhD dissertation, Ruhr-Universität Bochum, 2014.

Walsh, Maurice. *The Long Discourses of the Buddha: A Translation of the* Dīgha Nikāya. Boston: Wisdom Publications, 1987.

Wan Laiming 萬籟鳴. *Wo yu Sun Wukong* 我與孫悟空. Taiyuan: Beiyue wenyi chubanshe, 1986.

Wan Qingchuan 万晴川 and Zhao Mei 赵玫. "Xiyou gushi zai Ming-Qing mimi zongjiao zhong de jiedu" 西游故事在明清秘密宗教中的解读. Huaiyin shifan xueyuan xuebao (zhexue shehui kexue ban) 淮阴师范学院学报 (哲学社会科学版) 3 (2006): 327–331.

Wang Dingyong 王定勇. *Jiangsu daoqing kaolun* 江苏道情考论. Beijing: Shehui kexue wenxian chubanshe, 2013.

Wang Fang 王仿. "Wushu, yishu de jiehe yu fenli—Nantong tongzi xi diaocha" 巫术、艺术的结合与分离一南通僮子戏调查. *Minjian wenyi jikan* 民间文艺季刊 (1989): 122–154.

Wang Huimin 王惠民. "Dunhuang xieben *Shuiyue guanyin jing* yanjiu" 敦煌写本《水月观音经》研究. *Dunhuang yanjiu* 敦煌研究 3 (1992): 93–98.

Wang Shifu 王實甫. *Xi xiang ji* 西廂記. Translated into English by Stephen H. West and Wilt L. Idema as *The Story of the Western Wing.* Berkeley, CA: University of California Press, 1995.

Wang Xiangxu 汪象旭 and Huang Taihong 黃太鴻. *Xiyou zhengdao shu* 西遊證道書. Shanghai: Shanghai guji chubanshe, 1990.

Wang Xiyuan 王熙远. *Guixi minjian mimi zongjiao* 桂西民间秘密宗教. Guilin: Guangxi shifan daxue chubanshe, 1994.

Wang Xuan. "Reading the *Journey to the West:* How Fiction became a Sacred Scripture." *Chinese Literature: Essays, Articles, Reviews* 41 (2019): 25–57.

Wang, Yuanfei. "Genre and Empire: Historical Romance and Sixteenth-Century Chinese Cultural Fantasies." PhD dissertation, University of Pennsylvania, 2013.

Wang Zhideng 王穉登. *Ding zheng Wu she bian* 訂正吳社編. In *Siku quanshu cunmu congshu: zibu* 四庫全書存目叢書: 子部 241. Jinan: Qi Lu shushe, 1997, 727–733.

Ware, James. "The Fairyland of China I." *East Asia Magazine,* part I, vol. IV (1905): 80–89.

Wei Wenbin 魏文斌 and Zhang Liming 张利明, eds. Xiyou ji *bihua yu Xuanzang qu jing tuxiang* 西游记壁画与玄奘取经图像. Nanjing: Jiangsu fenghuang meishu chubanshe, 2019.

Wenyuange siku quanshu (dianzi ban) 文淵閣四庫全書 (電子版), 3rd edition. Hong Kong: Zhongwen Daxue and Digital Heritage Publishing, 2007.

Werner, Edward Theodore Chalmers. *Myths and Legends of China.* New York: Brentano's, 1922.

Wheelock, Wade. "The Problem of Ritual Language: From Information to Situation." *Journal of the American Academy of Religion* 50, no. 1 (Mar., 1982): 49–71.

Widmer, Ellen. "I-yu Cheng-tao Shu in the context of Wang Ch'i's publishing enterprise." *Hanxue yanjiu* 漢學研究 (Chinese Studies) 6, no. 1 (1988): 37–63.

Wilhelm, Richard. *Chinesische Volksmärchen.* Jena: Eugen Diederich, 1914. Translated into English as *The Chinese Fairy Book.* New York: Frederick A. Stokes Company, 1921.

Wivell, Charles J. "The Story of How the Monk Tripitaka of the Great Country of T'ang Brought back the Sutras." In *The Columbia Anthology of Traditional Chinese Literature,* edited by Victor H. Mair. New York: Columbia University Press, 1994, 1181–1207.

Wong, Dorothy. "The Making of a Saint: Images of Xuanzang in East Asia." *Early Medieval China* 1 (2002): 43–95.

Woodbridge, Samuel I. *The Golden-horned Dragon King: Or, The Emperor's Visits to the Spirit World.* Shanghai: North-China Herald Office, 1895.

———. *Fifty Years in China: Being an Account of the History and Conditions in China and of the Missions of the Presbyterian Church in the United States There from 1867 to the Present Day.* Richmond, VA: Presbyterian Committee of Publication, 1919.

Wu Cheng'en. *The Journey to the West,* 4 vols. Translated by Anthony C. Yu. Chicago: University of Chicago Press, 2012.

Wu Dianlei 吴电雷. "Wenhua dili shiyu zhong de Qiandi nuo wenhua xingtai yanjiu" 文化地理视域中的黔地傩文化形态研究. *Chongqing wenli xueyuan xuebao (shehui kexue ban)* 重庆文理学院学报 (社会科学版) 37.1 (Jan. 2018): 1–10.

Weiwei budong Taishan shengen jieguo baojuan 巍巍不動泰山深根結果寶卷. MQMZ, vol. 1.

Wu Xiaofang 吳曉芳. "Duoyuan zongjiao de duihua: lun Hailun M. Haiyesi dui *Xiyou ji* de jieyi (1930)" 多元宗教的對話: 論海倫·M· 海耶斯對《西遊記》的節譯 (1930). PhD dissertation, The Chinese University of Hong Kong, 2018.

Wu Yong 吳永. *Gengzi xishou congtan* 庚子西狩叢談. Beijing: Zhonghua shuju, 2009.

"Xitian daxiaosheng jinglü lun bing zai Tangdu shu mulu" 西天大小乘經律論並在唐都數目錄. Stein 3565v. Reproduced in *Yingzang Dunhuan wenxian (Hanwen Fojing yiwai bufen)* 英藏敦皇文獻 (漢文佛經以外部份). Chengdu: Sichuan renmin chubanshe, 1990, vol. 5.

Xia Zengyou. "Xiaoshuo yuanli" 小說原理. In *Wan Qing wenxue congchao wu juan: xiaoshuo xiqu yanjiu juan* 晚清文學叢鈔五卷: 小說戲曲研究卷. Liang Qichao et al. Taipei: Xinwenfeng, 1989.

Xie Jian 謝健. "Difang yishi yu yishi ju—yi Guangxi Cenxi diqu Nandu zhen weili" 地方儀式與儀式劇—以廣西岑溪地區南渡鎮為例. PhD dissertation, Chinese University of Hong Kong, 2015.

———. "Local Community Ritual Theatre in Guangxi, South China." *Asian Theatre Journal* 36.1 (Spring 2019): 205–220.

Xie Mingxun 謝明勳. "Hanguo Jingtian si Yuandai shita 'Xiyou' gushi fudiao tujie" 韓國敬天寺元代石塔「西遊」故事浮雕圖解. *Zhongyu zhongwen xue* 中語中文學 12 (2013): 163–214.

Xiyou ji 西遊記, 2 vols. Hong Kong: Zhonghua shuju, 2007.

Xu Shuofang 徐朔方. "Mulian xi san ti" 目连戏三题. *Xu Shuofang shuo xiqu* 徐朔方说戏曲. Shanghai: Shanghai guji chubanshe, 2000.

Xu Wei 許蔚. "*Xiyou ji* yanjiu er ti" 《西遊記》研究二題. *Huaren zongjiao yanjiu* 華人宗教研究 6 (2015.12): 87–135.

Xuan Ding 宣鼎. "Wu xian 巫仙." *Ye yu qiu deng lu* 夜雨秋燈錄. Shanghai: Wenming shuju, 1910s (exact date unknown).

Xuanzang 玄奘. *Da Tang xiyu ji* 大唐西域記. T51, no. 2087.

Xue Ruolin 薛若鄰, Chen Hongren 陳宏仁, and Yu Daxi 余大喜. *Zhongguo wunuo mianju yishu* 1 中國巫儺面具藝術. Taibei: Nantian shuju, 1996.

Yakushi-ji 藥師寺. *Genjō sanzō shūhōroku* 玄奘三藏聚芳錄. Nara: Yakushi-ji, 1991.

Yan Changhong 嚴昌洪. "1930 niandai guomin zhengfu fengsu diaocha yu gailiang huadong shulun." 1930 年代國民政府風俗調查與改良活動述論. In *Zhonghua Minguo shi yanjiu sanshi nian (1972–2002)* 中華民國史研究三十年 (1972–2002), vol. 3. Beijing: Shehui kexue wenxian chubanshe, 2008, 1150–1166.

Yan Pingjing 嚴苹菁. "Zhihu Dashiye ji qi yishi de tantao: yi Xinpu fangliao yimin miao 2009 nian Zhongyuan weili" 紙糊大士爺及其儀式的探討: 以新埔枋寮義民廟 2009 年中元為例. MA thesis, Guoli tongjiao daxue, 2011.

Yang Donglai xiansheng piping Xiyou ji 楊東來先生批評西遊記. In *Xuxiu siku quanshu,* vol. 1766. Shanghai: Shanghai guji chubanshe, 1995, 161–201.

Yang Jun 杨军 and Bai Xiaolong 白晓龙. "Yan'an shi Baota qu Shiyao shiku diaocha jianbao" 延安市宝塔区石窟石窟调查简报. *Kaogu faxian yu diaocha* 考古发现与调查 no. 6 (2019): 84–96.

Yang Hongming 杨宏明. "Ansai xian shiku si diaocha baogao" 安塞县石窟寺调查报告. *Wenbo* 文博 no. 3 (1990): 64–70.

Yang, Mayfair Mei-hui. *Gifts, Favors, and Banquets: The Art of Social Relationships in China.* Ithica, NY: Cornell University Press, 1994.

Yang Sai 楊賽. "Dongting hu yuanqu Fojiao daochang sangzang yinyue yishi 洞庭湖垸區佛教道場喪葬音樂儀式." In *Zhongguo minjian chuantong yishi yinyue yanjiu (Huazhong juan)* 中国民间传统仪式音乐研究 (华中卷), edited by Liu Hong 刘红. Beijing: Wenhua yishu chubanshe, 2011, 255–326.

Yang Shixian 楊士賢. *Shenzong zhuiyuan-tushuo Taiwan sangli* 慎終追遠— 圖說台灣喪禮. Taipei: Boyang wenhua shiye youxiangong, 2008.

———. "Taiwan Shijiao sangzang badu fashi ji qi minjian wenxue yanjiu—yi Minnan Shijiao xitong weili" 台灣釋教喪葬拔渡法事及其民間文學研究— 以閩南釋教系統為例. PhD dissertation. Guoli donghua daxue, 2010.

Yang Ti 楊悌. *Dongtian xuan ji* 洞天玄記. Beijing: Beijing Airusheng shuzihua jishu yanjiu zhongxin, 2011.

Yang Xuanzhi 楊衒之. *Luoyang qielan ji* 洛陽伽藍記. T51, no. 2092. Translated by Yi-t'ung Wang as *A Record of Buddhist Monasteries in Lo-Yang.* Princeton, NJ: Princeton University Press, 1984.

Yang Yanling 楊彥泠. "Kejia Shijiao sangzang yishi 'qu jing' keyi yanjiu" 客家釋教喪葬儀式「取經」科儀研究. MA thesis, Guoli zhongyang daxue, 2017.

Ye Mingsheng 葉明生. "Daojiao Mulian xi Sun Xingzhe xingxiang yu Song-Yuan *Mulian jiu mu* zaju zhi tantao" 道教目连戏孙行者形象与宋元《目连救母》杂剧之探讨. *Xiqu yanjiu* 戏曲研究 45 (1998.1): 156–172.

———. *Fujian sheng Shaowu shi Dafugang xiang Heyuan cun de "tiao fan seng" yu "tiao ba man"* 福建省邵武市大阜崗鄉河源村的 "跳番僧" 與 "跳八蠻." Taipei: Shi he zheng minsu wenhua jijinhui, 1993.

———. "Zhangping daotan posha sai yishi zhi yinyue ji xiju gaoshu" 漳平道壇破砂寨儀式之音樂及戲劇概述. *Minsu quyi* 民俗曲艺 117 (Jan., 1999):1–48.

———. *Zongjiao yu xiju yanjiu conggao* 宗教與戲劇研究叢稿. Taipei: Guojia chubanshe, 2009.

Yegŭrin Kŏnch'uksa Samuso 예그린 건축사 사무소. *Wŏn'gaksaji sipch'ŭng sŏkt'ap: silch'ŭk chosa pogosŏ* 圓覺寺址十層石塔:實測 調査報告書. Seoul: Munhwajae Kwalliguk, 1993.

"Ying shen saishe lijie chuanbu sishi qu gongdiao" 迎神賽社禮節傳簿四十曲宮調. *Zhonghua xiqu* 中華戲曲 3 (1987): 2–50.

Yoshimura Makoto. "Genjō no nenji mondai ni tsuite" 玄奘の年次問題について. *Komazawa Daigaku Bukkyōgakubu ronshū* 駒沢大学仏教学部論集 46 (2015): 183–205.

You Tong 尤侗. *Genzhai zashuo* 艮齋雜說, j. 5: 2b. In *Xuxiu siku quanshu* 1136. Shanghai: Shanghai guji chuban she, 1995.

Yu, Anthony C. trans. *Monkey and the Monk: A Revised Abridgment of* The Journey to the West. Chicago: Chicago University Press, 2006.

Yu, Anthony C. "Liu I-ming on How to Read the *Hsi-yu chi* (*The Journey to the West*)." In *How to Read the Chinese Novel,* edited by David Rolston, 295–315.

Yü, Chun-fang. *Kuan-yin: The Chinese Transformation of Avalokiteśvara.* New York: Columbia University Press, 2001.

Yu Huiyuan 余惠媛. "Kejia Shijiao sangzang yishi ji qi yinyue zhi yanjiu—yi Miaoli xian 'Guangfu tan' zhi wuye gongde yishi weili" 客家釋教喪葬儀式及其音樂之研究~ 以苗栗縣「廣福壇」之午夜功德儀式為例. MA thesis, Guoli Xinzhu jiaoyu daxue, 2011.

Yu Mong-in 柳夢寅. *Ŏu yadam* 於于野談 vol. 2. Ch'op'an 초판. Kyŏnggi-do P'aju-si: Tol Pegae, 2006.

Yu Shuo 于硕. "Shanxi Qinglong si qu jing bihua yu Yulin ku qu jing tuxiang guanxi de chubu fenxi" 山西青龙寺取经壁画与榆林窟取经图像关系的初步分析. *Yishu sheji yanjiu* 艺术设计研究, no. 3 (2010): 28–34.

Yu Songqing 喻松青. "*Xiaoshi zhenkong baojuan* kao"《销释真空宝卷》考. *Zhongguo wenhua* 中国文化 11 (1995): 109–117.

Yuanliu famai 源流法脈. MQMZ, vol. 8.

Zavidovskaya, Ekaterina. "Celestial and Human Audience of the Traditional Opera xiqu in Modern Shanxi and Shaanxi provinces." *Papers of the St. Petersburg State University Conference Issues of Far Eastern Literature,* vol. II, 2012, 485–497.

Zeitlin, Judith T. *Historian of the Strange: Pu Songling and the Chinese Classical Tale.* Stanford: Stanford University Press, 1997.

Zhang Baoxi 张宝玺. *Guazhou dong qian fo dong Xixia shiku yishu* 瓜州東千佛洞西夏石窟藝術. Beijing: Xueyuan chubanshe, 2012.

Zhang Bing 张兵. "Beisong de 'shuohua' he huaben" 北宋的 "说话" 和话本. *Fudan xuebao (shehui kexue ban)* 复旦学报 (社会科学版) (1998.2): 85–92.

Zhang Heng 張恆. "Zai Nanjing faxian de Tang Xuanzang yigu" 在南京发现的唐玄奘遗骨. In *Jiangsu wenshi ziliao xuanji,* vol. 10 江苏文史资料选辑, 第十辑. Zhongguo Renmin Zhengzhi Xieshang Huiyui Jiangsu Sheng Ji Nanjing Shi Weiyuanhui Wenshi Ziliao Yanjiu Weiyuanhui 中国人民政治协商会议江苏省暨南京市委员会文史资料研究委员会, document no. 312. Nanjing: Jiangsu renmin chubanshe, 1982.

Zhang Junhua 章軍華. "Yuanxing de zaisheng: Sun Wukong yu Fangxiang shi" 原型的再生: 孫悟空與方相氏. *Dongnan daxue xuebao (zhexue shehui kexue ban)* 东南大学学报 (哲学社会科学版) 8 (2006): 83–86, 93.

Zhang Qi 张琦. "Gudai zangli zhong de Kai lu shen, Xian dao shen tanyuan" 古代葬礼中的开路神, 显道神探源. *Sichuan daxue xuebao* (*zhexue shehui kexue ban*) 四川大学学报 (哲学社会科学版) 5 (2008): 134–139.

Zhang Qingyu 张庆玉. "Yuan qinghua *Xiyou ji* yuanda xianglu shoucang ji" 元青花《西游记》圆大香炉收藏记. *Shoucang* 收藏 15 (Aug., 2015): 81–83.

Zhang Shinan 張世南. *Youhuan jiwen* 游宦紀聞. SKQS.

Zhang Shushen 張書紳. *Xin shuo* Xiyou ji 新說西遊記. Shanghai: Shanghai guji chubanshe, 1990.

Zhang Xiaogang 张小刚 and Guo Junye 郭俊叶. "Wenshu shan shiku Xixia《Shuiyue Guanyin tu》yu《Molizhitian tu》kaoshi" 文殊山石窟西夏《水月观音图》与《摩利支天图》考释. *Dunhuang yanjiu* 敦煌研究 156, no. 2 (2016): 8–15.

Zhang Yanyuan 張彥遠. *Lidai minghua ji* 歷代名畫記, 3:23b. SKQS.

Zhang Ziying 张子英. *Cizhou yao ci zhen* 磁州窑瓷枕. Beijing: Renmin meishu chubanshe, 2000.

Zheng Binglin 郑炳林. "Huangling xian Shuanglongyu cun Qianfo dong shuiyue Guanyin zaoxiang" 黄陵县双龙峪村千佛洞水月观音造像. *Zhongguo Chongqing Dazu shike guoji xueshu yantaohui lunwen ji* 中国重庆大足石刻国际学术研讨会论文集. Chongqing: Chongqing chubanshe, 2013, 634–647.

Zhengxin chuyi wu xiuzheng zizai baojuan 正信除疑無修證自在寶卷. MQMZ, vol. 1.

Zheng Yinan 郑怡楠, "Guazhou shiku qun Tang Xuanzang qu jing tu yanjiu" 瓜州石窟群唐玄奘取经图研究. *Dunhuang xue jikan* 敦煌学辑刊 4 (2009): 93–111.

Zheng Yiwei 郑轶伟. *Zhongguo huaqian tudian* 中国花钱图典. Shanghai: Shanghai wenhua chubanshe, 2004.

———. *Zhongguo huaqian tudian xuji* 中国花钱图典续集. Shanghai: Shanghai wenhua chubanshe, 2006.

Zheng Zhenduo 鄭振鐸. *Xidi shuhua* 西諦書話. Beijing: Xinhua shudian, 1983.

Zheng Zhizhen 鄭之珍. *Xinbian Mulian jiu mu quanshan xiwen* 新編目連救母勸善戲文. In *Xuxiu siku quanshu,* vol. 1774. Shanghai: Shanghai guji chubanshe, 2002.

Zhisheng 智昇. *Xu gujin yijing tuji* 續古今譯經圖紀. T55, no. 2152.

Zhongguo Minzu Minjian Wudao Jicheng Bianjibu 中国民族民间舞蹈集成编辑部. *Zhongguo minzu minjian wudao jicheng: Fujian juan* 中国民族民间舞蹈集成: 福建卷. Beijing: Zhongguo minzu minjian wudao jicheng bianjibu, 1996.

Zhongguo shehui kexue yuan jindaishi yanjiusuo "jindaishi ziliao" bianji zu 中国社会科学院近代史研究所《近代史资料》编辑组, ed. *Yihetuan shiliao* 义和团史料, vol. 2. Beijing: Zhongguo shehui kexue chubanshe, 1982.

Zhongguo shiku diaosu jinghua: Shaanbei shiku 中国石窟雕塑精华: 陕北石窟. Chongqing: Chongqing chubanshe, 1998.

Zhongxi cuyan baojuan 眾喜粗言寶卷. Beijing: Beijing Airusheng shuzihua jishu yanjiu zhongxin, 2011.

Zhou Guomao 周国茂. *Mojiao yu Mo wenhua* 摩教与摩文化. Guiyang: Guizhou renmin chubanshe, 1995.

Zhou Kai. (*Daoguang*) *Xiamen zhi* (道光) 廈門志. Beijing: Beijing Airusheng shuzihua jishu yanjiu zhongxin, 2009.

Zhou li zhushu 周禮注疏. SKQS.

Zhu Hengfu 朱恒夫. *Mulian xi yanjiu* 目连戏研究. Nanjing: Nanjing daxue chubanshe, 1993.

———. "Mulian xi zhong de Sun Wukong gushi xukao" 目连戏中的孙悟空故事叙考. *Ming-Qing xiaoshuo yanjiu* 明清小说研究 (1993.1): 260–269.

———. "Wu Cheng'en *Xiyou ji* yu nuoge 'Tang chan' zhi guanxi" 吴承恩《西游记》与傩歌 "唐忏" 之关系. *Ming-Qing xiaoshuo yanjiu* 明清小说研究 4 (1994): 136–148.

Zhu Hengfu 朱恒夫 and Huang Wenhu 黄文虎. *Jianghuai shenshu* 江淮神书. Shanghai: Shanghai guji chubanshe, 2011.

Zhu Songying 朱松瑛. *Zhonghua wudao zhi: Guangdong juan* 中华舞蹈志: 广东卷. Shanghai: Xuelin chubanshe 学林出版社, 2006.

Zhuo Zuoren 周作人. "Ren de wenxue" 人的文學. In *Zhongguo xin wenxue daxi* 中國新文學大系, vol. 1, edited by Zhao Jiabi 趙家璧 and Hu Shih 胡適. Xianggang: Xianggang wenxue yanjiushe, 1962, 219–227.

Zuo Yibing 左怡兵. "*Yujia qu jing daochang* he *Fomen qu jing daochang* diaocha zhengli" 《瑜伽取经道场》和《佛门取经道场》调查整理. *Wenxue jiaoyu* 文学教育 (2013.08): 132–133.

Zürcher, Erik. "Prince Moonlight: Messianism and Eschatology in Early Medieval Chinese Buddhism." *T'oung Pao* 68.1–3 (1982): 1–75.

Index

Page numbers in boldface type refer to illustrations.

Protocol for the Festival for Welcoming the Spirits, with Forty Musical Pieces (Protocol): "The Bodhisattva Mañjuśrī Subdues the Lion" (Wenshu pusa xiang shizi) included in, 82; dating of, 168n42; dramas listed in, 81–82, 168n47; "Guanggong Beheads the Demon" (Guangong zhan yao)included in, 82; Mañjuśri battling a lion featured in, 82–83; "Mulian Rescues his Mother" included in, 82; *nuo* ritual compared with, 81–82; Obtaining the Scriptures narratives linked to, 81–82, 97; performance of, 81, 92, 97, 168n42; "Spirits kill the Disobedient Child" (Shen sha wunizi) included in, 82–83
Pu Songling, 119, 120

Qian Daxin, 33, 35
Qin Yanjia, 105, 174n55
Qing dynasty (1636–1912): images of Xuanzang on coins and amulets, 161n40; Obtaining the Scriptures associated with civil unrest during, 23, 122, 137, 140; persecutions of salvational associations, 134–136; Taiping Rebellion, 165n14. *See also* Boxers and the Boxer rebellion
Qiu Changchun: authorship of *Journey to the West* attributed to, 25, 36, 129, 153n6, 180n44; Christianity associated with, 32; Complete Perfection school of Daoism associated with, 129; Sun Wukong identified as his invention by Pu Songling, 119–120

Ramanujan, A. K., 88
Rawski, Evelyn Sakakida, 9
Record of the Western Regions (Record). *See* Xuanzang—*Record of the Western Regions (Record)*
Richard, Timothy: abridged version of *Journey to the West* translated and published by, 31–32; Liang Qichao as his secretary, 36; Nestorian Christian message detected in *Journey to the West* by, 31–32, 154–155n32

Righter, Anne, 164n5
Rites of Zhou (Zhou li), Great Exorcism (*da nuo*) described in, 70
Ritual Manual for the Buddhist Obtaining Scriptures (Ritual Manual): as a mortuary rite, 104, 105, 174n47
The Ritual of Requesting Scriptures in Western Heaven as Spoken by the Buddha, as a version of, *Ritual Manual for the Buddhist Obtaining Scriptures (Ritual Manual)*, 107
Ritual of the Buddhists Who Compassionately Saves Those in Distress, 107
Ritual of the Compassionate Precious Scroll of the Buddhist's Journey to the West (Buddhist's Journey): dating of, 110–111, 177n76; recitation during mortuary rites, 105
Road Opening Spirit (Kai lu shen), 68, 70, 165n7, 165n16
Rolston, David, 16
Rösch, Petra, 160n36

Śākyamuni Buddha: Cao Shun of the Teachings of Former Heaven as his incarnation, 136; claims of the Incense Smelling sect regarding, 134; claims of the Vast Yang sect regarding, 120, 123; decline of the present *kalpa* after his entering nirvāṇa, 127; depictions on stupas featuring Xuanzang and his companions, 76, 167n28; and Patriarch Luo, 123; Tang Monk's request of repentance texts from, 175–176n64; transmission of scriptures to Xuanzang celebrated at the Ghost Festival, 143, 172n15; "wordless scriptures" given to Xuanzang, 145, 183n3, 183n3
Samantabhadra: depiction on a stele at Thousand Buddha Hall in Henan, 167n28; veneration by Xuanzang and his companions depicted at Yulin, 51, 159n21; white horse given to Xuanzang as a manifestation of Mañjuśrī and Samantabhadra, 60
Sangren, P. Steven, 11
Seidel, Anna, 127

Taiwan: Ghost Festival, 92–93; *lingqian*
divination systems employed in,
160n31; modern funerary rituals
featuring the Tang Monk and his
companion, 22, 89, 89–92, 102–103,
173n38, 175–176n64, 177n78; Rituals
of Merit (*gongguo*) involving Tang
Monk and his companions, 109–110,
176n66, 176n69, **Plate 10**; Tang Monk
and his companions venerated in, 25;
Xuanzang and his attendants studied
and venerated in, 2, 7, 12, 28–29
Tanaka Issei, 79, 167nn34–35
Tanaka Tomoyuki, 164n56
Tang dynasty (618–907)–Gaozu (r. 618–626),
Lady Xue, 46
Tang dynasty (618–907)–Taizong
(r. 626–649), 160n30; hell visited by,
5, 29, 76, 85–86, 93, 106, 170n65,
172n12; *tongzi* ritual established by,
85–86, 170n64; Water Land Assemblies held by, 85, 93, **94**, 95; Xuanzang's pilgrimage to India allegedly
ordered by, 5, 85, 86, 93, 106, 170n65.
See also Xuanzang—*Record of the
Western Regions* (*Record*)
Tang dynasty (618–907)–Gaozong
(r. 650–683): painting of Xuanzang
commissioned by, 46, 158n9; on
Xuanzang's travels, 44
Tang dynasty (618–907)–Zhongzong
(r. 684 and 705–710), 46, 158n9
Tang dynasty (618–907)–Xuanzong
(r. 712–756), 163n54; *Heart Sūtra*
offered to, 61, 163n54
Tang Monk: contemporary veneration of,
19–20; correlation of his five pilgrims with the five phases, 131–132,
180–181n52; as a divine ancestor in
the Yellow Heaven sect, 129; Dunhuang cave depictions of, 41, **42**;
historical Xuanzang distinguished
from, 6–7, 42–43; historical Xuanzang
popularly fused with, 41–43, 146;
Mulian closely aligned with, 96–97,
97, 101–102; participation in *tongzi*
ritual, 86–87; presence within the

body, 117–118, 129–132, **131**, **133**,
180–181n52; as Pujing's true identity,
129–130, 139; as the Sandalwood
Buddha, 125; self-cultivation associated with his pilgrimage, 118; spirit
possession of the Tang Monk and his
companions by the Boxers, 114, 119,
120; in Triad lore, 137–138. *See also*
mortuary rites and traditions–Tang
Monk featured in; Obtaining the
Scriptures narratives
Taylor, George, 28–29, 154n16
Teachings of Vast Yang: Patriarch Piaogao,
120–121, 122, 125–128; persecution
of, 122; *Primordial Chaos-Vast Yang
Scripture of the Descent of Piaogao,* **126**
Teiser, Stephen F., 95
Ten Kings of hell: depiction on a stele at
Thousand Buddha Hall in Henan,
167n28; journey of the dead through
the courts of, 55, 104, 167n28; *Sūtra of
the Ten Kings*, 55
Thierry, François, 161n39
Tibet: divination practices centered on
Avalokiteśvara, 53; sites associated
with Obtaining the Scriptures narratives commemorated by Tibetans, 147;
Sun Wukong venerated in, 33, 155n43
tongzi rituals: contemporary staging of, 84,
86–87, 171n71; feats of bravado and
self-mortification, 87; origin story
traced to Taizong, 85–86, 170n64;
participation of the Tang Monk and
his companions, 86, 87; *tongzi* mediums, 84–85; Yangyuan Hongmen rite,
85, 170n64
"Trepiṭaka Obtains the Scriptures" (Sanzang qu jing) ritual: as the origin story
for texts and rituals during Ghost
festival, 96; performance at funerals,
109; staging of, 90
Triad groups: criminal activities associated
with, 137; Hong Child, 137, 182n70;
Tang Monk in Triad lore, 137–138

Ullambana Sūtra, Mulian legend contained
in, 95, 96

Xuanzang—images and portraits (cont.)
92–93, **Plates 7–8**; textual descriptions by his disciples, 45; textual
references to portraits, 45–46
Xuanzang—images with Water
Moon Avalokiteśvara, 149; at the
Avalokiteśvara Pavilion in southern
Shandong province, 52, 149; at Dayun yuan, 149, 183n11; depictions of
his entourage, 49; at Eastern Thousand Buddha Caves complex cave,
49, 149, 183, **Plate 2**; generic-render-
ings of pilgrim-monks venerating
Avalokiteśvara, 51–52; from Khara
Khoto, 54–55, **Plate 3**; at Mount
Zhong cave 4, 49, **50**, 183n3; at Shihong si, cave 2, 49, **50**, 149, 183n7; at
Yanfu si cave 8, 49, 149, 183n7; at
Yulin cave 2, 54, 149, 183n10, **Plate
4**; at Yulin cave 3, 49, **51**, 149, 159n21;
at Zhaoan cave 3, 149, 183n1
Xuanzang—*Record of the Western Regions*
(*Record*): compilation by Bianji,
151n8; emperor Taizong's ordering of,
4; Mount Potalaka described in, 52;
publication of, 2; translation by Julien,
41; Xuanzang's life described in, 2
Xuanzang's otherworldly pilgrimage: attainment of nirvāṇa, 141–142; early
conceptions of, 5; Xuanzang's power
to pass between heaven and hell, 23,
62–64. See also *Moralistic Tale*; Obtaining the Scriptures narratives

Yang Ti, 117
Yang Xuanzhi, *Luoyang qielan ji,* 169n49
Ye Mingsheng, 12, 68, 69–70, 173n32,
173n34
Yellow Heaven sect: path to Western
Heaven identified within the body,
129, 130, **131**, 132; Pujing, 129–130;
Puming, 129–130, 134, 181n66;
Tang Monk as a divine ancestor of,

129–130, 180n49; Tang Monk's travels
as an allegory for self-cultivation, 129
Yinzong, authorship of *Xiaoshi Zhenkong
baojuan* attributed to, 176n75
Yogācāra tradition: texts preserved in Japan
returned to China, 41; treatises and
commentaries translated by Xuanzang, 4, 144; Xuanzang as a patriarch
of, 20
Yoga Monks (Yujia jiao seng), 109
Yongle dadian, 73, 81, 93
Yoshimura Makoto, dating of Xuanzang's
leaving the capital, 151n6
You Tong, 33, 34
Yu, Anthony C.: scholarship on *Journey to
the West*, 26, 152n20, 153n9; translation of *Journey to the West* (*Xiyou ji*),
5, 26, 151n11
Yu Huiyuan, 165n10, 173n38
Yu Mong-in, 78
Yu Songqing, 176n75

Zhang Shengzhe, 57, 161nn42–44
Zhang Shushen, 178n19
Zheng Binglin, 160n38
Zheng Zhenduo, 39, 40
Zheng Zhizhen. See *Moralistic Tale* by
Zheng Zhizhen
Zhou Kai, 176n66
Zhu Bajie (Xuanzang's pig attendant), 6, 17,
43, 66; buddhahood attained by, 124;
in exorcistic rituals, 34n35; and the
five phases, 131–132; in the *Hell
Volume* narrative of the Mulian story-
cycle, 100–101, 173n35; inclusion
among Xuanzang's companions, 143;
Ming dynasty roof tile of, **78**; partici-
pation in *tongzi* rituals, 86, 87; as
"Pigsy," 24; presence within the body,
117–118, 132, **133**, 180–181n52;
veneration in northwestern China,
148
Zhu Youdun, 82

About the Author

Benjamin Brose is professor of Buddhist and Chinese studies and chair of the Department of Asian Languages and Cultures at the University of Michigan. He is the author of *Patrons and Patriarchs: Regional Rulers and Chan Monks during the Five Dynasties and Ten Kingdoms* (2015) and *Xuanzang: China's Legendary Pilgrim and Translator* (2021).